The New Hampshire Village Book

Mummy

With much love
on you birthday
from us all
Sue, Trevor
Julie & Simon

xx

12. 3. 92.

The New Hampshire Village Book

THE VILLAGES OF BRITAIN SERIES

Other counties in this series include

Avon*

Bedfordshire*

Berkshire*

Buckinghamshire*

Cambridgeshire*

Cheshire*

Devon*

Dorset

Essex*

Gloucestershire*

Herefordshire*

Hertfordshire*

Kent

Lancashire*

Leicestershire
& Rutland*

Lincolnshire*

Middlesex*

Norfolk*

Northamptonshire*

Nottinghamshire*

Oxfordshire*

Powys Montgomery*

Shropshire*

Somerset*

Staffordshire*

Suffolk

Surrey

East Sussex

West Sussex

Warwickshire*

West Midlands*

Wiltshire

Worcestershire*

*Published in conjunction with County Federations
of Women's Institutes

The New Hampshire Village Book

Compiled by the Hampshire
Federation of Women's Institutes from notes
and illustrations sent by Institutes in the County

Published jointly by
Countryside Books, Newbury
and the H.F.W.I., Winchester

Countryside Books
3 Catherine Road
Newbury, Berkshire

ISBN 1 85306 091 7

Cover photograph of East Meon taken by Jean Wheeler

Produced through MRM Associates Ltd., Reading
Typeset by Acorn Bookwork, Salisbury
Printed in England by J. W. Arrowsmith Ltd, Bristol

Foreword

Hampshire is a County full of history and early beginnings, with many Roman roads running through and the biggest Roman town, Winchester, as its capital. We have a coastline known for its two great ports, Southampton and Portsmouth, and the New Forest, created by William the Conqueror, and now one of the oldest stretches of woodland in the country.

There are large estates within our boundaries: two are widely known, Broadlands in the south of the county, with its trout and salmon streams, and Stratford Saye to the north, the home of the Dukes of Wellington. As well as fishing streams, we have the famous watercress beds in the Alresford and Bourne Valley area, Hampshire strawberries are well known for their flavour, as are our apples and Hampshire wines.

But it is our villages that contain much of our history, and I am sure you will enjoy reading about them and their famous sons, in this edition of 'Hampshire Villages'. All the material has been compiled by members of the Women's Institutes, some members having lived all their lives in the village they write about.

June Brooks
County Chairman

Acknowledgements

The production of this book has only been possible by the enthusiastic research of the contributors and the untiring efforts of Mrs. Betty Wilson who co-ordinated the whole. To all these and to others who helped in any way the Hampshire Federation Executive offer their grateful thanks.

Illustrations for the following villages were used by kind permission of the artists:

Hamble	– Nicholas Robinson
Kings Somborne	– Keith Chapman
Littleton	– Dorothy Deane
Longstock	– Anna Stone

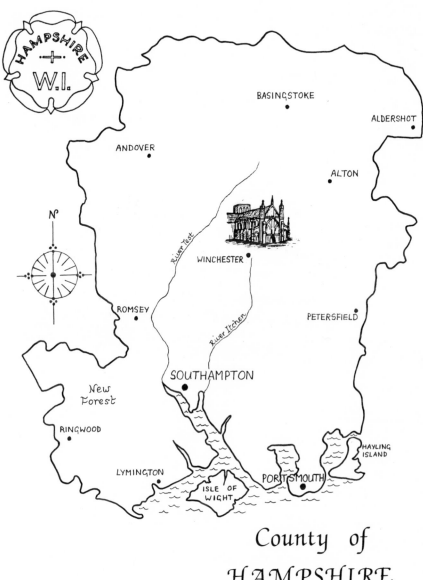

County of
HAMPSHIRE

Anna Stone

Abbotts Ann 🦋

The village of Abbotts Ann lies in the north-west corner of Hampshire on the edge of Salisbury Plain, just three miles south-west of Andover. It is picturesque with its many thatched cottages, avenues of chestnut and lime trees and a peaceful trout stream flowing through water meadows. Most of the village is now a conservation area.

Originally known as Anna, the name Abbotts Ann was given to the village in AD 901, after King Edward the Elder granted 15 hides of land from the valley to the Abbey of St Peter at Winchester.

As far as is known, the first settlement in the area was circa 50 BC when the Atrebates or Belgian Celts arrived by way of the rivers Test and Itchen. It appears to have been an important area during the Roman occupation, for a large Roman villa was discovered in the village in the 19th century. One of the fine mosaic floors is now displayed in the British Museum.

Abbotts Ann flourished as a farming area and was recorded in the Domesday Book as having five mills.

Bellarmine pots, dating from the medieval period, have been found under hearths and doorsteps. These pots had been filled with pins and noxious substances including urine, presumably to ward off evil spirits.

The most famous tradition in Abbotts Ann is the awarding of Virgins' Crowns, made to mark the death of men or women who were chaste in all senses, providing they were born in the village and were full members of the village church. The crowns were made of hazel twigs decorated with paper rosettes and had five parchment gauntlets hanging from them. At the funeral they were carried in front of the coffin by two girls dressed in white, and following the burial were hung above the font for three weeks to allow time for anyone to challenge the right of the deceased to this honour. The crown was then hung in the nave of the church, a small plaque being placed above with the dates of the Virgin's lifespan. The most recent crown was awarded in 1974.

The church was rebuilt in 1716 by Thomas Pitt, lord of the manor. He had returned from India with a large diamond which he sold to the Regent of France and consequently he was known as 'Diamond Pitt'. He was a relation of the Prime Minister, William Pitt.

In 1806 a young blacksmith named Robert Tasker came to live in the village. His invention of an improved plough in 1859 was such a success that he and his brothers built their own foundry in neighbouring Anna Valley. Amongst their famous achievements were many local wrought-iron bridges. During the Second World War, Taskers were famed for their long trailers – not least the 'Queen Mary', invaluable for transporting aeroplanes. A philanthropist, Robert Tasker founded the village school.

In the early 1930s, the Government bought Little Park Farm on the edge of the village and formed the Land Settlement Association. Families from the depressed areas of the North-East where unemployment and near-starvation were rife, were settled, each being given ten acres, a bungalow and a pig. The produce was sold by a central co-operative. During the 1970s this system was no longer considered viable. Settlers were given the option of buying their holdings and the remaining land was bought by the Hampshire College of Agriculture.

Farm workers are now in the minority. Since the growth of Andover, the village has become popular amongst professional, industrial and service people and of course is a pleasant area for the retired.

The nursery school has a waiting list and the primary school, threatened with closure a few years ago, is now flourishing. This, with a busy post office/village store, and two public houses, are proof enough of a thriving, friendly community.

Ampfield ᘔ፼

Ampfield derives its name from the spring that still rises within the church's grounds. 'An-felde' was the village's earliest name, 'an' being a Celtic word for a spring.

On the site of Gosport Farm stood a pilgrims' inn called 'God's Port', drawing its business from the old Saxon road running between Romsey and Winchester, and drawing its water from the ancient spring at Washers Well. The route of the main road has changed, however, and now the busy A31 carries its traffic well away from the site of the old inn. In 1610 a man named Wooll hanged himself at Gosport Farm. As the law demanded, he was buried as far from hallowed ground as possible, down by the railway bridge off Pound Lane – with a stake driven through his heart, to stop the Devil stealing his soul.

The original 'Morleys', pulled down at the turn of the century, was so-called because Richard Morley, the 17th century 'Hedge Poet', lived there for much of his life. A scythe was placed in the thatch 'to stop witches from frightening the children at night'.

Around the Potters Heron motel and restaurant were many pits from which local inhabitants once extracted clay to supplement their meagre incomes. A potter's treadle wheel can be known as a 'hern', because of its dipping motion, and hern is an old name for a heron.

St Mark's Day in April 1841 saw the consecration of John Keble's beautiful 'church in the wood', an event attended by many other leading

St Mark's church, Ampfield

members of the Oxford Movement, including J. H. Newman himself. This event coincided with the formation of the separate parish of Ampfield, but today the village shares its vicar with Hursley once more.

The village boundary with Braishfield still cuts through the middle of the lake at Wooley Green. At the turn of the century, May Day would see the local lads wading through the 6 ft of water and under the dividing chain, in the hope of receiving a kiss from the girls waiting for them on the other side.

The Rev W. Awdry, author of the *Thomas the Tank Engine* books, lived as a small boy in Ampfield, where his father was vicar of St Mark's. His earliest recollection is of going down Pound Lane, climbing up the embankment, and strolling along the old London & South-West Railway line.

The two World Wars did not pass Ampfield by. During the First World War a 'holding camp' was established here for horses on their way to France, but one day 20 of them vanished into the bogs off Pound Lane when a noisy train caused them to bolt into the undergrowth. The same area was used as a decoy aerodrome during the Second World War, complete with lights and what looked like a control tower. The Old Thatches public house became a First Aid post and the White Horse a mortuary (though it was never used). Considerable damage was caused to property by a parachute mine dropped just north of Body Farm, Pound Lane, but the many heavy air raids on Southampton left the village otherwise unscarred.

11

Until the 1930s Ampfield was a village predominantly feudal in character, dominated by the Ampfield House and estate, which comprised some 1,600 acres. In 1902 the Faber family took possession of the house and all the surrounding farms, and David Faber's death in 1931 led to the final break-up of the estate the following year.

Today Hilliers, the company of nurserymen, owns the house and some of its land. Agriculture employs very few of the villagers now, and the village is increasingly a dormitory for the businesses of Romsey, Eastleigh and Southampton. The village shop and its post office have gone, the school is under threat, and the old heart of the village at Knapp has been designated a conservation area.

Amport

Amport is a small village four miles west of Andover and over 300 ft above sea level, in the valley of Pillhill brook. William the Conqueror gave the land to Hugh de Port and since 'an' or 'anne' was a Celtic word for 'brook', so the village was called Anne de Port. Later this became Amport.

Evidence of man's occupation here stretches back over 5,000 years. Twenty-four Neolithic burial grounds are recorded in the parish. Beside the brook is the site of a Saxon Christian village. Today there are still tracks to be found which were once straight Roman roads. The Roman exports from this area included boy slaves, and near here a burial ground has been found containing the bones of over 60 girl babies.

Until the beginning of the 20th century sheep fairs were held in Weyhill, at the end of Sarson Lane. These were large fairs with over 140,000 sheep being sold in one day. Cornishmen also came to sell gold to Londoners, who travelled to Weyhill to buy the bullion. Thomas

Cottages at Amport

Hardy once attended a Weyhill fair and saw a drunk selling his wife and babe, for £5. He recorded this in his book *The Mayor of Casterbridge*. There are still some sheepfolds left at the site of the fair.

St Mary's church was built about 1320, probably on the site of a wooden, thatched church. It has been extended and altered several times. In 1988 it was re-roofed and now will stand for many more decades.

The present Amport House was built in 1857 and replaced two earlier houses built on the same site. In 1957 is was purchased by the Ministry of Defence and is now the home of the RAF Chaplains School. It is an impressive building set in beautiful gardens laid out by Sir Edwin Lutyens.

The village is mostly centred around the green by the Church of England school. The green is used for school games and local events such as maypole dancing and fetes.

The Hawk Conservancy in Amport is said to have the greatest collection of birds of prey in Britain. It is owned by Reginald Smith and family who train and breed the birds. Flying demonstrations of hawks and falcons are given daily throughout the summer months.

On the meadows beside the brook live several flocks of geese, which loudly announce their arrivals and departures. From the brook many brown trout find their way into the river Test, which provides some of the best trout fishing in Britain. A heron knows the brook well and can often be seen searching for his breakfast in the early morning. Nearby forests are the homes of deer. They can be seen in seasons of drought when they come to drink in the brook.

Horse breeding has been a local industry for centuries. Many successful racehorses have been born and trained nearby. It is a joy to see a string of racehorses, perhaps 20 or 30, pass through the village.

Amport is a beautiful village containing several thatched cottages, some of which were built in the 15th and 17th centuries.

Ashford Hill 🐌

Before the common was enclosed there were only two houses here, Brook Farm and Woodhouse Farm, together with a few squatters' cottages, tiny places with wattle walls and thatched roofs. Two of these cottages remain today. There was also a tiny wooden church, standing on Tuckers Hill. It was burned down in the late 1700s or early 1800s, during the common's enclosure.

Ashford Hill as a village began in the years 1800–1810 in the Old Cow Pen Lane, when most of the thatched cottages were built. The church and vicarage were built in about 1824 and the school soon after.

In the early 1900s Mr Cressor (Queen Victoria's dressmaker) came to the village, purchased some land from the Hopkins family and built Holt End House. Mr Hopkins was the village blacksmith at that time, while Mrs Hopkins ran the post office and shop. When Mr Hopkins died, his son Raymond took over and ran the forge until tractors replaced horses. He had the first petrol pump in the village. The old forge is now the post office and store.

When Mr Cressor died, Mr Driver bought Holt End House. He must have had the first car in the village, a canary-coloured Hispano Suiza. He used to roar up over the hill with his chauffeur sitting beside him!

Edwin Piper was the carrier. Every Thursday (market day) he would set off with a few passengers, collecting orders on the way. If anyone needed a new coat, hat, or anything at all, the shops in Newbury would send him back with boxes full of items on approval. Things not needed or not suitable would be returned next market day, along with the money to pay for any goods kept.

Ashford Hill had a turnpike at one time. The toll gate and house was on the Hampshire-Berkshire border, near the Pineapple Inn.

After the Second World War, London was looking for more sources of water and it was feared that Ashford Hill might be drowned to make a huge reservoir, with the head dam across the valley from Enborne Way to Brimpton. The scheme was abandoned, but during the geological survey the water meadows behind the Ship Inn were found to be so interesting in the mixture of soils and variety of plants that grow there, that the area is now a nature reserve.

The brick kiln has been here for centuries, since long before the village started. In the 1600s the kiln belonged to the Goddards of Blacknest estate, Brimpton, who also owned Ashford Hill Farm and Pineapple Farm. The estate was split up and sold in the late 1800s.

The biggest farmers in the village were the Mundys. Robert Mundy lived at Malt House, son Bertie at Dairy House, and another son, Teddy at Cary Lodge. Tommy Mundy, son of Teddy, was the last of the Ashford Hill Mundys when he died, at a very great age, in the 1980s.

The first council houses were built in 1927, those near the school a few years later, and Holt Cottages after the Second World War.

The bridge over the ford was built in 1828. The first one had only one arch, but another arch was added about 100 years later.

Ashmansworth

This small village in the north of the county stands on a high ridge very near the Berkshire boundary and has wonderful views of both counties. It is a long scattered village mostly devoted to agriculture and has at least five farms of some size. There has not been a great deal of modern building and there is a pleasant mixture of old thatched cottages and Hampshire flint houses. Ashmansworth has recently been designated a conservation area.

In the 10th century the ancient manor of Ashmansworth was granted to the Church in Winchester for the maintenance of the monks there and it remained for the most part in church ownership until the beginning of the 19th century, when it passed to the family of the Earl of Carnarvon.

The 12th century church of St James has some medieval murals although only a small section of these are now visible. In the porch there is a 20th century engraved window 'In praise of music' in memory of the composer Gerald Finzi, who lived in the village for many years.

There is no longer a school or a shop and the post office is only open five mornings a week. There is a modern, active village hall and the pub is popular with locals as well as long distance walkers on the Wayfarers Walk, which passes the edge of the village. In August the annual Flower Show and Fete attracts entries from all the neighbouring villages.

Ashurst & Colbury

Visitors to the New Forest who travel along the A35 from Southampton to Lyndhurst pass through Ashurst village. Some may discover it on a visit to the Ashurst Butterfly Farm or Longdown Dairy Farm. Others come by train to the local station, 'Lyndhurst Road', or stay at the well-equipped Ashurst campsite. All are within the administrative area of the newly formed civil parish of Ashurst and Colbury (1986).

Originally there were four villages: Colbury, Foxhills, Longdown and Ashurst. The name 'Ashurst' does not go back beyond the 1920s but was in general use in the 1930s. Prior to that it was known simply as Lyndhurst Road from the adjacent railway station, built in 1847. As its name denotes, this station was intended to serve Lyndhurst residents, gentry staying at Lyndhurst hotels or country house parties. This was the nearest approach permitted by local landowners and the line was nick-named 'The Weymouth Wanderer' from its circuitous route! The arrival of the railway is the explanation, perhaps, of the residential and commercial development of Ashurst in that location.

Colbury village centres round the church in Deerleap Lane and the Memorial Hall on Hunter's Hill. The name allegedly goes back to the 13th century when land was granted to the monks of Beaulieu Abbey to build a chapel at Colbury. Development here was helped by one family in particular, the Barker-Mills, who were benefactors and whose descendants still figure in local affairs. Their connections date back several centuries.

In 1870 Frank Ibbotson built the church at Colbury and endowed the living. He also built two schools at Colbury and Longdown. Marianne Vaudrey Barker-Mill, daughter of Frank Ibbotson, is a local legend. She built the Colbury Memorial Hall in 1928 in memory of her son Claude and other young men who died in the First World War. She made her home in Colbury, building Langley Manor where she administered her estates with charity and charm. She initiated a clothing fund for her estate workers which she personally supervised, and her annual tea-party and fete was a social highlight. The school fete was held in her field in Wharton's Lane and on Good Friday each child was given a hot cross bun by one of the Barker-Mills ladies on their return from church.

What is now Ashurst Hospital was formerly the New Forest Poor Law Institution, with 13 officers and 110 inmates in 1921. It catered for the destitute and needy children and was a night refuge for gentlemen of the road. In the Second World War it was used as a military hospital, helping with wounded from Dunkirk and later blitz victims from Portsmouth and Southampton.

Another feature of the village, St Joseph's House of Prayer, was once a large residence built for Mr Wharton, who gave his name to Wharton's Lane. The Dene, now St Joseph's, is currently presided over by Dominican sisters and a brand new chapel has been added. The Dene's boating lake has been drained to provide a recreation ground, which is occasionally waterlogged!

The character of buildings and status of residents has changed considerably. With the advent of 250 bungalows on ground previously owned by St Joseph's and many other modern residences, there are now more middle class, professional and retired residents. Previously the owners of large houses, their employees and workers on the Barker-Mill estates were typical, plus a few shopkeepers and railway employees. The earliest marriage certificate issued at Colbury church had to be signed with a cross because of illiteracy.

Some of the well-known landmarks have gone. There used to be a sign saying 'The Happy Cheese' on one side of the road near the station and one saying 'The Angry Cheese' on the other. Sadly only one remains. The Happy Cheese Restaurant, now a Beefeater Inn, has retained its sign but the Angry Cheese has gone forever!

16

Once ponies roamed freely along the A35 before the cattle-grids were installed. Now the traffic moves unhindered and the ponies have retreated from the fenced roads. But the Forest is still a feature and is not far away. Within minutes one can wander across open heathland where ponies dominate and in early morning and at dusk see rabbit, hare and deer. Ashurst and Colbury are within the Heritage area and feel part of the New Forest still.

Avington 🐚

Along the road from the lychgate of St John the Baptist's church at Itchen Abbas, lies the adjoining village of Avington with its fine old mansion of Avington Park.

The mansion is mentioned as early as AD 961 in the reign of King Edgar and some evidence suggests that its history goes back to pre-Roman times. Many Royal visitors have lived there including Charles II with Nell Gwynne, for whom a bathing pool was made, and later the Prince Regent and Mrs Fitzherbert. It was bought in 1848 by Sir John Shelley and remained in the family until 1952. Today the house is divided into flats and part of it is opened to the public at weekends. The call of several resident peacocks can often be heard across the valley.

Adjoining the medieval to 18th century parkland is the church of St Mary. It has old, high box pews made of Spanish mahogany – timber taken from an Armada galleon, and the pulpit is domed. It is said to be one of the most perfect Georgian churches in the country.

Worthy of note is the Pinder Centre in Avington which provides hydrotherapy, physiotherapy and remedial swimming and is fully equipped for the disabled. It was opened in 1973, converted from the 18th century coach house and stables of Avington House.

Awbridge 🐚

Awbridge (pronounced Aybridge) can lay no particular claim to fame. Its main attraction is its lovely rolling countryside. The beech woods and rhododendron-lined roads are a delight in spring. One boundary follows the river Test and there are several trout lakes. The lake at Awbridge Danes was made in the 1920s to provide work for the local unemployed, each man receiving one shilling a day and a loaf of bread.

Roman occupation in the area is suggested by a villa found on aerial survey, and tiles, pottery and coins have been found at Awbridge House dating from AD 307. The Saxons, and later the Normans, had hunting lodges at nearby Stanbridge Earls (whose estates until recently covered large parts of the village) and Awbridge Danes, and the village is still well wooded.

The names Danes Road and Awbridge Danes record the troubled times of the Danish occupation, and there is a Danish fort just outside the boundary. A battle may have been fought against them on Awbridge Common. Sadly the common has been enclosed and partly built on but a present inhabitant recalls that his grandfather had the right to graze two heifers, six sheep, pigs and twelve geese there in the 19th century. There is evidence of Cromwell's armies camping on the common, as Italian prisoners of war found a Cromwellian pike-head during the Second World War.

For many centuries Awbridge was a very small settlement. By the 1600s there were only half a dozen substantial houses, of which four still stand. By 1800 there were about 40 houses and a population of some 400. Recent building has raised numbers to 661 (1988). Present inhabitants are mainly commuters to nearby large towns but there are still half a dozen farms, a mushroom farm, golf course, nurseries and smallholdings, builders and small engineering firms, as well as the local shop/post office. Contrast the present with 1878, when the village could boast its own shoemaker, blacksmith, baker and brewer.

Several main routes once went through the village. From Romsey, minor roads still go to Salisbury, Andover and the garrison town of Tidworth (B3084). The railway to Bristol and Southampton skirts the village edge. The Andover road was once a turnpike road and has several tollhouses. Stories are told of how canny villagers carried their sheep through to avoid paying a farthing!

A local WI member recalls how her grandmother remembered villagers using 'rough justice' on errant wives. The offender's house was surrounded by women banging saucepan lids, hurling abuse and stones in an effort to get her to mend her ways. This was called 'scimmering' and was apparently a widespread local practice.

The parish itself is relatively modern, having been carved out of surrounding parishes in the 1870s. The church was built in 1876 at a cost of £2,800 and is a pleasant, unpretentious building in pretty surroundings. The village school dates from 1877.

Electricity first reached the village in 1939 but the last house was not connected until 1963. Mains water was installed in 1951 and many older houses still have their own wells. Awbridge is still waiting for mains sewerage, but then in a village things never do happen very quickly!

18

Barton-on-Sea 🍂

Barton-on-Sea looks out to Christchurch Bay, with a frontage over a mile long between Milford-on-Sea and Highcliffe. It has earned fame by giving its name to a type of fossil found in its cliffs and clay.

In addition to fossils many palaeolithic implements have been found in the area, mainly around Chewton Bunny. There is a collection of these implements in the Ashmolean Museum in Oxford.

In the late 18th and early 19th centuries smuggling was rife. Barton's cliffs, with their commanding views of Christchurch Bay and the Isle of Wight, provided excellent facilities for surveying the coast and making sure all was clear for a landing. Forest ponies were often used, with sacks on their backs to hold the kegs of brandy and other goods, to take the cargoes all the way from Barton cliffs into the New Forest. The hiding places were cleverly concealed 'under the hearth' and 'under the horse's belly', which meant under the flagstones of a fireplace or where the horses were stabled. Situated on the cliff top at the west end of Barton was Naish Farm. A tunnel ran from the farm to Chewton Glen (where the well known luxury hotel now stands).

During the First World War Barton Court Hotel, situated on the cliff top and now gradually slipping into the sea, became a convalescent home for British troops. Later, huts were erected along the cliff top of Barton Drive and, much to the surprise of the residents, hundreds of Indian troops were sent to convalesce there. An obelisk stands at the bottom of Barton Court Avenue to commemorate their stay.

Repeated falls have, over the years, reduced dramatically the area of the cliff top. The 'slumping' of water seeping through the gravel and sand of the cliffs until it reaches the impermeable clay, together with the waves whipped up by the strong winds over the bay which carry away the debris brought down by the slumping, are the main causes of the falls which present a constant problem for the local council.

The golf course at the eastern end of the cliffs had its origins in 1897 when a nine hole course was made on the cliff top. This was followed by an inland course in 1909 and the present course in 1932. Cliff erosion has presented problems here too and extra acres have been purchased at times. The erosion continues – so do the problems.

The novelist Elizabeth Goudge lived for a while with her parents in Barton Lane. In her autobiography she described Barton as 'a flat green plateau that is now a vast bungalow town'.

Barton House was taken over by the British Council for Aid to Refugees in 1956. It is a large, red-brick house facing Christchurch Bay which became home to many refugees, mainly from Eastern European countries, though help is now extended to the whole world. In 1961 an Orthodox chapel was built in the grounds and consecrated by Bishop Nikodem. The oldest refugee on arrival was a Russian woman of 92, who came to Barton with her 70 year old son.

Bashley ✒️

The New Forest is to the north of the village, and the sea two miles to the south, past the now large urban area of New Milton and Barton-on-Sea. The B3058 runs through the village from the Forest, passing the Rising Sun pub at Wootton and further on the shop, garage, cricket ground and the village hall and recreation ground. The little church, built before the First World War, is along St John's Road to the east.

The Danes had a great battle with the Saxons to the east of the village in the area called Wootton Rough, and the stream known as Danestream, that runs alongside, is said to have run red with blood. The new housing etate to the south-east of the village is called Daneswood.

Roads have changed little except to be widened and not much new building has taken place, although the south-eastern area, where there was a nursery garden, orchard and wood, has now been developed. One of the oldest lanes in the district, Cull Lane, has been closed to through traffic. Another, Stem Lane, has sunk over the centuries so that it lies below the level of adjoining fields.

Road names come from inhabitants who used to live there, eg Marks Lane from Mark Whitcher who lived in the corner cottage, formerly known as Mark's Cottage. Some roads are named by what went on there, eg Marlpit Lane – where marl was dug for the local handmade brick-works. At the corner of Smithy Lane and Bashley Cross Road there was a blacksmith's.

Mr Ernie Rickman lived on the main road not far from The Rising Sun and made his own motor cycle – he later moved and opened the Ashley Garage. He was one of the first speedway riders, riding for Southampton. His sons opted for motor cycle scrambling and were of international fame, and made and rode the 'Matise'. They now have a factory in Gore Road, New Milton.

Being comparatively near the sea, a great deal of smuggling went on in years gone by. Contraband was taken from the coast at Barton to Hoburne House, thence to Buffalo Cottage at Wootton via Smugglers Lane and a pub situated at Beehive Hill, now no longer there.

Early in the 20th century there was a washhouse at the back of the house known as 'Gilpin's' in St John's Road. Windmill House (and other large houses in the area) had a windmill and the power was used to pump water and make electricity. Cottages used their own wells and had candles. Pigs were kept at the corner of Cull Lane and Sway Road and this small area is still known as Pigsty Corner.

On the corner of New Lane and Bashley Cross Road are two cottages. The one known as 'Missioners' was a chapel. The one known as 'Taverners' was a wayside inn.

The original village shop was part of the cottage known as 'homestead' by the smithy. It has two front doors – one of which was the shop door. It did a roaring trade whilst the railway line was being built in 1887 to 1888, selling goods to the Irish navvies. Of course, there was no New Milton then – just a country road through trees and fields.

The Football Club have gone from strength to strength in recent years. They lease the recreation ground for matches and training and have built a clubhouse next to the village hall. The team were the Wessex League Champions from 1987 to 1989, before joining the Southern League. There are three teams of youngsters who play regularly.

Years ago skilled workmen in the village produced scaffolding, wattle fences, hurdles and besoms.

Basing 🐚

Basing is one of many small villages in the north of Hampshire situated on the Berkshire/Surrey borders. It has many traditional activities, such as the annual carnival. The lovely 11th century church of St Mary has a flower festival, and a horticultural show attracts many exhibits in the village hall. All of these are always extremely successful.

The ruins of Basing House are a great tourist attraction. It is said that the Marquis of Winchester held out in this house for two years during the Civil War, until it was stormed by Cromwell's army and captured in 1645. Also Queen Elizabeth I is believed to have visited Basing in 1601 and slept the night in the house. Excavations are still in progress on the site.

The main roadway through Basing is named The Street. Today it is a busy thoroughfare, but going back to the 1930s this was a street where everything happened, but at a much slower pace. The ruins of Basing House at one end where children loved to explore the mysterious tunnels, and the peaceful river Loddon at the other where children often splashed about in the clear water are, alas, no longer available to enjoy.

The rows of cottages were homes for farm workers on the Hackwood estate. There was a forge which was manned by Richard Hall and his partner, Mr Wiggins, where the farmhorses came to be shod and farming implements were repaired. There were three small shops, a post office, a reading room and a village hall where all social functions took place, such as dances (when the back of your hand was date stamped if you wanted to go outside for a while!), whist drives and WI meetings.

On the wall of Vine Cottage an unusual sign once read 'Well Borer and Dew Pond Marker – Jack Smith'.

Bartons Mill and Lower Mill are on the banks of the river Loddon which flows through the village and these mills gave employment to a few, but most people walked or cycled into nearby Basingstoke to work.

A small charabanc was the first public transport from Basing into Basingstoke and this ran each Wednesday and Saturday operated by Mr Reynolds, who lived opposite The Crown Inn.

Since those days, changes have taken place and there are now four shops and a post office at the centre of the village and a large food store, with doctors' and dentists' surgeries at one end, and a veterinary surgeon and shop at the other.

If you are really lucky, you may see a ghost dressed in a long blue dress and dark cloak walking from the recreation ground along The Street and vanishing near the river Loddon. Yes, Basing is a lovely village to look at, and it also has an air of mystery!

Baughurst ❧

Baughurst, pronounced Borg-hurst, is situated on the north Hampshire/ Berkshire border in the middle of the Newbury/Basingstoke/Reading triangle. Baughurst means 'bog wood' and although there are still a number of gravel pits around the surrounding district to account for the excess water, the woods have long since been cleared for housing development.

Aldermaston Park became Aldermaston Aerodrome during the Second World War and was used by the Americans. Thereafter it became the Atomic Weapons Establishment employing a large number of people. To accommodate these people, large areas of Baughurst and Tadley Commons were transformed into award-winning housing estates. Although many light industries have since moved into the area, AWE is still by far the main employer.

The building of a replacement village hall has been a major project in recent years, with numerous fund raising events organised by an extremely hard working committee of villagers. It was finally opened in October 1988 by the Duchess of Wellington, whose grandparents, the McConnells, gave the land to the village for the original hall, scout hut and green. The McConnells lived in Heath End House and had a small church, Little St Mary's, built near them to save travelling to St Stephen's.

Baughurst Road is about four miles in length and the village can boast four public houses, a post office and a parade of shops including two 'take-aways', a newsagent's/food store, off licence and hairdresser's.

A derelict bus depot in Baughurst Road has recently been saved from demolition by developers when a local planning officer from Basingstoke & Deane Council noticed it had a unique feature. The timber-framed building had been built in the earlier part of the century in a style favoured for a great many factories and warehouses, but featured the largest single-span roof in Western Europe – the roof trusses span some 80 ft from end to end without support underneath. The roof has been carefully rebuilt by a local builder and when complete, the building will be used as offices.

The present St Stephen's church was built in 1845 on the site of a Saxon church which has burned down. It is Gothic in style with an unusual octagonal tower. The church contains a 15th century choir screen which is now at the western end, screening part of the organ. The screen is rich in carving and is said to have been the gift of a Lord Chancellor of England, Archbishop Warham, who rose rapidly to power under Henry VII but lost his influence to Cardinal Wolsey. The old church contained a Jacobean oak pulpit which was removed from the ruins.

As well as the annual church fete, the church hosts an annual flower festival which is held over a weekend in early summer in aid of charity. A team of talented parishioners decorate the church and entrance with beautiful floral arrangements based on the nominated theme for that year.

Beaulieu ❧

The Cistercian village of Beaulieu grew out of the abbey, founded by King John in 1204. Its mill, wells and High Street fascinate visitors as they walk on its uneven and ancient stones. The Beaulieu estate came into the possession of the Montagu family in Henry VIII's time. Beaulieu village has a population of 860. There is a staff of 16 on the estate; Montagu Ventures has a staff of 18 in the winter and 267 in the summer!

Lord Montagu has opened his house to the public since 1952 and very much enjoys meeting his many visitors. Together with the Abbey and the Motor Museum, Beaulieu is well placed in the country's 'league' of stately homes. The famous Montagu Motor Museum was founded in memory of his father, John Montagu, who successfully persuaded Parliament to abolish the 12mph speed limit, and obliged motorists to register their cars and obtain licences to drive them. It was he who equipped the Army in India with mechanical transport during the First World War. Edward, the present Lord Montagu, is a vintage car enthusiast. He also takes an active part in the House of Lords. Edward's mother, the Hon Mrs Pleydell-Bouverie, has lived in the village since 1920. She now lives in the Lodge, which is the dower house of the estate. She always takes an active part in village life and is a founder member of the Beaulieu Women's Institute.

Beaulieu Abbey Church has a fine monument in the chancel of great interest to visiting Australians. It is to Bishop Tyrrell, one-time vicar of Beaulieu, who went to Newcastle, Australia, and eventually became their first bishop.

The village fire brigade was one of the earliest in the county of Hampshire, and before the Second World War was the private fire brigade of the Beaulieu estate. The village shops, the centre of village life, include the newsagent where messages are frequently passed on, a high class couturiere, an art gallery, a craft shop which replaced the butcher, and the Ruth Liversedge Chocolate Parlour, whose hand-made chocolates are sold worldwide. The village hall hosts lectures, dramas, bingo, elections, weddings and many other events. A vineyard flourishes on the south facing slopes above the museum.

One could not leave Beaulieu without mentioning the river, with Bucklers Hard so near to the centre of the yachting world, together with the riverside farms, woods, bird sanctuary, and the estuary shores so abundant with wildlife.

Beauworth 🦮

Beauworth lies on a sweep of high ground, the Millbarrows Ridge, on the northern side of the Hampshire downs in what has been designated an Area of Outstanding Natural Beauty. Despite the prehistoric long barrows, which are evidence of early occupation, the village only became a separate parish in 1879. However, according to charters dating from AD 909, its boundaries lay within the Saxon manor of Tichborne and the village was recorded in the Domesday Book.

The area, mainly chalk with clay caps and many natural springs, is agricultural, although the majority of the inhabitants no longer work on the land. There are now less than 50 dwellings and the population, in 1987, was estimated at 100. The earliest cottages, Church Terrace (once three but now two homes) date from the 16th century. In the early 1800s the centre room was used as a school room. A number of the cottages are thatched and several had indoor wells. Only one house has been built in recent years.

The Saxon church has disappeared; the only remains are stone heads in Cheriton churchyard. The present church of St James was built in 1833 by Mr H. Mulcock, who owned a brick kiln at nearby Shorley Farm, in Cheriton, where local clay was used to make tiles, flower pots and extra-large bricks.

Beauworth school, built in the 1840s, by 1907 could not cope with the number of children so a new school was built on a site opposite the Fox and Hounds public house. The old school then became the village hall. Gradually the number of pupils declined until the new school, in turn, was closed in the late 1960s and is now a private house.

The Fox and Hounds, recently enlarged by the addition of a restaurant, has been renamed the Milburys, a corruption of 'Millbarrows'. It is famed for its treadwheel, which drew water from a well said to be 365 ft deep and which was worked by manpower, one of very few of its kind in the country. Fifty years ago the landlord was also the village carpenter and undertaker.

One day in June 1833, some boys were playing near the village pond, now drained and forming part of the garden at Manor House Farm. One boy stumbled over what appeared to be a piece of lead pipe. His companions scrabbled in the ground with their fingers and discovered what they thought was an old metal box full of buttons. They hastily filled their pockets then ran home to tell their parents. The 'buttons' were in fact coins, about 6,000 in all and in mint condition, dating from the reigns of William the Conqueror and William II. They were declared treasure trove and are now in the British Museum. The lead coffer in which they were found is in Winchester Museum.

Another find was made in 1957 when, in an area of heavy undergrowth, Roman tiles and building materials were found. These led to the discovery of the site of a Roman villa covering some two and a half acres – further evidence that this has long been considered a desirable place to live.

In 1926 a lady named Miss Watts, who lived in one of the cottages by the green, decided to start a pottery, hoping to use local clay. Unfortunately this proved unsuitable for her purpose. Even so, the pottery was established and she produced some blue and yellow ware, marked with a Greek pi (π).

Bedhampton 🌿

Bedhampton was once merely a straggling parish one mile from the town of Havant and, in spite of the growth and development of the village, it still retains an attractive look where it lies close to the foreshore of Langstone Harbour.

There have been various mills in the vicinity. One, the Upper Mill, was owned by a John Snook, who is said to have provided flour for biscuits made in its own ovens for the troops in the Crimean War.

The manor appears to have existed as far back as the 9th century. It is now in the caring hands of a charitable trust set up in 1967. The manor house is now an excellent environment for the elderly. Close to the manor is the 12th century church of St Thomas.

A turreted house named The Elms (18th century) was acquired by Sir John Theophilus Lee and a room within named the Waterloo Room. Sir John was a friend of the Duke of Wellington, who was reputed to have dined there, and the room has been beautifully restored in white and Wedgwood blue. The house is also owned by the Manor Trust.

At the old Mill House in 1819, John Keats the poet stayed with the master baker Mr John Snook and his wife. He had walked from Chichester for a house party, and this is where he finished his poem *The Eve of St Agnes*. He also spent his last night in England here when his ship was delayed in Portsmouth because of a storm. Subsequently he left for Naples, only to die there in 1821. The house is well preserved.

Bedhampton had its share of smuggling in the past. Langstone Harbour was the haunt of smugglers during the 18th and 19th centuries and there was many a skirmish with the Revenue officers chasing after such men. A then nearby inn, the Cat and Fiddle on Bedhampton Hill, is said to have been used by them. The Golden Lion along the main road to Havant was the first stage coaching inn out of Portsmouth and some older villagers say that it has been known to be haunted!

Bentley 🌿

Bentley is on the A31 between Farnham and Alton. It lies in the middle of an area which has been inhabited at least since Roman times and there are the foundations and floors of a Roman villa in a field at the western end. In the forest of Alice Holt is the site of one of the largest Roman potteries in the country which produced goods for the occupying forces and also for export.

The name Bentley means 'green by the forest' and this is still a mainly agricultural area, although the fields, and fields of hops for which the district was famous, are now nearly all gone and comparatively few people are employed on the land.

In Norman and medieval times the houses clustered nearer to the 12th century church of St Mary which is on a hill about half a mile north of the main road. The Pilgrims' Way, which led by the shortest route from church to church from Winchester to Canterbury, passes through Jenkyn Place courtyard, where it is said the pilgrims used to stop and drink from a well called 'Jancknes's Well', from which the house gets its present name.

The church itself was much restored in the 14th and 15th centuries and again in the 19th. It plays a prominent part in the life of the village. Jane Austen's brother Henry was perpetual curate of Bentley from 1824 to 1838 and lived at the 'old' rectory on the main road. With others in the parish he subscribed to the setting up of the cage, which was built for the 'temporary imprisonment of the drunk and disorderly', formerly detained in a public house. Nothing of it now remains except the name, given to a row of cottages near the site, nor of the stocks, whipping post or ducking stool once situated between the main road, pond and Grafton Cottage!

Bentley must have been a very prosperous place in Tudor times, judging by the fine houses which have survived, though in many cases obscured by 18th century façades. One of the most beautiful is Marelands, where the naturalist Gilbert White stayed on occasions. A ghost is said to haunt the house.

Bentley village sign

The Eggar family have played a prominent part in the village and its surroundings since the 16th century and at one time owned Jenkyn Place and much of the surrounding land and properties. A Mr Sanderson, who was a director of the White Star Shipping Line, owners of the *Titanic*, was holding a dinner party at Jenkyn Place the evening he was told of the disaster in 1912.

Another famous Bentley resident was the Chief Scout, Lord Baden-Powell, who bought Blackacre in 1919 and changed its name to the world-renowned 'Pax Hill'. Since his death in 1941 the house has had various uses but is now one of two nursing homes, the other being at The Quinta. He was also mainly responsible for the design and construction of the Memorial Hall which he opened in 1920, on land given by the Eggar family, and of the village sign with its archer.

Bentley has its own railway station with a good service to London. It was once an important junction serving a branch line for the military at Bordon. Station Road itself was originally known as 'Pickling Lane', as it was used for 'pickling' the sleepers when the lines were laid.

Bighton ૐ

In the 10th century the settlement of Bighton was known as 'Bykingtune', and an even earlier reference in AD 701 mentions a grant of land including the manor and greater part of the parish, made by King Ine to Winchester Cathedral.

The church dates back to 1196, but Saxon traces have been found in an old window and it is thought a wattle and daub building stood on the site in Saxon times. In olden times all the cottages housed agricultural workers who were employed mainly by the owner of the manor farm, but in recent years these have been sold to professional people who travel away from the village to their place of work.

The public house is named The Three Horseshoes, believed to stem from three real horseshoes which were nailed up on the outside fabric of the house. This was the sign of the Farriers' Guild, and a blacksmith's shop did once exist in the village.

A tragedy recorded in 1743 states that an Edward Weekes was buried on 5th November; 'His skull was fractured in a well by ye bucket falling in upon him and he died in ye hospital at Winchester.'

There are several old houses in the village. The manor is a scheduled historic building with a William and Mary frontage. The Old Rectory is a compact Georgian house, and High Dell House is a double-storeyed colour-washed house with a thatched roof. The older houses in the village are of mellowed brick, or flint with thatched roofs. At Bighton House, part of which is late Georgian, a donkey treadwheel was used to supply the house with water.

Bighton is not without its ghost, named Kate Neville. She was supposedly brutally murdered in a lonely spot between Alresford and the village – the quiet lane is still known as Kate Neville's Walk.

Many changes have taken place in village life, especially since the Second World War. In earlier days the large houses employed a staff of up to 15 or 20 servants. The old village bakery has been gone for many a year – the bread, freshly baked, was delivered by pony cart, together with orders from the village store. The children would open the bakehouse door and tease the old baker and a large lump of dough would hit them on the ear – happy days! The area in the village which has changed most is Gundelton where, after the First World War, a hamlet sprang up, built mainly of galvanised tin bungalows (smallholdings) known locally as 'Tin Town' – a name which much annoyed the inhabitants there. These have now been replaced by modern bungalows and houses.

Few of the old field names remain, such as Mutton Hangers, Church Lands, Saintfoin and Gattage; the hedges have been uprooted and all fields swept into one.

Binley & Wadwick 🌿

Situated about two miles from St Mary Bourne, Binley and Wadwick are two hamlets closely connected by two footpaths and a minor road.

Since Binley has the only inn, the Hurdlemakers Arms, it is not surprising that the Wadwick dwellers trod the nearest routes on thirsty evenings.

The name of the pub gives the clue to what was once the major industry, since the whole area is surrounded by hazel copses, which supplied the hurdles for folding the sheep. Now the sheep are fenced by electric fences, and the hazel copses supply only pea sticks, bean poles, clothes props, and ample cover for the deer and pheasants.

Wadwick was once two farms, and Upper Wadwick and Lower Wadwick still each have a 'big house', and three cottages. Upper Wadwick houses the workers: a game-keeper, a woodman and a farm tractor driver; while Lower Wadwick is reserved for those who have retired. There is one barn remaining, which has been converted for the rearing of day-old partridges and pheasants, a substantial source of income.

There is also a reserve for young spruce trees, which are dug up every few years for Christmas, and then the area is replanted with new ones. Most of the hazel woods have been augmented by conifers, but in the last few years mixed deciduous and coniferous trees have been used for afforestation. These jobs keep the woodman employed, and there is also a lively trade in logs for wood burning stoves. The great storm of 1987 supplied, sadly, a lot of timber for this purpose.

The tractor driver is kept busy on the arable fields of the surrounding farmland. The crops are mainly barley, but wheat and also peas and tic beans are grown, and a few strips of maize as cover for the pheasants.

Binley has a couple of smaller farms with sheep on one and dairy and store cattle on the other. It also has a telephone by the side of the inn, while each hamlet has a letter box, one let into the wall of a barn, the other attached to a post. There is no public transport, although Binley once had a weekly bus to Newbury.

On the outskirts of the hamlet, going towards Stoke and Lye Farm, is a derelict piece of land known as 'the garden'. A middle-aged man built himself a house here, and planted the land as a smallholding. However, apparently he was not a good carpenter, because he did not build a staircase, but installed a ladder which he pulled up at night when he went to bed. His poor wife could not have been as agile as he, because she was forced to sleep downstairs. Whether or not she disapproved of this idea we do not know. But one night the house caught fire, and the master could not get the ladder down to escape and was burned to death. Since then no one has lived there, but the foundations can still be seen. It seems that the old man's spirit cannot rest, because when anyone trims the hedges and lights a fire, his ghost appears in the smoke.

Bishops Sutton ॐ

Should you be a passenger travelling on the Watercress Line steam train from New Alresford to Alton, the first village you will see from the right-hand side of the train is Bishops Sutton – or as written in the Domesday Book, 'Sudtone' meaning South Town. In 1136 King Stephen exchanged Sudtone with his half-brother Bishop Henry de Blois of Winchester for another manor in Surrey, hence it became Bishops Sutton.

Over the railway bridge you will see the 'faire great fermhowse' – Western Court – described by the surveyor of Edward IV in the 15th century as belonging to the Lord Chief Justice. It is now the home of the Coles family, who have in their possession a beautifully written account of two Beatings of the Bounds in 1745 and 1747, when men and boys of the village set up boundstones around the parish for Mrs Catherine Venables, lady of the manor of Westerncourt. The boundaries, together with the names, ages and occupations of the 'beaters' are faithfully recorded – occupations such as coachbuilders, wheelwrights, blacksmith, carpenters, farmers, labourers, maltsters, woodmen, yeomen, servants, and an ex-'tythman'!

Next you will come to Sutton Manor, lying close by the 12th century church of St Nicholas, whose vicar in 1796, one William Howlett, became Archbishop of Canterbury in 1828. From the church you will see that the village runs alongside the cress beds where workers in their high, green rubber boots are tending the watercress in the streams, a major industry of the area.

The big garden of Whitefriars (formerly 'The Ruins'), which is in the centre of the village, is where, in the mid to late 1800s, zebra, llamas, emu, peacocks and many other rare animals and exotic birds roamed free – for this was the great racing stables of Arthur Scotland Yates, the gentleman trainer who lived opposite Whitefriars in a large house called Lacklands. It was at these stables the fine horse *Cloisters* was trained, and you can imagine the excitement in the village when it won the Grand National of 1893. William Dollery was the winning jockey, and it is said that he built his house in the village named 'Cloisters' with his proceeds from that memorable race.

With a great racing stable and many horses working in harness, the village had a very large blacksmith's forge and shop, which in 1874 lay on either side of the road through the village. The old custom of 'Firing the Anvil' used to take place near what is now Parkers Cottage. Believed to have been performed in the 1600s to ward off evil spirits from the forge, it later became the customary climax to festivities marking national or local events, and to the completion of farriers' and blacksmiths' apprenticeships. Suffice to say that the method of 'firing the anvil' is still known to some blacksmiths; it is in fact a controlled explosion sounding like cannon fire, a loud bang, flash, and clouds of smoke – it has been called 'playing fireworks on the anvil'.

Bishopstoke ✣

The village of Bishopstoke, which today forms part of the borough of Eastleigh, has a recorded history going back to Saxon times. The water-mill which stood astride the river Itchen at the bottom of the village was mentioned in the Domesday Book. There was still a working mill until 1934 when the last building was demolished. Its memory remains, however, for locals boarding the bus in Eastleigh still ask for The Mill.

The river Itchen is a famous trout and salmon river and local boys can have permits to fish in certain stretches. During Victorian times water carnivals were held on it. Also running through the village is one of the oldest canals in the country – the Itchen Navigation. The men who worked the barges were given a certificate of exemption from 'salt water experience' to protect them from the press gangs, but the last boat carrying goods between Southampton and Winchester was in the 1860s. Nowadays the path alongside the canal is a favourite walk, called by locals 'going along The Barge'.

There were two pubs facing the river, but the Anchor is now a doctor's surgery. The Anglers, marked on the 1825 enclosure map, is still in use.

A mix of old and new buildings is evident throughout the village. A pair of 17th century thatched cottages stands next to houses built in the 1930s. The late 18th century manor house, in grounds across the river from the Anglers, has been converted into flats, with a new, but harmonising second block built beside it. Tight planning controls are kept on this area of the village, as it is a conservation area, very pleasant with its open spaces, trees and running water.

The inhabitants of the village until the middle of the 19th century were farmers and farm workers. One of the wealthier farming families were the Twynams, whose charitable works are commemorated by a plaque in the church. The Lavingtons were another well known family, farming at West Horton Farm since 1786 and their descendant, Arthur Lavington is still there.

Another distinguished resident was Admiral of the Fleet, Sir Henry Keppel, who died in 1904. He acquired a large neo-Gothic house, inappropriately named 'The Cottage', later known as Itchen House as the river runs through its grounds. The Admiral experimented with breeding trout there, and some of the rivers in Tasmania were stocked with fish from Bishopstoke.

The opening of the railway line from London to Southampton in 1840 marked the beginning of many changes in the village. Land was advertised for sale to newcomers and 'highly desirable residences' were built, such as Longmead House, a red-brick mansion with 23 bedrooms, set in grounds of 46 acres. This estate was put up for auction in 1928 and some of the land was sold off in small plots upon which houses were built in the 1930s. The former carriage drive to the house is now East Drive, bordered by the original line of tall trees. Stoke Park Road, which ran along one edge of the estate was a mustering point in the Second World War for American soldiers before D-Day. Their field kitchen was set up on the site where bungalows were later built.

Another large Victorian mansion is 'The Mount', later converted to a sanatorium and now a geriatric hospital. Nearby are two other Victorian buildings. St Mary's church was built in 1890 to 1891 to replace the old church which was near the river. Fierce controversy raged for many years because some of the villagers wanted to retain the use of the old church, but it was finally abandoned, although the yew tree planted in 1694 is still growing there. Opposite St Mary's is the village school of 1880.

Eastleigh became an urban district in 1894 and Bishopstoke was amalgamated with it in 1899. However, it is hardly necessary to make the two mile trip to Eastleigh, for grouped near the mill are all the shops and services necessary for daily life. It is also a point of pride with villagers that their history is longer than Eastleigh's. Even the railway station was originally Bishopstoke junction (for Eastleigh).

Bishop's Waltham ༄

Bishop's Waltham is known as a small town but many residents still think of it as a village. It was, and still is, a nice place to live, but gone are the days when children could walk anywhere in safety and roam the woods and fields. It was a hard life, when, to make ends meet, the women went stone picking, pea picking and strawberry picking; but everyone seemed happy and always ready to help each other. Children made their own entertainment, playing in the road with tops and skipping ropes. We had a flourishing Salvation Army band and I seem to hear the chant 'Penny on the drum' now!

There was a railway station but this has now gone to make way for a new road across the Pond. There were also two brickyards employing many local men. Progress is not always a bad thing but so many hedgerows and fields have been lost, where wild flowers and mushrooms grew. There are now two good council schools in the village, three churches and a Gospel hall, two Women's Institutes, cricket and football teams and a youth club.

Bishop's Waltham House is a home for the frail built in ideal surroundings. The Priory was a seminary run by the White Fathers; after it was sold it became a police college but is now derelict and awaiting redevelopment. Holm Oak, a large house in Bank Street, was demolished to make way for flats for the elderly, and is now known as Roman Row. Cromwell knocked down the Bishop's Palace; the ruins still remain and are a great attraction. The Pond provided fish for the Palace but now the Fishing Club has taken over and fish themselves. The Pond is also home for wildfowl.

There are a number of footpaths where the public can escape from the busy roads. The old railway track is now a public footpath, thanks to the Bishop's Waltham Society who worked hard to make this possible.

We have a good variety of shops and two car parks, but a whole street of houses had to be demolished to make one car park. St Stephen's Castle Down was once an open space but it is now used for training racehorses.

Bitterne 🌿

Bitterne on the river Itchen has been a village for many centuries. The name means 'bend in the river' and is not, as in general belief, named after the bird. Since the early 1900s, Bitterne has been gradually spreading, losing its village status to become just another suburb of Southampton. The final blow came in the early 1980s when the heart of Bitterne was literally taken out. The Bitterne by-pass was opened and this cut the village in half, connected only by the underpasses. To make way for the bypass many old established homes and businesses were demolished. It caused more havoc than the bombing during the Second World War, and Bitterne had its share of that.

One well-known local location went in the dramatic change – the animal pound situated behind the Methodist church was built over. A newsagent's now occupies the site. The village school, Methodist and United Reformed churches lost their battle for survival, although one must add that they have been rebuilt at different locations. The village playing field completely disappeared, taking with it memories of where many a young lad learned to kick a ball.

The parish church has stood the test of time and is still the centre of many community activities. In its grounds are the bowling green, tennis courts and church hall. There are still many old Bitterne families living in the area and the community spirit is very much alive, so much so that a Bitterne Local History Society has been formed. Several books have been written and also displays of local memorabilia are often held.

Life has not wholly changed for the worse, as there is now a shopping precinct, two supermarkets, a leisure centre, a bowling alley and a modern health centre. Bitterne, like the phoenix, is rising from the ashes. The stone lion that stood for 150 years over the small parade of shops in Bitterne Road, has been restored and now stands on a plinth in front of the Red Lion public house. Another landmark, the horse trough, stands at the Lances Hill end of the precinct.

Blackfield 🌿

Blackfield is a large semi-industrialised village in the parish of Fawley, on the very outskirts of the New Forest. It still has some of the old rural atmosphere about it in that the New Forest can easily be reached on foot, and it is only a short distance from Lepe beach, used by the Allied forces for embarkation on D-Day. There is a regular bus service to Hythe and Southampton.

In the 1920s it was a truly rural area. The roads were unmade with wide ditches and hedges; they were also gated to keep out the New Forest ponies. There was no public transport except the carrier's cart, which would take passengers to Hythe on a Tuesday to catch the 10 am ferry to Southampton. The carrier would also do any shopping required by local people which was unobtainable in Blackfield.

In those days Blackfield had a post office cum sweetshop, a small general store, an off licence and latterly two bakers' shops. The butcher, fishmonger and baker made regular deliveries by horse and cart. Milk was collected in a milk can, mainly by the children before going to school. There was great excitement when the first bus, called 'The Forest Queen', arrived in Blackfield. The old Baptist chapel was just a short walk away up in the Forest towards Exbury.

The building of the first oil processing plant (the old AGWI) in the 1920s brought the first influx of people into the area ('they foreigners and interlopers', so called by the local people in their strong Hampshire brogue) and with them came the amenities of gas, water, electricity and roads.

Blackwater 🦢

Situated in the north-east corner of Hampshire, Blackwater takes its name from the river which marks its boundary with the counties of Surrey and Berkshire.

In olden times a ford enabled people to cross the river easily, thus making the village an important changing stage for the coaches which ran along the main London to Exeter high road.

As well as two alehouses, there were three large coaching inns, of which one at least had its own brewery at the rear. While the horses were being rested or changed, the weary passengers could enjoy hospitality in the inns, heartened by the sight of rounds of beef, veal pies and hams, washed down with old port, burgundy or ale. Footpads and highwaymen abounded, making these journeys over the wild and desolate heathland, which surrounded Blackwater, extremely perilous. In 1839, 60 coaches a day were passing through the village.

Blackwater's greatest claim to fame must be its great two-day cattle fair. From the 13th century until after the First World War, it was held annually in November on the wide open spaces of commonland round the great crossroads to the south of the village. It was always mentioned in Old Moore's Almanac as the largest cattle fair in the south of England. Hundreds of cattle, horses, pigs and sheep were bought and sold. For days they would be arriving until all the nearby land was full of animals. Horses were brought up from the New Forest, cattle were driven hundreds of miles from the West Country and from Wales. On the great days one can imagine the hustle and bustle, the noise and excitement, as buyers and sellers haggled over prices, and farmers and drovers jostled with onlookers. Travelling musicians supplied the entertainment for the villagers, while the blacksmiths plied their trade, and gypsies and cheapjacks sold their wares. Taverns and inns did a roaring trade. Later in the day everyone enjoyed the delights of the 'pleasure' fair, stalls and sideshows were set up along Blackwater Street (now the A30), there were boxing booths and swing boats and so on. At night the jollity continued by the glaring light on naphtha flares.

Blackwater was an outer tything of Yateley until 1857, when a church was erected here and it was incorporated into the new parish of Hawley. Later a school was built nearby, and the almshouses which face onto the village green.

The pine scented 'healthy' air attracted many people to settle here and gracious houses were built, each on its individual estate, with attractive lodges for the employees. More new villas and cottages housed the men who worked on the railway line which was laid in 1849, with a level crossing at the station in Blackwater.

Hawley House (now called Hawley Park) is the oldest large house in the vicinity and has a chequered history. It was possibly a hunting lodge in the Middle Ages, then it was enlarged in the 18th century. There is, in the magnificent stable block, a clock dated 1743, still in perfect working order. These stables were used by Sir Francis Dashwood, the founder member of the notorious Hell Fire Club.

In 1860 Wilkie Collins, the author, stayed at Frogmore Park, another house in Blackwater. Did he see the ghost reputed to haunt it? It is said that his novel *The White Lady* was inspired by his visit there, others say he actually wrote the book during his visit. Another resident, in the 20th century, was Admiral Sir Charles Denniston Burney, a great designer of airships and the inventor of the paravane, a device for protecting ships against mines.

Botley

'Botley is the most delightful village in the world, it has everything in a village that I love, and none of the things I hate.' Thus wrote William Cobbett, author of *Rural Rides*, who farmed here for 13 years from 1805.

Botley Square in 1908

Vice Admiral Phillip Howard Colomb, who is buried in Botley churchyard, was not so well known. He introduced an important new worldwide system of signals and tactics upon the advent of steamships in the Navy in 1858. His work merits an entry in the Encylopaedia Britannica.

About 200 years ago the square was an area of turf and the market was held there. After a period of disuse the market was revived in 1830. On one occasion 1,280 sheep, 150 lambs, 250 cattle and 200 pigs were sold; each owner selling his own beasts. By tradition at the end of the market farmers sat down to a meal which always included Botley Plum Pudding.

The village grew around the square and it is said that there were 13 public houses, so it is not difficult to imagine a grain of truth in the story that a man was hanged without judge or jury in the Catherine Wheel public house. This was later made a Temperance house and is now a bakery which still uses flour from Botley mill. During alterations the old wall revealed wattle and daub, which has been glassed over and is still on display.

Botley mill still produces flour. The first mill was built in Saxon times and the water wheel was supposed to be the largest in Hampshire. The river has been of great importance to Botley; grain, coal etc used to be poled up to the mill.

In 1850 a large number of small industries existed in the village – chain maker, watch and clockmaker, chair maker, boot maker, broom maker and barrel makers. These have all disappeared. At the turn of the century strawberries were grown on a huge scale and train loads were despatched all over the country.

Artefacts in the Manor Farm area show occupation from the Stone Age to Roman times on both sides of the river Hamble. This area is now the Upper Hamble Country Park, a Hampshire Recreational Centre, with a working farm, farmhouse, old barns, wheelwrights and forge. The old church looks down on the ducks swimming on the pond and the animals in the farmyard.

All Saints' church is only 150 years old but the early Norman font which was dug up at Fairthorne was removed from the old church in 1835, as was the recumbent figure of John de Botteley.

Today in the square facilities include the bakery using Botley flour, two hairdressers, a post office, chemist, shoe shop, children's wear, ladies' fashions, a butcher's and a French restaurant, as well as three pubs. Still at the centre is the Market Hall, which is heavily booked by local groups.

Bramdean ✤

Even before Bramdean was known in Saxon times as 'Bradandene', loosely translated as the 'broad valley', there were various settlements in the area. The Iron Age farm site a few hundred yards from Woodcote House was probably started around 200 BC and superseded 300 years later by a Romano-British villa. During excavation in 1823 a beautiful tessellated pavement was discovered in a good state of preservation.

Although the village name is of Saxon origin, no evidence has yet been found that Bramdean's church of St Simon and St Jude is earlier than the Norman period. The oldest details are that of the chancel arch and the north doorway of the nave which are circa 1170. In 1989, Bramdean celebrated the 700th anniversary of its first recorded clergyman, Giles the Englishman, who was appointed to the living in the reign of Edward I.

In Bramdean church are two stained glass windows in memory of Field Marshal Sir William Gomm, whose grandfather was rector of the parish for 38 years until his death in 1831. There is a house in the village called 'Gomms' and next door to it is Bramdean Cottage, reputed to be one of the oldest houses, if not the oldest, in Bramdean. In the walled garden of Bramdean Cottage is the grave of Sir William and Lady Gomm's favourite Arab horse, *Pekin*, which died on 17th October 1865.

Pekin is not the only horse to have been reverently laid to rest within the parish. When he owned Brockwood Park, Colonel George Greenwood (1799–1875) buried his favourite hunter, with which he had performed a remarkable jump. Colonel Greenwood was a keen horseman and author of *Hints on Horsemanship*, published in 1839. A mound of flint stones marks the grave of his trusty steed on the small triangular piece of ground at the junction of the A272 road and the leafy lane going up to Brockwood Park.

Colonel Greenwood also wrote *The Tree Lifter*, published in 1884, in which he describes a method of transplating forest trees up to 25 or 30 ft in height. In the book, he claimed that he had transplanted trees of this size every month of the year without a single failure. The beeches that line the leafy lane, now somewhat denuded by the great October storm of 1987, give testimony to his prowess. In all probability, he was responsible for the planting of the magnificent copper beech trees alongside the A272 near Brockwood. Travellers along this strip of road can also glimpse a pile of huge stones, reminiscent of a scaled down Stonehenge. These stones were erected by Colonel Greenwood at some time around 1845.

Past wars have touched Bramdean perhaps more than the average village. Certainly during the Civil War, at what has become known as the battle of Cheriton of 1644, Bramdean in company with Hinton Ampner shared as much of the conflict as Cheriton. Indeed, among the casualties was a Royalist officer who died of his wounds, and whose memorial at Oxford – being the headquarters of Charles I at that time – states that he was mortally wounded in the 'Bramdene' fight.

It is only by luck that no civilians were killed within the parish during the Second World War, because bombs fell in the field at the back of Bramdean church and at Cheriton Wood. One enemy bomber, a Dornier Do 17, crashed in a field not far from Wood Lane and exploded on impact.

The Americans arrived as the war continued. Their presence saturated Bramdean. Shortly after their arrival the A272 road through Bramdean was permanently widened to cope with the escalating military traffic in readiness for D-Day. This alteration in late 1943 was the biggest village development since Bramdean was introduced to electricity in 1936. The village is still waiting for mains drainage and gas!

What shops there were in Bramdean have gradually dwindled as village car ownership has increased to bring Alresford, Winchester and Petersfield within just a few minutes journey from home. On the other hand, Bramdean Garage is prospering – thanks to the motor car. It is nice to think so, as it has evolved from the village's most traditional trade, the village forge.

Bramley 🌿

Known as Brumelia in the 11th century, Bramley lies five miles due north of Basingstoke and is very much a linear village, stretching for about two miles along the road and bisected halfway by the railway crossing. In the old days the Bramley line was part of the GWR broad gauge system and the railway is today still an important link for villagers. An important character in the village was Joseph Jibb, whose persistence was instrumental in persuading the Great Western Railway to open the station in Bramley in 1895.

Another event which had a great effect on Bramley was the commandeering of a large area of land for a prisoner of war camp during the First World War. Subsequently the site became the Central Ammunition Depot and provided a good source of employment for residents. With the closure of 'the camp', there is now no local occupation and Bramley could therefore be said to have become a dormitory village. Development has added to this situation. Since 1984, when there were only about 400 dwellings, building has been taking place and numbers will soon reach nearly 800.

Popular events bring everyone together and the annual Church Fair is such an example. On its 70th anniversary it was opened by a member of Bramley's oldest family, John Clift, who was present at the first fair in 1919. Harvest Festival is always celebrated with a grand spread at the village hall following evensong at the parish church. In olden times two events brought visitors from other villages. In the 16th century 'The King's Ale' was a week of feasting and dancing, and in Victorian times the Village Maying was held on the green at Stocks Farm. Into this century on Hospital Sundays there would be a great gathering with a service and bands to raise money for the Royal Berks Hospital.

Passing through the village one cannot help noticing the incidence of attractive cottages with distinctive small leaded windows and tile-hung first storeys. These were part of the building programme of the Welch-Thornton brothers who as owners of the manor of Bramley in 1885 changed the face of the village. Probably the last and largest of their buildings is the Six Bells Hotel.

The year 1922 was a milestone in the history of Bramley when Colonel Welch-Thornton, then owner of the Beaurepaire estate, disenchanted by the loss of much of his property to the military authorities, put the estate on the market. It was broken up and sold in 64 lots. Thus the semi-feudal regime that had existed for hundreds of years came to an end.

Bramley has several listed buildings, the most notable being the 12th century parish church of St James with its remarkable wall paintings, the oldest of which portrays the martyrdom of Thomas Becket. The beautiful windows, particularly in the Brocas chapel, contain 16th century glass and the work of Flemish artists. These works escaped destruction during the Civil War by being buried in the moat at Beaurepaire House, then the home of the Brocas family.

Among the graves in the burial ground is that of Lise Meitner, a refugee scientist who was working in Germany on experiments on nuclear fission at the beginning of the Second World War. She is buried next to her nephew Walter Meitner, whose son farmed at Sherfield-on-Loddon.

Not far from the church is the Manor House, previously the Old Manor House, a 16th century timber-framed dwelling with brick infilling on a brick base. The old school which is behind the church was converted into dwellings some years ago and the modern school built in Moat Close.

The village green is at the eastern end of the village towards Sherfield-on-Loddon and it is around here that most of the expansion of Bramley is taking place on land released by the Ministry of Defence. The pond which occupies a corner of Bramley Green has recently been rescued from its neglected state and residents have helped to make it again an attractive feature habitable by fish and wildlife. At this end of the village also, on a slight rise in woods beside the road to Sherfield, there are traces of a triple-walled Iron Age fort.

One name without which no record of Bramley would be complete, is that of Clift. Since John Clift came to Bramley in 1673, nine generations of the family have lived and farmed in the village and become well known benefactors. The latest gift, fulfilling the wishes of the late Will Clift and of his surviving brother John, is of the seven acre field next to the Six Bells Hotel, which will permanently commemorate the name of Clift in a leisure area known as the Clift Field.

Bransgore

Not perhaps the most beautiful of Hampshire villages, although it has its gems tucked away, Bransgore, just south-west of the New Forest, is nevertheless remarkable for its liveliness and friendly outgoing character. This may be partly due to a considerable influx of people over the last 25 years or so to fill the new housing estates which have proliferated around the village, blending the urban with the rural.

In some instances a large house of the older type, designed to meet yesterday's needs of families with a number of servants, has had to go to

~AUDREY ALDEN~

Bransgore House

make way for today's developments of varied, relatively small dwellings set in appropriately sized gardens.

In Bransgore, however, there is at least one case of what might be called compromise where a country house has managed to survive, whilst most of its land has been sold off for building purposes.

Originally Bransgore House, an elegant Edwardian mansion of some 36 rooms, stood in grounds of 57 acres of garden, pasture and woodland, which also included three thatched cottages, a coach-house and stabling with accommodation above. In the care of a head gardener and about eight under-gardeners, there were orchards, a walled kitchen garden with a pond and a number of greenhouses in which peaches, nectarines, grapes, carnations, orchids and alpines were grown. There was also a sunken rose garden and a Dutch garden with geometric flower beds, each enclosed by a low box hedge. Border beds alongside the brick-walled terraces, numerous herbaceous borders, together with lawns, yew hedges and a grass tennis court were also featured. The lawns were cut by horse-drawn mowing-machine, the horse's hoofs being encased in leather shoes to protect the grass.

But this way of life could not be kept up. Although the terraces and Dutch garden remain today, most of the rest has gone. No longer are vegetables grown in the kitchen garden; instead, imaginatively constructed within its remaining walls, there are six pairs of houses arranged in an open plan of front gardens. And this is only part of a change that had already begun.

By the end of the Second World War much of the land, and outbuildings, had fallen into neglect and parts of it were subsequently sold at intervals for development. For a period a few acres of the estate were cultivated by a market gardener who lived in one of the cottages. Then this was demolished and five houses were built, followed by ten bungalows. Thirteen more bungalows came later on the old greenhouse area, making a total of 40 new homes built on the old estate. Add to this a remaining cottage, now modernised though still with its thatched charm, and the accommodation over the stables – previously inhabited first by a coachman, then by a chauffeur and finally by a caretaker – which, along with an acre of land, was sold and then demolished to be replaced by a substantial new house.

Bransgore House itself, becoming run down, was left by the end of the 1950s in about six acres of deteriorating gardens, surrounded by a further 20 acres of woodland. Salvation came in the shape of a property company which converted the house into nine owner-occupied leasehold flats with communal responsibility for the gardens. Thus today the flats, together with the new houses and bungalows, provide pleasant homes for around 50 families where once there was only one!

Bransgore House, the work of a distinguished Bournemouth architect, is so well hidden amongst the trees between the village crossroads and Thorney Hill that not many people are familiar with it. Roughly L-shaped, it has an imposing entrance of decorated Portland stone surmounted by a fine oriel window. The walls have an unusual hand-applied finish of pebbles from Dorset's Chesil beach, while curved stone lintels above the windows are echoed in the elegant sweep of the roofline. Everywhere, both inside and out, there are numerous features of artistry and fine craftsmanship.

Breamore

The present village of Breamore (pronounced Bremmer from its original Saxon name) lies along the busy B388 Salisbury/Ringwood road. The rosy brick cottages are mostly 17th century, built along the turnpike road by families whose descendants live locally to this day. Villagers worked on the Breamore House estate or leased farming land from the estate and there were carpenters and undertakers, laundry workers and farriers.

It is a pretty village with colourful gardens and flowering trees by the road, but life is difficult for residents as the road cuts it in two. The school and shop lie on one side and the village hall and the Bat and Ball pub on the other. Seventeenth century stocks stand very near their original site opposite the pub. Villagers must have been fairly well behaved as records show the stocks were seldom used. Perhaps people were too tired after working for themselves and for the estate.

The original village of Breamore is much older and lay to the west of the road across the marsh, where people have grazing rights for geese and cattle and one is often held up while a procession of geese cross the road. It was centred round the Saxon church and is worth exploring to find old hidden cottages, and to take time to visit the church.

Here too is the gateway to Breamore House park. The house is an Elizabethan manor house built in 1583 by Queen Elizabeth's Treasurer, William Doddington. It stands in a splendid position on the hill slope, backed by sheltering woods and looking out across a stretch of farmland and 17th century water meadows. The house is still a family home but is open to the public in the summer season. There is much to see – even a ghost, or two, if you are lucky (or unlucky).

You will not find any traces of the major battle that took place in the 5th century near the house but, if you walk up through the woods you come to the medieval maze, known as the Miz Maze. It consists of raised turf circles and its purpose is not known, nor if it was connected with the 12th century priory that stood in the water meadows on the east side of the B388.

The early village 'street' led down from the church area, across the marsh, across what is now the B388 to the mill, and beyond to an area known as the Shallows. The mill is mentioned in the Domesday Book and has played its part in history. You will see the brick gun emplacements from the Second World War still in place. The mill was working commercially until quite recently. And it was here that the village children learned to swim, and children today come to feed the ducks.

You can drive very quickly through the village of Breamore, but it is rewarding to stop a while and perhaps stroll up to the marsh and feel that time, for a moment, stands still.

Brockenhurst 🦌

Brockenhurst, named in the Domesday Book as Broceste, is in the heart of the New Forest. Surrounded by everything rural, it is still within easy reach of Southampton, Winchester and Bournemouth, with a fast main line train service to London and a branch line to Lymington with connections to the ferry to the Isle of Wight.

The village shops provide all the necessities of life. It is said that it was an ancestor of the present Purkiss the grocer who discovered the body of William Rufus, after he had been killed in the Forest in 1100 by an arrow. In about the year 1087 Rufus had his horses shod and his armour, pikes and his arrow tips all made at the smithy which stood on the site of the present 'Island Shop', now a grocery store.

There are several churches including a Roman Catholic church completed in 1939 and St Nicholas', mentioned in the Domesday Book of 1086. In the churchyard is an old yew tree known to be at least 1,000 years old, an Anzac war memorial and several graves in memory of New Zealanders who died in the First World War. Also buried in the churchyard is 'Brusher' Harry Mills who died in 1905. He was the local snake catcher and his gravestone was subscribed for by the people of the parish. One villager well recalls that her grandmother and grandfather often met him whilst out walking in the Forest. 'Brusher' would be carrying his sack full of snakes, and he would say to her 'Put your hand in, Mother' – an offer she hastily declined! Another church, St Saviour's, was privately built by the Walker Munro family in 1910 (and finally completed in 1961). They lived in Rhinefield House, now an hotel.

In the summer the village is filled with visitors and parking then can be a problem. Hollands Wood holds about 2,000 campers in caravans and tents, and nearby Beaulieu also has a large camp site on the old wartime aerodrome. There are very many delightful walks, ponds and streams in the area.

There are still many attractive cottages, some of them thatched. One of the latter, Ash Cottage, once the home of Miss Bowden Smith, was the first village school and pupils paid 1d a week to attend! Shops, garages, hotels, guest houses and rest homes provide work for local people. There is also an engineering works and, of course, stables. One public house, the Rose and Crown, provided the village with its first bus service. There are four pubs and several builders. Many of the villagers work at the Esso oil refinery at Fawley and other establishments connected with the oil industry.

Years ago, before the coming of television, the tennis courts were quite famous and all the well-known players of the time came here to play. Freddie Grisewood came to commentate for the radio! Alas the courts are no more and their site is now a housing estate, where one owner called his house 'Centre Court'.

The first council houses were built just after the First World War in Addison Road and Fathersfield Cottages came soon afterwards. These latter were in a field owned by Mr Fred Keeping, who was always known as 'Father' – it is not known why, as he never had children. He was a real village character and was once a candidate for the Parish Council. He posted notices around saying 'Why is Brockenhurst like Port Wine?

Because it is improved by Keeping.'! He kept the only bicycle shop and one could hire a machine for 6d an hour.

The Morant Hall, at one time the hub of the village, was knocked down and where it stood is now a housing estate. Its famous dance floor, said to be the best in the South of England, is now the floor of the Football Club's social hall. Brockenhurst now has a new and thriving village hall, built on the site of the first Brockenhurst grammar school. When this school outgrew those premises it was succeeded by new buildings in the grounds of Carey's Manor, formerly the home of the Bowden Smith family.

Brook & Bramshaw

Brook and Bramshaw are two villages situated just inside the New Forest. As they run into one another, most of the residents of Brook consider themselves part of Bramshaw, especially as the one and only post office and general store is in Bramshaw.

The villages have changed considerably over the last few years, with the M27 motorway just one and a half miles away. However, the area has certainly not lost its charm and character and the New Forest ponies still walk along the roads and graze the verges and commons. It is not only ponies that have to be avoided by passing motorists but cows, donkeys, pigs and occasionally deer.

There is still a working forge in Bramshaw. This has a long history and the cottage adjoining is dated 1793, with the initials 'W.H.' William Henbest placed an advertisement in the *Salisbury and Winchester Journal* on 1st September 1794, respectfully informing the public in general 'that he has erected a Foundery to cast iron of every sort'. In 1813 he made numerous cast iron safes for local churches at £3 13s 6d each. There is one in Salisbury Cathedral, embossed with the initials 'W.H.' and 'Bramshaw Foundery'. Bramshaw church was not supplied with a safe by Henbest although in 1967 one of his was given to the church.

Great attractions in the area are the two golf courses. One is over the open forest with spectacular views, but here the players have the added handicap of the ponies wandering on and off the greens. The main course is the venue for several tournaments, and the complex includes an hotel.

On the outskirts of Brook is the famous Rufus Stone. In August 1100 William Rufus, King William II of England, was shot dead by an arrow whilst he was out hunting in the Forest. The stone marks the spot where William Rufus died. Was it an accident, or was it murder by the hand of the French nobleman Walter Tyrell? The mystery remains to this day. Very near to the stone is the public house called the Sir Walter Tyrell.

High on a hill at one end of Bramshaw stands St Peter's church. Although tradition holds that a church stood on the present site before the Norman Conquest, there is no written evidence of a place of worship before 1158. The earliest part of the structure dates from the 12th century. There is a gallery which was built in 1829 'for the girls school and free seating for females only'. Among the features of interest are the framed Lord's Prayer and illustrations of the Ten Commandments which hang in the north transept. They were left unfinished by John Wells, a self-taught artist who died at the age of 32 in 1858.

Broughton ⚜

Broughton has had a very long history, as proved by the discovery of the skeleton of a Saxon warrior, found on Broughton Hill by a ploughman in 1875. The blond hair only disintegrated on being exposed to the air. A 'pig' of Mendip lead, weighing 156 lbs and dated AD 59, the time of Nero, was found in 1783.

Henry V's soldiers, en route for the battle of Agincourt, encamped in a field near Bossington, part of the parish of Broughton. Glassmakers from Lorraine were in evidence in about 1576, cutting the trees down in Buckholt forest on the edge of the village, in order to keep their charcoal kilns going, until the local people protested.

As recently as 1829, the owner of Bossington House, a Mr Penleasze, destroyed the hamlet around, and a broadsheet published in 1870 laments this destruction, beginning thus: 'Alas poor Bossington. What is thy village fled? Where are thy natives gone? None left, but sleeping dead?' Before this event, a Thomas South, also owner of Bossington House, and inventor, discovered that by covering a hot air balloon with a net, the difficulties of attaching a basket could easily be overcome. He also invented appliances for raising sunken vessels and keeping damaged ones afloat, and conducted experiments in the river Test.

Broughton honey-making has long been an important industry – it has been famous since Roman times. A Mr Ayles of Broughton tried to market his own invention to combat the dreaded 'Isle of Wight disease' which had wiped out 90 per cent of all bees in the country by 1918. As Mr Ayles's 'cure' consisted mainly of creosote, one feels it must have done the bees almost as much harm as the disease! Happily, bee-keeping is still active in the village, with a large number of hives kept there. The Hampshire Beekeepers' County Library, which is the second largest and most comprehensive in the country, is housed in the village.

Education has always been important in Broughton and children benefit from a trust that is still in existence today, started by Thomas Dowse in 1601.

One year, it is said, when the Christmas bullock was being driven to the village to be killed, so many people went out to help bring him home that the bullock took fright and ran away up into the Downs. To this day there is on the Downs a hollow – wooded and quite deep. Any day you look at Bullock Hole and see steam or smoke spiralling up from its centre you may be sure rain is certain. A round barrow burial mound is called 'Plum Pudding' – a hawthorn tree just looks like a stick of holly in the centre!

In the 13th century, John Maunsel, lord of Broughton manor, was granted a charter by Henry III to hold an annual fair. Six hundred years later the reputation of the fair had sunk to 'a nasty mixture of beer and gingerbread'. In July 1871, the fair was discontinued, much to the annoyance of the landlord of the Greyhound Inn, who protested at the thought of losing so great an income. However, in modern times it has been resurrected and still the ale and gingerbread are present in the form of competition. A procession from the village hall stops at St Mary's church to obtain dispensation and renewal of the charter.

However, the ancient custom of carrying a man on a hurdle and depositing him on the doorstep of newcomers in the parish, when he would start brushing the step and refuse to go away until he had been given food and drink, has not been revived!

Burghclere ❧

Burghclere was for many centuries a prosperous farming area. Sheep and barley were the chief sources of income with their associated products, wool, meat and beer. Skilled craftsmen were needed for the making of leather shoes and harness, tools and carts. Dairy cattle, fruit, fish and honey were additional items of diet.

In recent years the small mixed farms have mostly disappeared. Farmhouses and cottages have been modernised and have become homes for commuters or retired folk. Some dairy cattle, a few sheep and light riding horses can still be seen, with a few mixed cereal crops.

Ladle Hill is an Iron Age earthwork on the southern ridge. Far bigger and more interesting is Beacon Hill on the western side of the road. These were human settlements 4,000 and 3,000 years ago. They later became look-out posts guarding the important route to the coast, then called the Salt Road, now the busy A34.

Old Burghclere has its ancient manor and All Saints' church, the former mentioned in the Domesday Book. Two ornamental doorways can still be seen in the church though neither is now used. The modern church of Ascension, built two miles to the north in 1838, is attractive but of no historical interest.

In the main village the chief centre of interest is the Sandham Memorial Chapel. It was built in memory of a soldier killed in the First World War, but its main claim to fame is the series of paintings executed by Stanley Spencer on its inner walls. The general effect of the work is macabre because the human figures are stiff and wooden but details are beautifully drawn. The scenes are from behind the Gallipoli war front.

Down in the south-east of the parish is Earlstone House. Its foundations are Norman but the present house dates from the time of James I. Also in the south-east is Watership Down, a pleasant hilltop with literary associations.

There are three schools in the village. The excellent primary school has a brass band which has achieved considerable success. The Grange, which for some years served as the rectory, is now run as a school for underprivileged boys.

Most of the land in the area belongs to Lord Carnarvon, so the village feels it shares in the fame of the 5th Earl who, with Howard Carter, uncovered the wonderful treasure of Tutankhamen.

The roads of Burghclere are a mixture of old and new. The A34, once the Salt Road, was a very early route to the sea and so to Europe. The Ox Drove, Well Street and West Street were probably cattle roads to the hills to link up with the Ridgeway. The loop road, on which the main village stands, is modern. A single line railway ran through the village for a century (1860–1960) and served the inhabitants well, carrying people, milk churns and animals to Newbury or Winchester. It is now closed and overgrown with only a few lengths accessible for walking.

Buriton 🌿

Buriton has come a long way since it was the easternmost settlement beneath the escarpment of the South Downs, where prehistoric people took advantage of the abundant natural springs with downland pasture and light arable soils. Within the village are signs of Bronze Age, Iron Age and Roman occupation, while the church wall holds stones which could be Neolithic.

The church of St Mary we see today is Norman, built between 1150 and 1200. It stands on high ground on an old site at the east end of the village high street, and the only way to do justice to this fine village church is to pay a visit. It is a beautiful place and was the Mother Church of Petersfield and Sheet when it served a parish of 6,000 acres, until

The Old Hop Kilns at Buriton

1886. History has turned full circle and the vicar of Petersfield is now rector of Buriton. A previous church on this site is listed in the Domesday Book of 1086.

Perhaps this village churchyard is a fitting resting place for John Goodyer (1592–1664) who was one of the first great botanists. He is buried in the churchyard in an unmarked grave. He lived in Goodyers, The Spain, Petersfield, his house being in the tithing of Weston in this parish.

On the north side of the church is the historic manor house. It has seen much history and was mentioned in the records of St Swithun's monastery at Winchester in 1325. Many famous people like Thomas Hanbury and Edward Gibbon, the 18th century historians, have lived here.

Across the pond from the church stands the old rectory, another old and very interesting house. The pond is fed by sadly depleted descendants of the original abundant natural springs.

Burley 🐾

Standing on the edge of Cranesmoor and looking up towards the old smugglers' road, it is still possible to mistake sudden movements of a grey or brown forest mare amongst the heather, for the flash of Lovey Warne's petticoats as she ran to warn smugglers of the imminent arrival of the Excise men. At night she would hang a lantern in a tree near Picket Post as a warning, for Burley was the centre of the old smuggling trade.

The Queen's Head Inn is the oldest building in Burley, dating from the middle of the 17th century. The queen of the title could have been Elizabeth I, although no one knows for certain. In 1848 a village smithy and forge were mentioned as being part of the inn, a meeting place in those days for the smugglers planning their 'runs', over jugs of ale.

At the present time there are more than 30 active organisations in Burley, catering for all ages and tastes, from a play group for the under-fives to a club for the over seventies.

One hundred and fifty years of Burley history was celebrated in 1989, commemorating the anniversary of the church of St John the Baptist, while the chapel has celebrated over 200 years.

Thomas Eyre (1752–1829) was one of the better known names in the village, and there was old Mrs Evemy who lived to be over 100. The Herberts (family name of the Earls of Carnarvon) came to the 'Old House' in the mid 19th century, and Auberon lived in his beloved forest until he died in 1906. Another long-lived lady who died in 1981 in her 108th year was Constance Applebee, who pioneered women's hockey in

America and who, on her 100th birthday received telegrams from the Queen and from the President of the USA. There is now a stained glass window dedicated to her memory in the church.

Burridge

In 1908 Samuel Wynn Hornby Hood, Esq, offered for sale the 'Burridge Estate' comprising '54 acres of Valuable Freehold Properties to plots of 1½ to 3 acres' as well as 'a desirable small Pleasure Farm known as Burridge with old Fashioned farm House, buildings, 49 acres of land and nearly quarter of a mile of frontage to the river Hamble'.

Among the rules regulating the use of the landing place on the river Hamble was that 'the landing place and the way leading to shall be closed between sunset and sunrise, and the landing place shall not be used for smuggling or other illegal purpose'.

The growers who bought the plots had a massive job clearing the trees and undergrowth using horses and carts and finally burning it over, before the planting up of stawberry plantations.

Swanwick and District Fruit Growers Association was formed at the turn of the century, and soon they were joined by Burridge Fruit Growers. Together they were a progressive group and by 1913 a sub-committee was formed to start a factory producing chip baskets to market the fruit. Poplar trees were grown locally to provide the raw material.

After the First World War the village set about finding a hut for social activities. They purchased an army hut and Miss Augusta Burrell of Fairthorne Manor, well known for her generosity, offered a field nearby of some six acres which could be used for a social and sports centre at a peppercorn rent, on condition that no alcohol should be served in the hut and no politics discussed. Here the hut was erected by local labour and was to be the centre of many activities until after the Second World War.

The village prospered. Strawberries were dispatched daily in the season to London and farther afield, and school holidays were arranged to fit into the picking times.

One of the leading growers, A. E. Roberts, took on seven acres of additional land after the war. After clearing the trees he grew black-currants and loganberries, some of the first to be grown in England. He took more land on each year until the total of 35 acres grew black-currants. Older folk in Burridge still remember the total involvement of everyone in picking the crop.

By 1928 the nearby coppice of Caigers Green was cleared and bungalows built. Burridge extended to cover that area, said to have once been a staging post, and sadly the name Caigers Green has disappeared.

As time went on the local strawberry growers drifted into other occupations. Development was rapid after the Second World War, and from 1950 to 1960 most of the strawberry plots disappeared.

Burridge as it is today is a most sought after place to live in, with the peace and quiet of the country, yet close to the motorway and the coast.

Bursledon

Early scribes were casual about spelling, and the place name was written variously as Brixenden, Burtlesden, Bristelden and Bussleton – in addition to the 12th century Brixedone, which is remembered in a farm and in the house which until recently was the annexe of Southampton Children's Hospital.

In 1154 Henry de Blois, Bishop of Winchester, allocated land to the French monks at Hamble, instructing them to build a church at Brixedona, 'to serve it well and maintain it'. By 1230 St Leonard's was completed, but it seems there may have been an earlier Saxon building on the site. When in 1888 Barney Sutton was digging foundations for a new vestry, he uncovered a mass grave which contained the bones of large men thought to have been killed in battle. They had damaged skulls and were not victims of the plague. These were considered to have been the crew of one of the Danish longboats from a fleet defeated by King Alfred in AD 871. Barney himself was a large, bearded man who lived in a shed in a field at Old Bursledon, and used a wheelbarrow in the doorway as his armchair.

Through the centuries ships were built at Bursledon, the first important launching being that of the man o' war *St George* in 1338, to which came King Edward III accompanied by Adam Orlton, Bishop of Winchester, and the Abbot of Netley. A great day for the village. Henry V's *Grace Dieu*, whilst laid up, caught fire in 1439. Whether this was caused by accident or lightning is not known, but when a 'son et lumiere' was staged in the church in 1975 the producers took the opportunity to include a very realistic thunderstorm.

The church was enlarged in the 19th century, but the Early English arch of 1230 remains, and the ancient font. There are murals to Philemon Ewer (died 1750) and George Parsons (died 1812). The latter was a very strong man, who could drive in a copper bolt at one blow. He built HMS *Elephant*, Lord Nelson's flagship at the battle of Copenhagen.

With bad roads, and no bridge until 1880, the river was the main highway, and sailing ships carrying cargo moored in the deep water off

53

the Jolly Sailor. There were several inns, and a fiddler came from Southampton to play for dancing. A May Fair was held on the green by the New Inn (now 'Greywell'). The picturesque black and white toll-bridge was replaced in 1934 by a concrete structure. The railway came in 1888, blocking the top end of Badnam Creek which formerly gave access to Hungerford, where bolts were made for the wooden ships. Lowford is the shopping centre, surrounded by housing, most of the inhabitants working elsewhere. Old Bursledon, which is a conservation area, has a High Street with no shops, but some interesting houses including the 'Dolphin' with a 16th century porch.

Mrs Shawe-Storey, who lived at 'Greyladyes' until her death in 1937, was responsible for the elaborate brickwork and chimneys around the estate. She also provided the richly decorated Roman Catholic chapel.

John Iremonger Eckless was a notable villager who lived at 'Upcott' from 1790 to 1869. He obtained pardons from William IV and George IV for agricultural labourers sentenced to transportation, and he was highly regarded by Lord Palmerston, who consulted him on such matters. He helped shipwrecked emigrants who were landed at Southampton, destitute, and obituaries in Hampshire newspapers testified to his great generosity and kindness.

There has been a mill on Providence Hill since 1767, marked on Admiralty charts. The present one, built in 1814, was worked until 1880 by George Gosling. Strawberries then became the chief crop.

During the Second World War the boatyards worked exclusively for the Navy, and there was a Royal Marines base in the Upper Hamble woods, from where landing craft operated. Afterwards the yachting business grew enormously, the river now being overcrowded with boats and marinas.

Calmore 🦊

Calmore, originally known as Calmoor, used to be administered by its near neighbour Netley Marsh, but today is incorporated into Totton and Eling Town Council.

Village life centred around the village hall, Calmore church, the school, post office and stores and the cricket ground. The church was also used as the village school. Today there is a new infants and junior school which caters for children from the new housing estate which was built in the area.

There is said to be a ghost in the village. Cook's Lane was named after the cook who was murdered at Testwood House, who is supposed to haunt the lane every year on the anniversary of his death.

The Misses Everett were responsible for having the village hall built and were organisers of many activities including flower shows, concerts, drama and lace classes. During the Second World War the hall became a social centre for the villagers, and sailors from nearby HMS *Safeguard* at Tatchbury Mount also patronised the functions. Today Tatchbury Mount is a psychiatric hospital but still retains the lawns which sweep down to the village. Now many activities and classes take place at the new community centre, built a few years ago when housing developments took place in Calmore.

Calmore once had a thriving industry of glove-making, called the Netley Marsh Glove Industry. It was organised by Miss Everett and employed only WI members. Over 1,000 pairs of gloves were made in a year and Royalty were supplied, as well as demonstrations and exhibitions at shows far and wide.

The village shop and post office was always a busy place and even today remains a focal point for residents. Most of Calmore now consists of a large housing estate with all the associated amenities and further development is planned to the north. Nevertheless the area still retains its rural atmosphere.

Catherington

Originally an isolated settlement in the heart of the Forest of Bere, which protected it from all but the most foolhardy of marauders, Catherington has developed into the more open area of downland beauty of today. In 1908 is was still described as an area whose 'road is rough and the scenery wild'.

Catherington is a wishbone-shaped development with the centre being the highest, where Catherington Down is 425 ft above sea level. The southern end of Catherington Lane drops to 290 ft and the two northern ends (Downhouse Road and Whitedirt Lane) are approximately 360 ft above the sea. For this reason it is a catchment area for the Portsmouth Water Company, but this is a comparatively recent development. Originally the only source of water for man and beast was the village pond.

By 1692 there is a mention of a 'Great Wheeled Well'. This possibly refers to the Catherington Well which was sunk on the Kinches Farm site. It went down to about 350 ft. The water was pure because it had been filtered by the chalk, but it took ten minutes to draw up one bucket, albeit holding around five gallons of water. The means of raising it was by a human treadwheel.

It wasn't until after the First World War that the area started to expand, when piped water, gas and electricity came to the village. The village today has a good share of smallholdings, farms, light industry and cottage crafts.

In 1750 the church tower was altered to take a peal of bells, and so today there is a village team of bellringers. The present All Saints' is thought to have been built during the last half of the 12th century. However, the walls, which were restored in 1883, are mostly Norman and are of knapped local flints. The tower is Norman, as are the columns inside the nave.

A well preserved timber roof is most likely 14th century and on the north wall is a mural depicting St Michael weighing souls. That is thought to date from 1350. There are various stained glass windows and commemorative plaques, and one large table tomb. The latter is of Sir Nicholas Hyde, a former Chief Justice of the King's Bench in the 17th century.

Catherington House is presently used as the Diocesan Retreat House. The church is at the top of the village, as are most of the older properties,

Catherington village sign

including Tudor Cottages. Near the church are Butts Cottages, named after the site where the ancient law decreed every man tall enough to hold a bow should practise on a Sunday after church.

Almost opposite the church used to be the Katryngton Inne, (or 'Anchor'). Today the Farmer Inn is on the same side as the church.

The village school is much appreciated by the community for its friendly atmosphere. It was first opened on 26th July 1852. The building is of brick and flint. Between the church and the school is the village pond. Until recently this was much neglected, but thanks to a team of young volunteers from the British Trust for Conservation, the pond is now restored, with seats provided to sit and watch the wildlife in it, or to admire the water irises around it.

Catherington Down is composed of very shallow, poor clay soil over solid chalk. It is a nature reserve with many flowers upon it. The poor soil ensures no one species dominates the others. It also has ancient lynchets, which are terraces cultivated by the Saxons. These doubled up for defence positions when required.

Chandler's Ford 🐿️

In the early 1920s Chandler's Ford was a small village surrounded by beautiful woods and fields. The main road running through the centre, linking Southampton to Winchester, was quiet and traffic free. Now the village has grown in all directions and is a very busy place.

There were many groups of thatched cottages, interspersed with large properties set in several acres of land, and a number of market gardens and dairy farms. The springs and little streams have mostly been piped, converging where the railway station used to be, under the name of Monks Brook.

The whole area was densely wooded, chiefly oak, yew and sweet chestnut. In the autumn lorries used to come to gather the fallen chestnuts to take to town for sale.

Before the railway works came to Eastleigh providing employment, the main industry was brick making. Bricks were taken from here by rail to London to build the Law Courts in the Strand.

In the 17th century, cherry trees grew in abundance throughout the village and each year people came from surrounding places to buy cherries (or merries as they were called). Oliver Cromwell's son Richard brought his wife from Hursley to enjoy the Merrifeasts.

During the Second World War, American troops were stationed in Chandler's Ford before D-Day. The men ate and slept with their vehicles which were parked under the trees along the roads. Many friendships were formed with local people and the children were given food they had never seen before – such as white bread, tinned peaches and tinned ham.

After the war, most of the large houses were sold, demolished and a close full of houses and bungalows built on the land. The west side of the main road was developed before the east, which was mostly farmland or smallholdings. Chandler's Ford is today quite different from the small hamlet of bygone years.

Charlton 🌿

When villagers were successful in separating Charlton from mighty Andover in the 1980s they were merely re-establishing an identity dating from before the medieval period. The name Charlton itself indicates association with the Saxons, while the older, western area of Foxcotte probably had a church before the Norman invasion.

Flint axes, tools and a rare stone mace are proof of man's existence and activities. Bronze Age round barrows were followed by a later large, complicated network of boundary ditches which, although intended to be demarcation lines for land ownership, carefully curved in and out between the burial mounds to avoid desecrating them.

The pagan Saxons, seeking good farming land, naturally settled down at Charlton and Old Down Farm, where their simple houses were excavated in the 1970s. Two of the more impressive cemeteries also touched the Harrow Way, and, since the Saxons were buried with their jewellery and weapons, provided evidence of their prosperity and physical well-being.

The conversion to Christianity may have followed a movement downhill to Foxcotte where there was easy access to the river and where a large part of the village is positioned. The Domesday survey records a total of 27 households. Archaeology has proved that beer and brewing were important.

It is said that the local flocks of sheep yielded excellent tallow for making candles, which found a ready sale in London. After one successful trip a villager returned carrying the dreaded plague. Since one way of reducing the rat population (the source of further contagion) was to burn the cottages, this was done, according to legend, and the villagers moved temporarily elsewhere. In fact, excavation did reveal a cottage destroyed by fire but the position of the remains suggested a mad dash outside to safety rather than deliberate arson!

Chawton

Chawton lies in the valley of the river Wey, two miles from Alton. The village was known in Saxon times and was described in the Domesday Book as the manor of Celtone.

Chawton, being on the main pilgrim route to Winchester, had need of a coaching inn, which later became the house in which Jane Austen spent the last eight years of her life and where she wrote *Pride and Prejudice*, *Sense and Sensibility*, *Mansfield Park*, *Emma* and *Persuasion*. She lived here with her mother and sister Cassandra, who are both buried in Chawton churchyard. Jane, who died in 1817, is buried in Winchester Cathedral. Before being officially opened to the public in 1949, the house was used as a working men's club. It was bought by a Mr Carpenter and given to the Jane Austen Society in memory of his son.

Another interesting house is Clinkers, which was the village blacksmith and wheelwright's for about 400 years. The family were protected from evil by a mummified cat and rat in the roof – reputed to be good luck charms! Another house, Baigens, is possibly one of the oldest houses in Hampshire. Elizabethan murals were found behind the plastered walls. It also has a slightly sinister past, as a Mr Baigen was found hanging from a tree in what is now known as Baigen's Copse, north of the railway line near Chawton Park Woods.

A church existed in the grounds of the manor in the 13th century. A subsequent church was partially burned down in 1871, but must have been rebuilt at once as St Nicholas' was reopened in 1872 by the Bishop of Winchester.

The Knight family appear to have held land here since the reign of Edward II and purchased the manor in 1578. From that year there have been Knights at Chawton until the present time. The house is a beautiful example of Elizabethan architecture. Jane Austen's nephew Edward Knight, who was lord of the manor in the 19th century, established the first school in the village in 1840. This was for 'both sexes' and was established some 30 years before the Education Act of 1870 made schooling compulsory.

Present day Chawton is somewhat different – Clinkers Forge is now a gift shop, the village shop and post office is an antiques and tea shop and the vicar is no longer a resident as he now serves two parishes and lives in a neighbouring village. The school is still flourishing, however, with 70 pupils on the roll, and the size of the population has not altered in 30 years.

Cheriton 🌿

Cheriton lies seven miles east of Winchester in an Area of Outstanding Natural Beauty. The first known mention of the village is in an 1167 Pipe Roll but, prior to that, it came within the boundaries of the Saxon manor of Tichborne. A Bronze Age bowl barrow and Celtic field system suggest much earlier occupation.

The church of St Michael and All Angels was built between 1129 and 1171 on the site of a prehistoric long barrow by Henry de Blois, Bishop of Winchester, the village growing around it and thereby acquiring its name 'the homestead by the church'. From then until the 19th century, when the title reverted to the Church Commissioners, the Bishop of Winchester was lord of Cheriton manor. In 1874 the Crown became patron of the living of Cheriton.

The river Itchen, famous for its trout fishing, rises at nearby Hinton Marsh and flows through the heart of the village. Water meadows, providing early feed for cattle, can still be seen but a well-known local industry, watercress growing, is no more. Cheriton is said to be the last place in England where truffle hunting occurred, dying out early in the 20th century. Farming, once the main means of livelihood, still plays an important role although the majority of the inhabitants no longer work on the land.

In 1644 the battle of Cheriton was fought between the armies of King and Parliament, a nearby lane reputedly running with blood. It was a victory for Parliament, proving to be a decisive turning point in the Civil War. Several mounds to the east of the village are said to mark the burial places of the dead soldiers.

Like most villages, Cheriton was once nearly self-sufficient with its church, Congregational chapel, school, shops, blacksmith, wheelwright, dairy, bakery, laundry, post office and three public houses. The first public telephone arrived in 1922, three years later a bus service was introduced, electricity arrived in 1935–36 and mains water in 1951–52. There is still no mains drainage or gas.

One public house, the Bricklayers Arms, closed in 1961 and is now a private house. Another, the H. H. Inn, built in 1894 on the site of a farmyard, closed in 1986 and also has become a private house.

A major employer today is the timber yard, established in 1874 on what was the site of the Hampshire Hunt Kennels. The siren, used during the Second World War as an air-raid warning, has reverted to its peacetime role of marking the start and finish of work. There are two garages, a post office and shop, a filling station and shop and one public house, the Flower Pots – a beer house until 1951.

Many of the cottages, the earliest dating from the 16th century, are thatched. The centre of the village is a conservation area but many new houses and bungalows have been built since the 1960s. Justifiably, Cheriton can boast of winning Hampshire's Best Kept Village Competition a record three times.

Chilbolton 🦋

Visitors to Chilbolton are intrigued to find a large 'Stars and Stripes', topped by a gilt eagle, adorning the village hall wall. A proclamation beside it declares that the citizens of Chilbolton have 'Honorary Citizenship of Montville, New Jersey'. What could they have done to have earned this honour? What connects this Test valley village with a town so far away?

The story began at the outbreak of the Second World War when Chilbolton was chosen as a suitable site for an airfield. In 1944, new craft were brought in, in preparation for the invasion of France. These were troop-carrying gliders: they were the size of small bombers, and had distinctive white wing-stripes. The men who would use them were the 17th Airborne (US) paratroopers and glider-troopers. In December, in atrocious weather, they were towed into the air, the men inside crammed in like sardines, and crossed the Channel into France. There they took part in the 'Battle of the Bulge' in the Ardennes mountains.

Every few years since the war a few veterans have revisited Chilbolton, but in June 1984 a large contingent of ex-servicemen and their wives and families, numbering over 100, came to the village at the start of their 40th anniversary celebrations commemorating the D-Day landings.

At the end of their visit, the veterans presented 'the citizens of Chilbolton' with an American flag, and a proclamation. The flag had been flown for a day from the Capitol in Washington in Chilbolton's honour, sponsored by the town of Montville, New Jersey (home of the 17th Airborne Division), and Honorary Citizenship of Montville bestowed on all citizens, in 'the interests of world peace'.

The flag now hangs in the village hall. An American lady, who had lived in the village some years previously, saw the flag during a return visit and on her return to the States, sent over a gilt eagle to top it. This transatlantic link is treasured by many in the village, and the striking emblem of the 17th Airborne has been incorporated into the Chilbolton panel of the Test Valley Tapestry.

Chineham ❧

In the 1960s the village consisted of approximately 70 dwellings, mostly bungalows, wooden shacks and railway cottages. At the bottom of the village was a transport cafe, a boarding house and a coal office, while in the middle of the village was a two-pump garage with a village shop attached, converted from the house's front room. Tiny though it was, the lady who ran it kept it stocked with a huge range of goods.

Just before you reached the little wooden church there was also a sweet and general store; this later became a tool shop. The coal office moved and the transport cafe closed and became a pet shop, which has in turn now become an Indian restaurant. The heart of the village was the village hall, a wooden building used for children's Christmas parties, the annual flower show and many other activities, but eventually the floor collapsed through dry rot and no money was available for replacement.

The appearance of the village began to change in the late 1970s with the building of a housing estate at the far end of the village near the old toll house. Then a bypass was built cutting the toll house off from the village and changes came faster. Most of the old cottages and shacks were knocked down (their elderly tenants either having died or moved) and two-storey houses appeared in their place. Once the estates were extended the old village disappeared into the general sprawl, much to the sadness of the old villagers. The old church was replaced by a brick built edifice across the road and two new houses were built on the site. The woods were bulldozed and built on and the fields are rapidly disappearing under brick. From being people working and living in the area, the vast majority of villagers are now commuters.

Clanfield ❧

Clanfield was in existence at the time the Domesday Book was compiled and in the 1086 survey was part of the Ceptun estate belonging to Earl Harold. It subsequently passed to the Duke of Beaufort who sold it to Clerke-Jervoise, in whose hands it remained until 1918.

Clanfield had many thatched cottages right up to the late 1950s and early 1960s, when a row of deteriorating cottages was pulled down to make way for a row of shops.

The village suffered a number of times from fire, probably due to the thatched cottages. A medieval barn and the local pub, the Rising Sun, were damaged by fire, the latter being reconstructed in a day by a prefabricated building in 1960. It still stands in the same form but is showing its age.

There is a forge still in existence but not sadly in use. It was built around a tree stump. A somewhat strange thing to do you might think, but in fact it served to make a perfect base for the anvil. During the First World War a German prisoner of war worked in the forge and carved on the door in German script, 'German Shoes'. Although the door has from necessity been replaced, the panel bearing this inscription was carefully cut out and set in the new door as a panel by the local village carpenter whose shop is opposite and who owns the forge.

Horses featured largely in the village at one time as forestry and agriculture were the main occupations. Large shire horses and Clydesdales were to be seen making their way down to the village pond at the end of the day for a drink. Nowadays the pond is fenced off from the road.

The village erected a wooden ex-army hut, originally from Liphook forest, in 1921 as a memorial hall to the Clanfield men killed in the First World War. Eventually it was replaced by the villagers' own fund-raising efforts, by a grand new large hall with three smaller committee rooms and large kitchen. This is regularly used by villagers for the local amateur theatrical group known as The Windmill Players (after the nearby windmill at Chalton village).

Clanfield is the proud possessor of a village well. Situated by the side of St James' church, with a thatched roof over the wellhead, it served the villagers for many years and it is easy to visualise a scene similar to those depicted in *Larkrise to Candleford* with women gossiping around the wellhead. Inevitably the arrival of piped water and strict controls resulted in the well being sealed off but it remains a well known local landmark and a listed Hampshire treasure. To many visitors it would seem an item of historic interest, to the villagers it is the subject of a long struggle to establish ownership. It was only in 1985 that the land was finally purchased outright by the Parish Council.

Colden Common

The present village of Colden Common was recorded in 1210 as Colvedene Hethe when a certain Arnoldo of Colvedene paid his dues to the lord of the manor. By 1528 it had become Coledown Hethe, to become eventually Colden Common.

Isolated farms and a few groups of dwellings have now become a growing dormitory for commuters working in the towns around, some even travelling as far as London. There is very little work to be had in the village itself.

Palaeolithic finds indicate early trade in the manufacture of flint implements using the Itchen waterway for transport.

Brickmaking from local clay is no longer carried out but has left its traces in the names of Brickmakers Lane and Kiln Lane.

The Welles family had a large house and land locally and left their mark on history during the time of the Reformation, Swithun Welles being martyred for his faith as a Roman Catholic. There is a window dedicated to him in Colden Common parish church of Holy Trinity and a school bearing his name in Chandler's Ford.

The Tyre Fire in 1974 really put Colden Common on the map, filling the newspaper headlines and causing fear and dismay in the village. In a roaring sea of flames a mountain of old rubber tyres burned and smouldered uncontrollably for days, some householders separated from the blaze only by a bank of trees. The pall of smoke over Colden Common could be seen at Portsmouth and the Isle of Wight. There were no deaths and no houses were damaged thanks to the heroic efforts of the firemen, some of whom were injured.

A stroll through Colden Common still gives an air of peace and quiet, the heavy traffic mostly travelling along the main road which runs past the village, not through it. Pretty, well kept gardens and the children and 'young ladies' riding their ponies and horses keep up the rural atmosphere which makes Colden Common such a lovely place to live in.

Compton & Shawford

As you can tell from its name, this is two villages in one. For the past hundred years it has been said, 'Compton is the one with the church and Shawford the one with the pub.' Unfortunately in recent years the village has been neatly divided into not two but four sections, largely owing to the presence of the dread A33 road – soon to become the M3 motorway.

There are traces of a Bronze Age settlement at Compton and parts of the Roman road still run through the village, whilst the busy Saxon road to the hamlet of Silkstead survives in the form of ancient tracks over the downs.

In 1836, whilst life in Compton continued to revolve round its fields and its Norman (previously Saxon) church of All Saints, the building of the Waterloo to Southampton railway was started and in 1882 a station was opened at Shawford. This resulted in the building of houses for the first commuters, who enjoyed the convenience of the railway and the beauty of the district. The house agents' expression 'this favoured residential area', which is still used, dates back to this period. Thus the hamlet of Shawford became a bustling village with shops and an inn. This hamlet had previously consisted of a few cottages on the banks of the Itchen Navigation Canal and the great house of Shawford Park, built in the 17th century by Henry Mildmay on the site of a much older dwelling.

The Navigation Canal was probably completed in 1729 and had been a busy commercial highway with a wharf near Shawford Mill and a regular passage of loaded barges, but with the coming of the railway the canal became a peaceful, reed-bordered waterway.

From this time Shawford continued as a residential area and at the turn of the 20th century more houses were built in fields at the top of the hill bordering the Roman road and separated from the village by Shawford Downs. Similarly, building was started on the top of the hill south of Compton village and separated from it by Compton Down. Between the two world wars these districts were particularly popular as residences for retired members of the armed services and many gruff colonels and breezy admirals are remembered by present inhabitants.

The four locations, consisting of two villages and two residential areas, remained an entity. The two tracts of downland, one of which was a golf course, far from separating them, served as the background for pleasant walks and to link them. However, with the increase of motor traffic, the problem of holding together a viable village has become increasingly difficult particularly with the advent of the fast road which cuts a swathe through its heart. Much work will be needed in the future to keep Compton and Shawford as a single village.

Copythorne 🌿

Copythorne (meaning 'cropped thorn' from the practice of pollarding trees hereabouts) was a large common on the eastern edge of the New Forest. Now the parish consists of Bartley, Cadnam, Copythorne, Newbridge, Ower and Winsor.

Many road names relate to the past, such as Pollards Moor, Pound Lane (the village pound), Whitemoor Lane (owing to the low-lying area attracting mist in the early morning and evening) and Barrow Hill (from the ancient tumuli). Many Romany families settled here from the Forest where they had lived for generations and brought their trade names to the area, such as Wytcher (withy cutter for hurdles, pegs and baskets).

Half Moon Common is known as Bartley Regis, the royal connection dating from the time that a certain charcoal burner by the name of Purkiss came across the body of King William Rufus in a Forest clearing

Sir John Barleycorn inn, Copythorne

in 1100. In transporting the body to Winchester on his cart he rested at this spot.

Paulton's Park at Ower, the home of the Sloane Stanleys (owners of Sloane Square, London) since 1646, played a large part in the life of the community. The cricket club, which in 1989 celebrated their centenary year, started life in the celebrated Horseshoe Gardens, designed by Capability Brown, at Paulton's. They now have a portion of Copythorne Common as their permanent site, whilst Paulton's Park is now a well-known wildlife and leisure park, with an extensive rural life museum.

In 1843 a Mr Andrew Saunders of North Eling granted half an acre of land for a school for the poor persons of the parish. Opened in 1844, this was Copythorne Church of England school. The early years had very poor attendance as the children were often required to help drive animals to market, pick potatoes, help with haymaking and so on. However, in 1882 things appear to have improved, as an infants school was built in Cadnam to relieve the pressure. This school is still functioning as a first school, whilst the Cadnam school is now a doctor's surgery amongst other uses.

Before 1939, Johnson's Brakes used to come out from Southampton on a Sunday evening, bringing people to the 12th century inn, the Sir John Barleycorn, for a ride and a drink. Now the M27 whizzes traffic past to the west, and this beautiful thatched inn, reputedly the oldest in Hampshire, sits isolated, surrounded by the earthworks made by the building of the motorway. It is still popular with those who know of its existence and whereabouts.

Barrow Hill was once so rutted with cart tracks that residents had to jump along it as best they could, earning it the name of 'Monkey Jump.' This necessitated their leaving their wellies in a shed at the corner shop before catching the bus into town.

A now dilapidated thatched cottage in Barrow Hill was once the property of one Henry Robinson Hartley. Upon his death his estate endowed the Hartley Institute in Southampton, opened by Lord Palmerston in 1862. After its closure in 1902, the money was used to start the Southampton University College, which in turn received the Royal charter to become Southampton University in 1952.

Cotton's pie factory at Cadnam was famous throughout the Forest for its tasty pies. Many craftsmen lived in the area. There was a blacksmith where the British Legion hall now stands, a local brickyard, several carpenters, and one Mr Deadman, who made coffins in a shed near the Compass Inn, Winsor!

Cove ✖

Cove is known to have been in existence in King Alfred's time; in the west of the village, earthworks were in use. Neolithic tools and remnants of pottery were discovered during the building of the M3 motorway, whilst on the Aldershot/Cove boundary gold coins of the 7th century were found.

Mentioned in the Domesday Book, Cove was the residential area of three yeomen farmers, a family of 'potters' and a manor house.

In those times Cove was a hamlet of the see of Crondal, but was later given to the monks of Winchester, in whose possession it stayed until the 19th century. It remained a small and rather isolated area, being surrounded by heathland and scrub.

Fernberga (which means fern on the hill), later known as Farnborough, the neighbouring village, was also isolated. The expansion of Cove/Farnborough took place on the arrival of the army in 1854 in Aldershot, four miles south of Cove.

In 1850 the population of Farnborough/Cove did not exceed 500 but changes followed with the setting up of permanent military encampments on its borders. During 1853 the government had bought most of the surrounding area and in the second half of the 19th century, aided by military development, Aldershot became the largest town in the northeast of Hampshire.

With the arrival of the railway, the area took on residential status. A station was built in Farnborough linking it with London and the south, and subsequently the population increased.

The start of the 20th century brought its first links with the Royal Air Force by the building of HM Balloon Factory in 1913. A large housing estate was built in Cove to house the employees of what was later known as the Royal Aircraft Establishment.

Farnborough absorbed Cove, and the area then became Farnborough Urban District. Despite this Cove has retained its sense of identity as a village unit within the now large town of Farnborough.

Crondall ﹏

The Saxons called it Crundellan, which refers to the local Celtic chalk workings. This name, together with Crundelas and Crundale, justifies the insistence by many, but not all, that Crondall should be pronounced 'Crundle'.

One's first impression is of a pleasing blend of houses of all ages, predominantly in mellow red brick. There are, in fact, 83 listed buildings in the village but it is by no means an 'ancient monument'. Two council estates and a high quota of infilling have doubled the number of dwellings since the Second World War.

Farmland entirely surrounds the compact community and imparts a rural atmosphere. As many tractors as men seem to be engaged in growing the crops of cereals, oil-seed rape, pulses, some maize and an occasional field of beautiful blue linseed. There are sheep, but now no hops are grown, neither are there dairy herds nor pigs. In the past there were spring-fed watercress beds, basket making, weaving, a malthouse – even tobacco growing, and an area of good clay gave rise to a brick industry. Nowadays the soils, whether clay or chalky loam, blessed with a high water table, make fertile ground for many lovely gardens. On occasions some of these are opened to the public. There is much riding and keeping of horses, and walkers enjoy an abundance of footpaths, which are ritually trodden on Rogation Sunday.

The Grade I listed Norman church of All Saints dates from 1170. It superseded a wooden Saxon building from which there only remains a fine stone font, still in use today. On view also is a small marble font, which a Puritan vicar had made to supplant the Saxon object 'profaned by Papal usage'. The present calm, uncluttered interior belies the vicissitudes of fashions and values. Parliamentary troops were actually quartered within the church during the Civil War, when skirmishes occurred in and around the village between Roundheads from Farnham Castle and Royalists from Old Basing and Alton. Fortunately no harm came to the famous brass of Nicholas de Caerwent, a 14th century rector. This is decorated with fylfot crosses, better known to us as swastikas.

On display is one of the country's few remaining 'pitch-pipes'. It was purchased in 1783 to aid the musicians who led the first singing of psalms and hymns. Curiously, it was the Church which bought the village hand-driven fire-engine in 1776, kept it at the back of the church for years and maintained it for a century or so. With leather pipes and buckets, it was still relied upon as the sole appliance in 1935! Now it has to be brought from its lodging in the museum in Winchester to be admired on very special occasions.

The distress wrought in farming communities by legislation in the 19th century was met in Crondall by several acts of charity. One trust which provided for the education of the sons of labourers predated the establishment in 1870 of what is today the County primary school. This Victorian building recently had an imaginative and colourful facelift. And so, the village flourishes, with a village hall, two sports pavilions, a boys club, two shops and four pubs.

Crookham Village 🦢

A visitor to Crookham Village in the mid 19th century would have found a rural area, consisting of small farms, with most of the workers on the land. Many local men found employment in the woods, cutting under-growth for hop poles and standards, and pea and bean sticks. There were several one-man brickmaking businesses in the area and the gravel pit at Beacon Hill was opened in 1876.

By 1911, Crookham had become a thriving little community with a wide variety of commercial interests. In fact, for the period of 60 years up to the 1930s, there was a marked change in the way of life in Crookham Village. At first, apart from the public houses, businesses were mainly basic, tied to the necessities of life. However, as more people came to live in the neighbourhood, and the area was opened up by the coming of the railways and the expansion of the motor industry, the commercial interests became more sophisticated, reflecting a more affluent, leisurely way of life. This expansion did not cease in the 1930s but is still continuing today.

The principal landowner in the area in 1935 was the Calthorpe Estates Company. Tobacco was grown to a considerable extent on the estate of A. J. Brandon, where there was a rehandling shed capable of preparing 100 acres of tobacco for the manufacturers. Tobacco was grown at Crookham from 1912 until 1937 and retailed under such names as Golden Queen and Blue Pryor.

At that time Crookham's facilities were still expanding to include the Anchorage Home for Aged People, Crookham Fire Brigade Station, Crookham Lads' Club, Crookham Rifle Club and the Hampshire and General Friendly Society. The local people were now able to patronise the local dyer and cleaners/ and market gardener. A further significant factor in the development of the area was the building of the railway, which had a station in Fleet in 1850.

Besides the normal development that many 19th century villages underwent, the Crondall and Crookham area was also affected by special circumstances connected with the army.

It was in 1853 that a decision was reached by the Government to make use of the extensive heath and commonland in the Aldershot area for military training purposes. Prior to the establishment of the camp at Aldershot in 1854, no garrison or camp existed in the whole country for the concentration or training of troops on a large scale. The British Army at home were stationed in recognised long established garrisons, most of which had been military centres from earliest times, and the garrisons occupied castles, forts and similar old defensive installations.

The contractors building 'The Camp' in Aldershot offered every inducement to labourers in the area to urge them to press on with the construction of the urgently required accommodation. There was no consideration of cost, and fabulous wages were paid to all classes of skilled workmen and unskilled labourers. This proved a great attraction, and carters, herdsmen and other agricultural workers left the farms for miles around to work as builder's labourers in 'The Camp'. One young man had worked as a farm labourer at 18 shillings per week, but his wages whilst working in the camp were at one time £1 per day.

This gives some idea of the economic changes which occurred in Crondall and Crookham in the 19th and 20th centuries – changes which obviously made themselves felt in the lives of the villagers.

Crowe Hill 🌿

Crowe Hill, as its name implies, is a cascade of houses on a hill, spreading onto the plain to the east of Ringwood. It boasts only a Methodist chapel over 150 years old and two farm shops, But on its borders is the Elm Tree Inn, which at the beginning of the 20th century was a thriving thatched farmhouse, and at the other end the usual petrol station stocked with everything from bread to beach balls, newspapers to chocolate.

A stream runs by the side of the road, flooding in winter and a muddy channel during the heat of the summer. A quiet sleepy place in the sun, until you pass the WI hut in its beautifully tended garden. Here is the hub of Crowe. Cars fill the parking area, with bicycles propped against the walls. For here most days, either for craft, patchwork, drama or choir, meet the women of Crowe.

In the WI hut take place whist drives, residents' meetings, coach teas, and in the winter evenings entertainments and buffets for the members, their husbands and friends.

When all is over and night falls and you climb the hill, you too may hear the neigh of a horse in the distance and wonder. For with the grandeur of the forest moorland on one side and the sea scarcely ten miles away, it is not hard to imagine that as the moon dances amongst the clouds a line of men can be seen crossing the hilltop, each leading a heavily laden horse with two kegs of brandy strapped to the saddle!

Crux Easton 🦌

The hamlet of Crux Easton appears in records as far back as the 11th century as Estune. Then it became Eston Croc when it was given by William the Conqueror to Croch the huntsman (warden of Chute forest), from whom the present name probably derives.

The site of Croch's manor house is now lost but a subsequent one was said to have stood at the western end of the avenue of lime trees, most of which are still standing. As late as the 1960s children were still able to explore a series of tunnels leading from this site; stories circulated that they were secret passages but they were probably drains.

A church is recorded in the Domesday Book. A Norman church, standing in the 12th century, was replaced by the present St Michael's in 1775 and restored in 1894, when a commemorative tree was planted at the crossroads.

The wind pump is said to be unique, being the only one of its kind remaining in Hampshire, if not the whole of southern England. It was certainly in use at the beginning of the 20th century, pumping water into a reservoir opposite where the Porchester estate cottages now stand, supplying only the present manor house. The original blueprints for this still survive. In 1920 the firm of Martin & Wilcox were employed to bore deeper; they hit stone a further 30 ft down but found no extra water. It took 20 minutes to winch the man from the bottom of the shaft.

In about 1692 Edward Lisle bought the estate and made copious notes of agricultural practices in the district. After his death his son Thomas, then rector of Burghclere, published these as the best-selling *Observations in Husbandry*. Edward Lisle had 20 children and his daughters built a grotto in what is now called Grotto Copse.

In 1897 when the Rev Charles de Havilland took the living, the village consisted of the rectory, church, school, farmhouse, pub and a dozen cottages. His son Geoffrey, who 'tinkered' with machinery, installed the first electricity into the rectory and in 1902 built a motor bike which crashed into the church wall when the brakes failed on the first run. Geoffrey was a pioneer of the aircraft industry and when he flew to Crux Easton to visit his parents all the children would rush out of school to watch him land; he parked his plane in a fenced area to keep the cattle away.

Since the Rev de Havilland's day the village has changed. Though the number of houses has risen the number of inhabitants has remained much the same. All the small cottages have been knocked together to make larger dwellings. The village policeman left in 1930, the school closed in 1945, the pub in 1950 and the generations of rural families who lived in the cottages have gone, but their names live on in the names of the properties – Faithfulls, The Alders, de Havillands, Three Legged Cross.

Curdridge 🦐

The parish of Curdridge, which nowadays embraces Curbridge, has a population of approximately 1,200 and is 2,956 acres in area. Like many Hampshire villages, it has no real centre, but it certainly has a heart! Depending on your leanings, the church, reading room or the local pub might be classed as the heart, but of course, as we all know the local post office and village store is the place to find out what is really going on!

Until 1838, Curdridge was a tithing of the parish of Bishop's Waltham where all church services and burials were held. It is said that once a party of pall bearers travelling to Bishop's Waltham with a coffin stopped at the Cricketers Inn, which at that time stood alongside the pond on the main road to Bishop's Waltham. It was a hot day and they stopped to slake their thirst. However, one drink led to another and in the end the bearers were too drunk to continue on their way. The luckless body in the coffin was put in the pub's coal cellar until morning, when after a good sleep the bearers completed the journey to Bishop's Waltham!

A claim to fame is the link with *Alice in Wonderland*. Rev Dodgson, who wrote under the pseudonym of Lewis Carroll, is thought to have spent time visiting Kitnocks House as the guest of the Liddell family. It was Alice Liddell who was Dodgson's model for the book.

St Peter's church tower, built in 1894, is unique in that all but one of the gargoyles can be related to the Southampton legend of Sir Bevois, a knight who travelled to the Holy Land, performing dashing deeds along the way! The odd gargoyle is the head of a woman on the south-east corner of the tower. There is some conjecture as to whether it is supposed to be Kate Knox, who was drowned in the then moat around Kitnocks House, toward which she is looking, or Kate Hunt, reputed to be a witch.

From 1933 to 1950, Curbridge was a separate civil parish and its church came under the jurisdiction of Sarisbury Green. Owing to a lack of enthusiasm for council work on the part of the populace, the parish was divided. Wickham got most of the rural area and Curdridge was given the hamlet around Curbridge Creek, which includes the Horse and Jockey public house, the parish quay (alongside) and St Barnabas' church, which is still administered by Sarisbury Green and not Curdridge.

No story of Curdridge would be complete without reference to the strawberry trade. In the early part of the 20th century strawberry growing was a way of life; even the school holidays were adjusted so the children could help gather them in. The fruit was then shipped off to London from Botley station, after children had packed the baskets on the train because children were smaller and took up less room while packing! The station house has long gone, as have three of the village's four ponds and the toll house which stood opposite Cricketer's pond. All that remains of the village pound is a wayside seat at the plantation, formerly the common, maintained by the Parish Council.

Denmead ✺

Denmead is on the main B2150 road between Waterlooville and Hambledon. Situated on the edge of the Forest of Bere, its boundaries are the parish of Hambledon, the Southwick estate (which for centuries has been owned by the Thistlewaite family) and Waterlooville, while just over Portsdown Hill is Portsmouth and the historic naval dockyard.

All Saints' church is in the centre of the village near the shopping area. It was not built until 1880 and the first vicar (Rev Green) took office as the vicar of Barn Green in 1881. Until that time the village was still part of Hambledon parish and most of the villagers were baptised and buried at Hambledon church. The old font in All Saints' was presented by the parishioners of St Peter and St Paul, Hambledon, in1880. There is also a Baptist church in the village, which started off as a chapel. It stands in its own grounds in Anmore Road. Having a church in Barn Green made life a lot easier for the village, which was beginning to grow. Rev Green decided that Barn Green should be renamed, and Denmead was the name given.

The green is the centre of the village and all royal and national events are celebrated there. Close by is a modern health centre. The church and shops are a little further on and the name of Restall's must be mentioned here as, for over a century, Restall's shop was, amongst other things, the post office, baker, butcher, grocer, off-licence and the general meeting place of the area.

There are four public houses – the Forest of Bere, the Harvest Home, the Fox and Hounds and the White Hart. It is said that the last bear in Hampshire was killed at the Forest of Bere pub. The Forest of Bere was ancient woodland, although very little remains today. Most of the timber was used to build ships in the naval dockyard in Portsmouth. There is an area left close to the village known as Creech Wood, which was opened to the public a few years ago and is now enjoyed by many villagers and their families.

There are still a few working farms round the village. One often sees a tractor go by with a load of hay and there are fields of sheep, cows and horses nearby. The village has never boasted large buildings or mansions, but there are still thatched cottages. These were very much in need of repair until the naval families came to Denmead to live and took them over, saving them from neglect.

There is also a growing industrial estate, the main industry being a pottery which also has a lake, aviaries and animal enclosure. It is a popular attraction for people from the nearby towns and cities.

Denvilles & Warblington ✣

Warblington Castle and the church of St Thomas a Becket have long been historical landmarks overlooking Emsworth harbour.

The then moated castle was destroyed by Parliamentarian forces during the Civil War in 1642 leaving only the tower and one side of the gatehouse. Believed to have been built in 1512, the castle was once occupied by Sir Richard and Margaret Pole, Count and Countess of Salisbury.

Warblington church (13th century) was at one time in the centre of a village which was wiped out by the Black Death. The houses fell into dereliction leaving only the church. The church has a partly Saxon tower and a fine 15th century timbered porch. Standing in the churchyard is a grand old yew tree which is reputed to be at least 1,500 years old. At the west and eastern ends of the churchyard are huts built to accommodate watchmen who were employed to prevent 'body snatching' when medical men, mainly students, desperate for cadavers on which to practise their profession, were willing to pay for a dead body.

Green Pond, Warblington, has ceased to exist but at one time was situated at the junction of Southleigh Road with the old A27, opposite the blacksmith's forge, which is now the site of the One Stop shop.

Prior to the Second World War, Warblington House stood in its own grounds bordering Pook Lane and was occupied by the Marquis of Tavistock. Within the estate, enclosed by high brick walls, was a small wildlife park kept by the Marquis, specialising in parrots. The secretary to the Marquis was none other than the notorious traitor, William Joyce, who, having absconded to Germany, regularly broadcast enemy propaganda as Lord Haw Haw.

Denvilles, by comparison, is a more recent development. In all probability the first houses were constructed in the late 19th century, the residents being mainly naval officers and businessmen who wished to live 'in the country'.

The more rapid growth of the area during the latter part of the 20th century has seen the disappearance of the majority of these large old properties, creating opportunities for developers. Denvilles has become a rather sprawling residential area with few facilities for the convenience of the residents.

Dibden ✍

Dibden is a little parish on the Southampton Water situated between Marchwood and Hythe.

All Saints' is a lovely little church, parts of which were built in the 13th century. It was the first local building to be bombed in the Second World War, but it lost nothing in the rebuilding in 1955. The Bishop of Winchester consecrated it and over the door is the commemoration stone with the inscription 'A joyful resurrection' – how apt!

There used to be several farms in the area. On the main road there still stands a house, 300 to 400 years old, purported to have been an inn, and nearby an old cottage. A creek that came up from Southampton Water leads the thoughts to smugglers, but the connection was never proved. The site of the brick kiln still carries the name Claypits Lane.

Within the last 50 years, up the Southampton Water would come the big, world famous liners and other shipping, so there was plenty to see if one took to walking along the bank to Marchwood. There was only one little shop and post office combined.

Now things are a little different. Entering Claypits Lane from the main Southampton Road you soon come to a well situated caravan site surrounded by trees and further on two large housing estates either side of the road. Shortly comes the modern Appelmoor School for senior boys and girls. On the same site is a huge successful sports complex. The

Southampton-bound buses now come off the main road and go through the lane to serve this and the many houses. This means one cannot get to Dibden church unless one has transport.

A new golf club and club house with restaurant has taken in many fields and there is another site for mobile homes on the main road as you go out of Dibden into Marchwood. This also looks attractive and is well tended.

Dibden Purlieu

Dibden Purlieu is in the parish of Dibden. In the Domesday Book Dibden was Deepdene, an Anglo-Saxon word for a deep valley. Purlieu is a Norman-French word meaning 'the outskirts of a forest', a place free from forest laws.

At the beginning of the 20th century Dibden Purlieu was little more than a hamlet, with unmade roads and few amenities. Many people today work in the petro-chemical industries and other smaller industries, a far cry from rural village life when inhabitants would have been employed on the land, in forestry and on the large estates of Exbury and Beaulieu. Others may have worked at Bucklers Hard, the 18th century shipyard, where Nelson's favourite ship the *Agamemnon* was built. It is interesting to note that the timbers of the old barn (once part of Butts Ash Farm, now a builder's yard), came from the wreck of a man-of-war at Bucklers Hard and have nautical markings.

Today's village centre is modern. Close by stands St Andrew's church, an unusual octagonal church with a copper spire. It was dedicated by the Bishop of Winchester in 1970. The original place of worship is now used as the church hall. The Methodist church is in North Road leading off the main road. The present building was opened in 1923 but prior to this in 1916 the first Methodists worshipped in a corrugated iron hut, known as the 'tin tab'. Some of the village shops were also constructed of tin before being modernised in the early 1960s.

At the end of Lunedale road is a Roman road which runs parallel with the borders of the Forest, with large banks of gorse on the right. There is a local saying that 'kissing is out of fashion when gorse is not in bloom'. Happily gorse blossoms can be found all year round! Years ago gorse was a wash-day aid; the blossoms were boiled, and the subsequent liquid used to 'cream' net curtains.

The Forest can be reached by crossing the busy Southampton road (A326), then through a 'kissing gate' into a wide grazing stip of pasture for the ponies.

Dibden Purlieu is proud to be associated with several distinguished people, one of whom is Richard Eurich RA, OBE, a talented artist who from 1941 was official war artist to the Admiralty. The village was also the home of Ron Lane, a wildlife wood sculptor, well known not only in Hampshire but throughout the United Kingdom. The Ron Lane Memorial Trust annually organises a wood sculpture competition for schoolchildren to perpetuate his memory.

Although Dibden Purlieu is frequently referred to as 'the village' it is a fast expanding area, with two large comprehensive schools, a sports centre and a busy shopping complex. Its shortest contact with Southampton is across the water via Hythe Ferry.

Drayton & Farlington 🪶

At the turn of the 20th century Drayton and Farlington were little more than hamlets, each with a manor house and some farms. For many years the church of St Andrew also served the people of Purbrook, who came across the hill on rough tracks, but in the 19th century they established their own church and the parish was divided.

The old Wesleyan chapel in Drayton gave way to a fine church in the 1930s which is an important centre, not only for the Methodists themselves, but as a meeting point for many organisations of all persuasions.

Being on the outskirts of Portsmouth there has always been a very close link with the Royal Navy, which was furthered by the building of a large housing estate on Portsdown Hill. The houses are just below one of Palmerston's follies, Fort Purbrook, one of the last castles to be built in Britain, and now a youth centre.

In the 1920s, as public transport improved, people moved out from Portsmouth to what was still mainly country. New houses and roads were built on the church glebe but there was little tarmac and few pavements. The squelching mud of First and Second Avenues was bright yellow-brown and viciously sucked off galoshes at the first opportunity. A few open-topped buses ran to and from Portsmouth and eventually as far as Brighton. For several years many people travelled on a little local train known as the Chichester Motor, which stopped on its way to Portsmouth at Farlington Halt, built to accommodate horses and racegoers for Farlington racecourse in its heyday at the beginning of the 20th century. After the First World War it was used for destroying ammunition, which caused a pall of strong smelling smoke to waft across the area.

In 1925 a new school was built in Solent Road on a former potato field. From the outside little has changed, the pastel-washed walls have a pleasant country look which leads some people to think it must be a farm, which it never was.

The villages of Drayton and Farlington have long been suburbs of Portsmouth but there are still fields with cattle around and the marshes are now the Hampshire Wildlife Park, attracting many seabirds. It is not uncommon to see foxes or squirrels in local gardens or hear cattle lowing on the marshes. There are many social clubs or organisations and plans for a Community Association to serve the area are well advanced.

East Boldre 🍃

Along the main road between Beaulieu and Lymington, lies the well known beauty spot of Hatchet Pond. This serene stretch of water reflects pine trees and is often marbled at sunset with pink, gold and the blood-red of a dying day.

When tired of idling here, take the turning sign-posted 'East Boldre'. The village is a long straggling one – a rural ribbon development, and the road leads eventually to East End, South Baddesley and the Lymington to Yarmouth ferry. There are two excellent shops in the village (one a sub-post office), a useful garage and the little Victorian church of St Paul. Most of the houses are built on the left hand side of the lane, with open forest and grazing animals on the right.

Further on is the old schoolhouse and the village school which are situated on the right, between clumps of pine trees. Today, the village school stands empty and has fallen into a sad state of disrepair. Grubby, pale pink paint flakes from the brick-work and mossy roof slates hang loose and occasionally drop on to the asphalt below. However, its interesting history is recorded in the school log books.

The school was built in 1842, on four and a half acres of land presented by the young Queen Victoria, together with money from the Crown and the Church of England.

Imagine those first pupils of Victorian days; the girls black-stockinged and pinafore clad, the boys in Eton collars and serviceable boots, all working at their slates. The log books of those early times bear witness to the strict discipline enforced by the use of the cane for such offences as untidy arithmetic, loitering outside the school, kicking a dog, and having dirty boots!

This, the smallest and oldest school in the Forest, was a sad loss when it was closed in 1985, but there was one happy outcome. When closure was first mooted because of falling numbers, a sub-committee of the Parish Council was formed and, after valiant fund-raising efforts, the playing field and infants classroom were purchased for the modest sum of £9,000. This amenity is now used by the Scouts, Beavers and Cubs, the under-16s football club, and the Mothers and Toddlers Club, not to mention the annual church fete and countless other activities.

East Meon 🌿

East Meon is a picturesque village, four miles west of Petersfield. There have been Bronze Age finds near Westbury House and Old Winchester Hill, now a nature reserve with extensive views over the countryside, was originally an Iron Age fort.

All Saints' church was built between 1075 and 1150 by Bishop Walkelin, who also organised the building of Winchester Cathedral. It is magnificently situated at the base of steeply rising, green Park Hill, overlooking the village. The most famous feature is a black marble font, from Tournai in Belgium, carved about 1150, depicting the Garden of Eden. There is also a curious stone inscribed 'Amens plenty' which at one time covered the grave of four men buried vertically, probably at the time of the Civil War.

The river Meon rises behind South Farm and wends its shallow way through the village. During past centuries flooding of the river became a worsening problem, with streets and houses annually under several feet of water, even preventing children attending school. As there was no mains drainage or piped water, this brought additional problems from privies. In 1955 the course of the river was changed and widened. It now flows over a concrete base with many small bridges.

There are two lovely Tudor houses in Workhouse Lane (where there was a workhouse between 1727 and 1910) and several Georgian and earlier houses and cottages in the village centre. The oldest of these is a pair of cottages and a shop, formerly a butcher's shop but now a dairy. It is unusual to find a group of small houses of as early a date as the mid 14th century. The Court House, now a private residence, has a large medieval barn from the same date. This was used by the Bishops of Winchester for the local manorial court and residence for the visiting bishop. It has five ft thick flint and stone walls, which are 50 ft high.

To the south of the village HMS Mercury – a naval communications school – occupies a sprawl of buildings over the hilltop by Leydene House. This magnificent mansion was the home of Eleanor Countess Peel, who, with her politician husband, built it in 1924, probably the last 'stately home' to be built in England. In its heyday there were brilliant weekend parties and shoots for political and titled guests. There were 14 gardeners – the kitchen garden alone was seven acres, and at least twelve

View of All Saints' church, East Meon

80

indoor staff were employed. When Lady Peel died in 1949, the Navy bought the house and some of the land.

Today East Meon is a very mixed community. At the beginning of the 20th century there were four bakers, three grocers, a paraffin and hardware store, a saddler's, two butchers, two mills, a wheelwright, a farrier, a post office and a fish and chip shop. Now there is one general grocer with butcher, one grocer with dairy, a post office and a blacksmith.

Easton ✤

This little village, of about 450 inhabitants, lies conveniently two and a half miles east of Winchester, as its Anglo-Saxon name Est-tun (east village) implies. The river Itchen, that renowned trout stream, flows past the outskirts and virtually on its banks stands the ancient church of St Mary, built between 1120 and 1170 on a Saxon foundation. You can approach it over the river, and turn left at the Cricketers Inn into the village street, which stretches for half a mile or more, lined with a varied collection of old thatched, half-timbered cottages, existing harmoniously beside 19th century villas and more modern houses. The street bends sharply twice, the second time just past the second pub, the Chestnut Horse, and eventually becomes a country lane leading to Avington. Of the three side roads, Chapel Lane and Church Lane contain the same attractive mixture of old and new, including a pleasant cluster of council houses and, off Easton Lane, there is Malthouse Close, a 1960s development of well-designed houses and bungalows.

All around is the lovely Hampshire countryside – the farmland, green in spring, golden in the autumn, the winding lanes, the backcloth of gentle wooded hills. Fortunately the village is situated on unclassified roads, with little through traffic, though less than half a mile from the Winchester/Alresford road. A few years ago the threat posed by modern transport became a reality when the M3 cut through this lovely valley. Villagers have learnt to live with it, though the sound of traffic is now a permanent background murmur.

Older residents look back wistfully to a time when Easton was a 'real' village, with two bakeries, a post office, a shoemaker, a laundry, a dressmaker, a corn chandler, a blacksmith's forge, a basket-maker (with a field for his reeds near the river), and a couple of general stores. Milk could be bought from the farmers, and there were two carriers, both ladies of indomitable spirit, one of whom went into Winchester three times a week with her pony and trap, and the other with a donkey cart. There are tales of wonderful Christmases, Sunday school treats in Cockett's Mead (now the cricket field), and hardships and pleasures enjoyed by a rural community which kept many of its old ways until after the Second World War.

Few people now work in the village, though farming, including a large bulb-growing business, does offer some employment. It is a familiar story. The village school closed in the late 1960s and is now a private house, the same fate overtook the Methodist chapel, and the post office and general store closed in about 1970. Easton is lucky still to have a local garage, two pubs and a small market garden run by an old-established family of the village, which sells fruit and vegetables.

East Tytherley 🦢

If you drive from Lockerley to West Tytherley, you will pass through one of the smallest villages in Hampshire – East Tytherley.

In 1335 Tytherley was given to Queen Philippa by her husband, Edward III. She loved the peaceful village, and when the appalling Black Death spread to London, she brought her court here for safety. Tragically, two of the young courtiers had already been touched with death's finger, and within a few days 70 per cent of the village died. Flemish weavers, who had been given sanctuary by the Queen from persecution in their own country, helped prepare the shrouds. Philippa created a semi-permanent court here, and names such as Queenwood and Queen's Croft remain to recall the days following the sorrows.

After the Civil War, the Rolle family became lords of the manor and until 1800 lived in the village. Each generation added something to the history of the place. In 1736 Miss Sarah Rolle founded a charitable school, and the charity exists to this day.

The beautiful old trees in the churchyard of St Peter's were planted by Dennis Rolle. In spring and summer the little church comes into its own, a most peaceful spot. Built in 1250, it remained unaltered until 1863 when a porch and bell-tower were added. The first resident incumbent was appointed in 1803. A shoemaker by trade, with his business in Broughton, he walked to church each Sunday through the woods, and the track still exists. At the west end of the building was a gallery where the 'church music' sat – clarinet, bugle, flute, bassoon and bass viol – all played by the villagers.

Of course, East Tytherley has had its share of eccentrics and historical oddities. Sir Robert Peel's uncle, General Jonathan Yates, became tenant of the manor house, and was much admired by the village in spite of rather dubious morals. Amongst his hobbies was cock-fighting, and in the grand salon of the manor, turf was laid instead of carpet for matches between his birds and those of other landowners. Though a great brandy drinker he lived to a ripe old age.

In 1849, a Mr Cooke bought half the estate, and while in Tytherley invented the electric telegraph. Telegraph Hill, and Telegraph House are reminders of those times.

Today, the village is as peaceful and happy as it has ever been, though of course the cricket pitch sees some good battles, and the skittle alley in the Star Inn is a popular rendezvous.

East Woodhay & Woolton Hill 🦥

East Woodhay and Woolton Hill are right in the country, five miles from the nearest town, Newbury. In the extreme north of Hampshire, some of the village is on the border with Berkshire.

There are two churches served by one rector. St Martin's, with a tower and six bells at East Woodhay, is right under the downs. The date of its foundation is unknown but in 1136 Wodehaye is named as one of the 'considerable rectories' giving an annual donation of 100 shillings to the hospital of St Cross, near Winchester. Its list of rectors goes back to 1546, one of whom was Thomas Ken (1669–1672), who later became Bishop of Bath and Wells. He planted a yew tree very close to the main door of the church and when it had to be cut down, a processional cross and alms bag handles were made with the wood and are in use today. There is a lovely east window, a memorial to those from East Woodhay who gave their lives for King and Country.

St Thomas's at Woolton Hill was built in 1849, a neat structure with a tower containing five bells and crowned by a spire. Woolton Hill once consisted of large houses and estates and these employed a large number of village people who lived in estate property, now privately owned.

Years ago there was a police station next to the post office. There was also a church hall, built in 1911, but many local activities were held in the working men's club. There are still two inns in Woolton Hill. Hollington House is now a nursing home and there is also a rest home at Broadmead and a shop at Broadlayings. The stud, which used to be known as Harwood, is now called Gainsborough and many famous racehorses have been stabled there. There are now housing estates in Woolton Hill and there has been quite a jump in population, especially of younger folks with children.

There used to be a forge and blacksmith's at East End, but that has gone. So too has the post office and stores at East End and North End. The nearest post office is now in Woolton Hill. The Prior family ran a bakery as well as a post office and stores. There is a small bakery in Ball

Hill. A lovely thatched cottage at North End is reputed to be haunted.

In 1644 Oliver Cromwell slept at Stargroves the night before the battle of Newbury. A bowl which he used is now in Newbury Museum for safe keeping.

East Woodhay has a splendid Silver Band, founded in 1884, with its conductor of over 40 years, Mr D. T Webb. An 'impromptu' band under Mr Bob Paton plays in church regularly for Family Service.

Elson ✍

In spite of the fact that the village has now almost been swallowed up by Gosport, at the turn of the 20th century, and even up to the Second World War, it was still a truly rural community. Somehow, in spite of all the new housing covering its once green fields and woods, the village atmosphere still survives.

Elson's history goes back to a time before either Gosport or Portsmouth had been founded, for it was mentioned in a Royal Saxon Charter of Alverstoke, dated AD 948. The boundaries are carefully decribed and at one point they run along 'the meadows of the people of Aethelswithetun', which was later corrupted to Elston, and finally to Elson. It means 'Ethelswith's town'. King Alfred is believed to have granted this peaceful little retreat on the western shore of Portsmouth harbour as a gift to either his mother or his wife or his daughter, all of whom were called Ethelswith!

Elson remained the only settlement between the harbour entrance and Fareham until the 12th century, when the Norman Prior of St Swithun's built the Priory Home Farm at Hardway, with a tide-mill across the creek at Forton. There was also a jetty, and wharfs convenient for transporting goods and passengers to and from Normandy. This was called Pope's Walk until it fell into the sea at the beginning of the 20th century!

Then, as now, the shortest route to Normandy was from Portsmouth Harbour. King Stephen's brother, Bishop of Winchester, Henry de Blois, having been rescued from shipwreck in the Solent by local fishermen, granted privileges of markets and fairs to 'Godsport' as he called the tiny peninsula near the harbour entrance. By a charter of 1204, Bishop Godfrey de Lucy endowed Winchester Cathedral with 'all the trading profits which can reasonably be derived from the village newly built upon the harbour in the manor of Alverstoke'. Thanks to Bishops Henry and Godfrey, nearly 800 years later the town of Gosport has managed to swallow up not only ancient Elson and Hardway, but also the villages of Alverstoke, Forton, Brockhurst, Rowner and Lee-on-the-Solent too.

Enham Alamein

Enham was a tiny hamlet at the turn of the 20th century. Enham Place was a large house owned by Lord and Lady Earle, and there were two smaller houses, Littlecote and the White House, each with a few servants. Some villagers lived in their place of employment, others in lovely thatched cottages, or chalk and flint cottages with tiled roofs dotted along the Newbury to Andover Road which ran through the grounds of Enham Place.

Tucked away on the edge of the village in Anton Lane, the main road in medieval times, a cottage still retains its original tie beam and many Elizabethan beams, and an inglenook fireplace with a wooden fire door to the bread oven. The partition walls are 17th century wattle and daub. Littlecote House, the dowager's house on the original Enham estate, was used from the early 1920s until it was demolished in the late 1950s, to accommodate tuberculosis sufferers.

In 1919 a consortium of London businessmen purchased Enham Place and started a rehabilitation centre for disabled men from the First World War. In 1939 Enham Place was demolished, and in its place Enham Industries was built, thus enabling victims of the war to help in the manufacture of Nissen huts and barrage balloons. Over the years several houses have been donated to the village by outsiders who have appreciated the work being done by the Enham Village Centre.

In 1942, after the battle of El Alamein, one of the turning points of the Second World War, some prominent Egyptians gave £100,000 to the Enham Village Centre as a mark of their gratitude to the men who had saved Egypt from occupation. It was then decided to rename the village Enham-Alamein. Plans were made to build 100 cottages, a hostel for the disabled, a church, a school and an inn. The houses were to be specially adapted for disabled personnel. The school and inn did not materialise, however, there being an excellent school in nearby Smannell.

Every year on Alamein Sunday in October, the young men of 1942 who turned the tide at the battle of El Alamein travel from far and wide to the village for a parade and service at St George's chapel to remember their colleagues who did not return. On 23rd October 1947 HRH Princess Elizabeth unveiled a stone commemorating Egypt's gift and opened the first pair of cottages built with some of the money.

Enham Industries has now diversified its products. Engineering, furniture making, book-binding, candle-making and wax items, electronics and horticulture give work for over 300 disabled men and women.

Eversley & Bramshill 🦢

Eversley has always been a forest parish of scattered hamlets. In Norman times it gave its name to a royal forest for deer-hunting and Hampshire County Council has recently made this a heritage area with the same title – the Royal Forest of Eversley

Long ago it was mostly heathland and pasture woodland like the New Forest. Later it had its own self-sown pine woods and now they are Forestry Commission plantations where many people enjoy walking and horse riding. There is pasture beside the Blackwater, which flows through Eversley and Bramshill and forms the county boundary with Berkshire. The bridge over it at Eversley Street is the latest of several bridges. At one time there was a toll bridge. There are four public houses in Eversley of which two are at Eversley Cross, where cricket has been played on the green for over 200 years.

Charles Kingsley was rector of Eversley for over 30 years from 1844 to 1875. It was here in the Old Rectory next to the church that he wrote *The Water Babies*. It is now a private house, but it can be seen from Church Lane and its appearance is little changed since the Kingsley family lived there. Charles and his wife are buried in the churchyard, their grave marked by a white marble cross with a passionflower entwined on it. Below their names and almost hidden in the grass are the Latin words he chose, 'Amavimus, Amamus, Amabimus', meaning 'We loved, We love, We shall love'. Charles Kingsley planted the avenue of Irish yews leading from the lychgate and the big Wellingtonia grew from a cone which he brought back from America and which his daughter planted a few days after his death. In the church is the pulpit from which he preached, now reduced from its former three-decker height. The church is the only one in Hampshire with an 18th century screen.

Charles Kingsley founded the village school which is called after him and which has Tom of *The Water Babies* represented on its wrought iron gates. Model cottages were built here and there in Eversley after Charles Kingsley's death by his devoted pupil, John Martineau. They are in rustic style with carved beams and barge-boards, some with texts and quotations on them.

Bramshill is closely linked with Eversley. Its name means 'broom-covered hill' and Bramshill House stands on the hill with splendid views. It is now the Police Staff College and therefore not open to the public. It is a beautiful Jacobean house built by Lord Zouche between 1605 and 1612. It is reputed to be haunted by several ghosts, among them a green man and a grey lady!

The Cope family lived there until 1936 and in their time mummers

Bramshill House

performed their ancient play in the great hall every Christmas, and sang the ballad of the Mistletoe Bough which was thought to be connected with the house. The mummers also walked over to Eversley and sang carols there, some of them unique and heard only in these two villages.

Ewshot

Ewshot is small and consists of five hamlets: Ewshot Village, Beacon Hill, Warren Corner, Doras Green, and the new complex, now known as Ewshot Heights, built by the late Charles Church. The postal address is Farnham, Surrey, the post code is based on Guildford, the telephone is via Aldershot, rates are paid to Fleet in Hart District, and the County Council is Hampshire at Winchester!

Many of the older houses were built with bricks made at the local brickworks, which no longer exists. Bricks were also supplied for the building of Ewshot Camp in 1900. Gravel from the local pits was used, much of which was transported on tramlines laid for that purpose, down the hill and through the woods and across fields. Sand too was required, and Sand Pit Cottages in Tadpole Lane mark an area where much sand was extracted.

The camp, when finished, was occupied by the Royal Artillery, and for many years the horses being exercised were a familiar sight in the village lanes. When Aldershot Camp was built in the 19th century, land known as Bourley Bottom became a catchment area. Five reservoirs were dug and water from the surrounding hills ran into them and was piped to form the water supply for the camp. It still does so today. The water bailiff's house is on the far side from Ewshot and in days past, the Ewshot postman had a long and bumpy ride across the common to take letters.

In the early 1920s, a local man started a bus service to Farnham, three miles away. If the passengers were lucky they rode all the way, but alas, they often had to get out and walk up the steep hills, as the bus couldn't make it when loaded. Later the Aldershot Traction Company took over.

Most people now find work outside the village, so that occupations are very varied. There is, however, a small haulage firm which has been in the village and run by the same family for five generations. There is also a small removal firm, various builders, plumbers and decorators, and a small equestrian centre.

Exbury 🙦

Exbury must surely enjoy one of the most favoured situations in Hampshire, being on the edge of the New Forest, just one mile from the Solent coast and having its fields and woods overlooking the Beaulieu river. Its fortunes have been much tied up with the owners of Exbury House, a fine neo-Georgian mansion which stands in Exbury Gardens, now famous for their collection of azaleas and rhododendrons. In the 18th century Exbury House was owned by the Mitford family and today the heir to the Mitfords, Lord Redesdale, has made a comfortable family home of the little stone school next to the church. The next owner was Lord Forster and on his appointment as Governor-General of Australia in 1919 he sold the estate to Mr Lionel de Rothschild, whose son, Mr Edmund de Rothschild owns it today.

All the cottages in Exbury village were built for workers on the estate. The earlier ones are built of distinctive yellow bricks made at a brick kiln on the estate. Supplies for the kiln were brought in by barge to a small hard at the brickyard. Later when the gardens and greenhouses were being established, a large army of labourers and gardeners was recruited and houses were built for them in the 1920s in red brick with inside toilets and, later, electricity. Mr de Rothschild also built an attractive bow-fronted shop and post office and a village club.

Exbury church was built in the early 19th century using some of the stones from a monastic chapel which had existed at Lower Exbury. Several members of the Mitford family are buried in the churchyard, their coffins having been reverently removed from the Mitford family vault when the church was renovated in 1907.

The most impressive monument is the Forster memorial bronze in the Memorial Chapel. This depicts the recumbent figure of Alfred Forster, son of Lord Forster who, as a lieutenant in the Royal Scots Greys, died of wounds sustained at the end of the First World War. A young sculptor, Cecil Thomas, was wounded at about the same time and for four months the two young men were in the same hospital and became great friends. After the war, Lord and Lady Forster commissioned Cecil Thomas to design a memorial to Alfred and his elder brother, John, who also died in the First World War. The bronze was so impressive that it was exhibited at the Royal Academy in 1924. It is remarkably life-like and shows such detail as the greatcoat folds, the Sam Browne belt and the lacing-up pattern of the boots. Four candlesticks surround the figure and these burn spiked candles on Remembrance Sunday each year.

Between the wars, Exbury was very much a self-contained community. Its cottages were all occupied by workers on the estate and in the gardens, and they made their own entertainment at Exbury Club and its adjoining cricket field. There were amateur dramatics, a dance band, whist drives, the WI, billiards, snooker and darts, and of course, the annual children's party. In the summer, there was tennis, cricket and the annual Flower Show. Only one or two people owned a car or a pony trap and could make the occasional excursion to Blackfield, Hythe or Southampton.

Today the cottages are still occupied by estate workers or their families. They have been modernised to some extent but most of them still have their open fires burning coal and logs. And every Christmas the owner of the Big House still brings round to each pensioner his gift of a brace of pheasants and a load of logs.

Fair Oak & Horton Heath

'The old order changeth yielding place to new' – Tennyson's words are an apt comment on the parish of Fair Oak and Horton Heath. Once a small cluster of cottages, it has developed into a village with a population of between 7,000 and 8,000.

For many years the parish was known just as Fair Oak, the name of Horton Heath being incorporated in 1983. The name derived from the fair that was held near the oak tree in the square on 9th June every year. The first person to erect his stall called at the front door of the Old George Inn to collect the 'key' of the fair. He then returned it to the landlord at the back door and received a quantity of beer, thought to be a gallon.

The fair was discontinued after the First World War and all that remains of the original oak tree is a chair made from its wood in Winchester Cathedral. A carving depicting it outside the George Inn is incorporated in panelling above a fireplace at Fair Oak Lodge in Allington Lane. The present tree was planted in 1843.

Inevitably, the surge in population has resulted in all sorts of changes, especially in amenities. The parish church of St Thomas has been extended. The church school was superseded by a large school campus on another site, with the original site now being used for sheltered accommodation for the elderly. When the church graveyard became full, a new cemetery was opened in 1942 and Mr Jesse Latimer was appointed gravedigger. Sadly, he died before he could start work and was accorded the dubious privilege of being the first person to be buried there. The latest amenity is a new village hall which serves a growing number of clubs and activities.

More and more people, more and more buildings. William Cobbett could never have foreseen the spoliation of this area on his frequent journeys between Winchester and Botley along what was then known as Cobbett's Road, but is now plain Winchester Road. He wrote of this route in his *Rural Rides* of 1832: 'a more beautiful ten miles there is not in all England'.

Yet some of that beauty still survives in what is so unromantically known as the Green Belt, and human habitation has not quite driven out the wildlife. The village has its own designated nature reserve, Knowle Hill, adjoining the deer farm. Administered by the Parish Council it was once part of a rubbish tip.

Not far from the reserve in Knowle Lane is a large private house called The Cockpit. Until about 1880 it was an inn where cockfighting flourished, and even when the sport was made illegal, the participants continued their activities in the cellars.

Farringdon ✦

Farringdon is a small village in the fold of the Downs between Selborne and Chawton. In his journal dated 13th February 1774, the naturalist Gilbert White mentions 'Great flocks of buntings in the fields towards Farringdon'. At the time he was curate of the 12th century church of All Saints at Farringdon as well as curate at Selborne. So he would have ridden over from his home at the Wakes on his old safe cob in all weathers to take the services and preach to the faithful, observing the habits of the wildlife on the way. There are still many beautiful thatched cottages which must have been seen by Gilbert White on his rambles round the village and certainly the present yews in the churchyard were already old by that time.

Later, about 1877, the eccentric rector Rev Massey bought an old boarding school opposite the church and, with only the help of one bricklayer and his labourer, proceeded to add a tower and a wing and gradually covered the building with red brick, ornamented with beautiful terracotta work of pomegranates and other fruits. Work went on and on for the next 20 years and when the puzzled villagers pressed the rector for an explanation for what use he intended the building he would tease them by saying confidentially: 'I believe I shall make a tea house out of it. Do you know of a secondhand revolving light for sale, such as they use in lighthouses? I want one. When it turns green it would be tea time!' 'Massey's Folly', as it is now called, was divided into the school and village hall. Sadly the school closed in 1988, but the hall is still used by village organisations.

At one time there was a blacksmith and a baker as well as a village shop. Even today there is a working blacksmith down at the crossroads of the A32, opposite the treasured post office and shop.

An unsolved mystery in 1785 is recorded in the churchyard where the tomb of Mary Windebank, aged 75, appears to tell of a murder in what is now Gilbert's Cottage. The top part of the stone is carved. It shows the old lady in a large fourposter bed, with a row of moneybags underneath. A thief is seen coming up the stairs and behind him is a curious winged figure thought to portray the Devil.

Simon Windebank married Mary in 1700. When he died he was quite well to do. The heir to the property was a certain John Heath. A stipulation in Simon's will stated that his widow was to be provided for and so, following the usual practice of the time, Heath mortgaged her house and its grounds. Mary's death is recorded in the burial register with no mention of murder. It is speculated that perhaps John came up the stairs simply to take charge of his own money and explain the new arrangements about the mortgage. But who put up the tombstone? Was it indignant Windebank relatives? John Heath lived comfortably in Farringdon until his death and the mystery was never explained.

Nationwide interest has been sparked by the discovery of a 14th century 'Doom and Last Judgement' wall painting in the church, dated about 1380, with another dated about 1400 painted on top, no doubt when a new patron commissioned it. It is the older of the two that is causing the most excitement, the blue pigment of the Saviour's robe making it a rare and very special find.

Fawley ❦

The heart of a village lies not in its picture postcard image, but its inhabitants. Among those who have enhanced the life of Fawley was the colourful character of Dr Eric Jones-Evans, who died in the 1980s aged 92. He came to the village as a young physician in 1922, and stayed for the rest of his life. His practice was far flung, Fawley lying between the New Forest and Southampton Water. Most of his visits were accomplished on horse-back, and he became a familiar figure galloping across the countryside, in broad-brimmed hat with black cloak flying!

In 1922 the AGWI oil refinery, the first modern industry to make its debut in the area, was so situated as to be completely out of sight, although not always out of mind! The locals spoke with dry humour of 'They dratted lavender-bags.' The smells emitted during the refining of crude oil were totally obnoxious! Twenty-eight years later Esso built their massive refinery. It was opened by the Right Honourable Clement Attlee, in 1951.

On the plus side, this brought a great deal of employment to the area, and the village shops benefited accordingly. But many older folk remember the beautiful house and surrounding estate of Cadland, home of the Scottish banking family of Drummond since the 18th century, which had to be totally destroyed to accommodate the refinery.

Fortunately, the family possessed a fishing lodge on part of their estate in the area of Stanswood, and in 1930 built a gracious house upon the foundations of the old lodge. This is now known as Cadland House.

Eaglehurst, another large residence looking across to the Isle of Wight, has in its grounds a building known as Luttrell's Tower, so called after Simon Temple Luttrell, a former owner of Irish descent. It is said that he may have been involved in smuggling, as a passage runs from the tower to underground caves nearby. That smugglers existed in the vicinity of Spratsdown is a known fact, and to this day it is alluded to as Lazy Town, presumably because its inhabitants were not early risers! Small wonder, no doubt catching up on sleep lost, unloading the previous night's haul!

However, Luttrell's Tower has a far greater claim to fame. Eaglehurst was purchased at a later date by a member of the Drummond family, who let it to Marconi. It was from this tower that the first radio signals were sent out to Marconi's yacht, *Electra*, anchored in Cowes Roads.

The church of All Saints, parts of which date back to Norman times, has many points of interest. In spite of a bomb scoring a direct hit on the chancel in November 1940, it has been lovingly rebuilt and restored to its former glory.

Fawley possesses two taverns, the Jolly Sailor and the Falcon. It was in one of these on VE night in 1945 that the local lads, in a moment of exuberance, turned the village 'bobby' upside down and filled his trousers with beer! It is reported that his only remark at the end of this horseplay was – 'Now lads, stand me the right way up!' No wonder the rural policeman was held in such affection!

Fleet 🦢

Until around the 1950s Fleet was still a village, but today it has grown into a small town.

The area of Fleet was once known as 'Fuglemere' (wild fowl lake). Londoners came to enjoy the beautiful scenery around the pond, also to skate when it was frozen. During the late 1830s the railway was constructed and the station was built not far from the pond.

Fleet pond is now a lovely expanse of water, owned by the local Council and preserved for its wild life. The Basingstoke Canal also runs through Fleet, constructed around 1793. At one time it was quite a busy waterway carrying bricks and timber to build new houses, also to carry coal until the railway was built. Now the canal is used for fishing, boating and many people enjoy a Sunday stroll along it.

One highlight of life in Fleet is the annual Carnival, which takes place in June, starting with a gathering on the dodgem track at the fairground for songs of praise.

During the week many attractions take place. Baby shows, fashion shows, a grand parade through the streets on the Wednesday and finishing on the Saturday with arena events, scouts barbecue and exhibitions of local groups in the area. The day ends with a firework display. The first carnival took place in 1955. From the funds raised many local charities have benefited, including an ambulance for the St Johns Ambulance Brigade as well as various items for the small hospital, built in 1897.

The 'Cottage hospital' has had many improvements over the years. Although it is no longer used for surgery it is now mainly for geriatric cases, with an out-patients department for x-rays and physiotherapy.

Several Residents Associations and other groups have been formed in the area bringing back the fellowship of village life.

Fordingbridge

Fordingbridge is situated on the North Hampshire borders, on the edge of the beautiful New Forest.

The outstanding feature of Fordingbridge must be the river Avon, one of the best fishing rivers in the whole country and one of the prettiest and cleanest. Most of the fishing rights on the river are strictly preserved but permits for some parts may be obtained. Salmon, trout, pike, chub and other coarse fish are plentiful and record catches have been recorded. The river flows alongside the recreation ground (as well as meandering round the houses) making this area a very pleasant place to wander. A statue of Augustus John the painter, who once lived in Fordingbridge, stands in a shady corner by the water.

The river at Fordingbridge is one of only five rivers in the world to freeze from the bottom to the top, owing to the underground streams from the chalkland coming out on to the gravels. The old medieval bridge has seven arches and the centre one is 14 ft 6 inches wide, possibly constructed about 1362.

From 1870 until the First World War, a regatta was held each year. The boats and riverside gardens were illuminated, trainloads of people came down from London to 'Hampshire's Henley' and much fun was had by all.

During the Second World War the 3rd Royal Tank Regiment was stationed in and around Fordingbridge and from here dashed to Calais to cover the retreat from Dunkirk. Under the threat of invasion, the Royal Engineers were asked to drill into the foundations of the bridge to place charges of explosive so the bridge could be blown up if necessary. The men found it extremely difficult to drill into the stonework placed there in the 14th century. Later, during the war, the 7th corps of the US Army were just outside Fordingbridge and General Patton stood outside Locks, the chemist, watching his troops march through.

Fordingbridge was a very busy place in bygone days and is still much the same today. The community centre 'Avonway', which used to be the village school, is the venue for numerous activities.

In the 14th century St Mary's was a very important church, Fordingbridge being the head of the Deanery which included Ringwood, Christchurch and the Forest parishes. It is very important to its parishioners today and the building itself is beautiful and such a peaceful place to worship. Every other year it has a flower festival with a floral carpet which covers the whole of the centre aisle. Members of the local Flower Club derive great pleasure from the hours spent in making the church beautiful for its visitors.

It is said of Fordingbridge folk, 'they are a funny race as they only get up every other day' – Is that why the population is increasing?

Four Marks 🌿

Many villages go back hundreds of years and have their roots in feudal times, but Four Marks is a unique self-made village, the result of the hard work and enterprise of its inhabitants.

In the late 19th century it was merely a name on the map to mark the place where the four parishes of Farringdon, Chawton, Medstead and Ropley met. As this was an important beacon site in the Napoleonic Wars and all four parishes claimed it (and the fee for maintaining it), the Bishop of Winchester decided to make it a special extra-parochial area bounded by four stone marks, and he himself would take the maintenance fee. In Telegraph Lane, near the highest point in Four Marks, there is a house called Semaphore Farm.

From then on Four Marks grew and established itself as a village. It was on the main stagecoach route from London to Winchester and Southampton, so development started on this road (now the A31). A garage was built by an enterprising mechanic and is now Chawton End

Garage, run by his sons and grandsons. Shops and a post office sprang up opposite the Windmill Inn.

The school in Lymington Bottom was called Ropley school as the site was given by a generous Christian lady from that village who specified that it was to be governed by the vicar and churchwardens of Ropley. She also gave a corrugated iron building which had been used as a mission for the navvies working on the railway. When the railway was finished and the gang moved on, she had the building re-erected in Lymington Bottom as a church served by the Ropley priest, and so it remained. Several older residents can remember worshipping there, but it is now derelict.

Many people settled here after the First World War, building colonial-style bungalows with large gardens where they could grow vegetables or keep poultry to be self-supporting. Many of the lanes were grass tracks and Blackberry Lane really did have lots of blackberries, which the schoolchildren gathered and sold to a factory in Romsey for 2d a pound. When people arrived at the station, their luggage was collected by Mr Deacon with a horse and cart; he later had a lorry and ran a transport business.

By 1930 the population had increased to such an extent that in 1932 a council was duly elected and the first Parish Council meeting was held. A new church was built in 1956.

Two things were still needed to complete the village amenities – a burial ground and a recreation ground, and both of these were made possible by the purchase of two and a half acres of land, with a bungalow, in Brislands Lane. The generous bequest of a local nursery-man made it possible to buy more ground and establish a sports centre with facilities for football, cricket, archery, tennis, bowls and a putting green.

On the top of Swelling Hill there is a pond which, when Four Marks had no mains water supply, was a great standby in times of drought. Local residents can remember seeing cows driven to the pond, and some remember how they swam in it when they were children. But it fell into disuse and became so overgrown that it was little more than a swamp. In 1974 a team of enthusiastic helpers was formed and they dredged the pond, cleared the surrounding jungle, planted shrubs and plants, put up seats and even a wishing well. So hard did they work that they won the Daily Telegraph National Award for the best rehabilitated pond!

Fritham ✒

In the north of the New Forest, a stone's throw from the Wiltshire border, nestles the ancient village of Fritham, a hamlet of less than 200 people, and mentioned in the Domesday Book as Thorougham or Truham.

For generations this Hampshire village slept happily at the end of a track which dwindled into the silent forest. Most farmsteads had a few cows, pigs and hens and an acre or two which supplied their needs, and villagers teamed up and helped each other with the harvesting at the end of the year.

The village shop with its clanging door bell and indescribable smell of freshly baked bread, shoe polish and smoked bacon, was the main shopping centre and post office, and as the towns of Ringwood and Lyndhurst were a fair old pony and trap ride away they were not journeys to be undertaken lightly.

At the top of the lane, the banks of which are still dotted with primroses and bluebells in spring, stood the Royal Oak, one of the oldest pubs in the forest. It was renowned for its beer from the barrel, drunk in the little front parlour, often in the company of a pony or cow's head peering in through the open door, and to the accompaniment of the grunting pigs in the adjoining sty.

The other main meeting point in Fritham was the little tin chapel where services held twice on Sundays were attended by everybody in the village. Every child, willing or reluctant, was washed and scrubbed for the weekly visit to the Sunday school in the hut beside the chapel, which served as the junior school during the week and meeting place for the Band of Hope, sewing circle and socials most evenings.

Many of the old cottages had Forest Rights, which entitled the owners or tenants to collect wood and turf, and to pasture their cattle, ponies and donkeys on the forest. Pannage rights also allowed pigs to forage and root for acorns from 25th September to 22nd November, thus preventing the ponies from eating too many, a practice which is too often fatal. These rights belong to the chimney and hearthstone of the cottage, not to an individual, and several cottages in Fritham still hold on to them.

When the Schultz Gunpowder factory was built in an isolated glade by Eyeworth lake, life for the village changed overnight. The factory, making ammunition for sporting guns, provided work for most of the men and many women in Fritham and surrounding areas. The grass tracks, unchanged for decades, were strengthened with gravel from the forest, and huge carts drawn by teams of heavy horses trundled along the once deserted lanes. The tin chapel was 'adopted' by the factory owners, and a handsome brick building was erected. The village had never been so prosperous.

In 1912 disaster hit this tiny hamlet when five of its young men perished in the *Titanic* and, when the factory closed a few years later, Fritham returned to its sleepy isolated existence. Today, although much is unchanged deep in the glades and marshlands, and animals still graze the green and wander down the lanes, life in Fritham has changed considerably.

The shop and post office closed a few years ago, and the only meeting place now is the travelling library which pauses briefly on the green every other week. The Royal Oak has never been busier, but the little chapel holds only two services a month for a handful of people and sits silent and withdrawn, remembering perhaps the days when its congregation spilled out on to the forest. It still comes to life at Harvest Festival and Christmas, however, when the villagers gather and sing and enjoy for a brief moment the old community bond.

Fyfield ⚜

The parish of Fyfield, which includes Redenham as well, is situated a few miles west of Andover, near the Wiltshire border. Fyfield has remained a small and rural village. It was once a mere handful of thatched cottages with three large houses – the manor, the Grange and the rectory. The small church of St Nicholas lies out of sight of the village street and dates from the 13th century. Records of Fyfield's past can now be found in the Bodleian Library at Oxford, in the diaries of its rector, Henry White.

The Rev Henry White, brother of the world-famous naturalist Gilbert White of Selborne, was rector in Fyfield from 1762 to 1788. He and his wife Elizabeth (née Cooper, from Oxford) lived and farmed here. They also kept a school for the sons of the local gentry at the rectory, known as the 'Fyfield Academy for Young Gentlemen'. Each pupil paid £100 a year and brought their own horses and items of furniture.

Henry White acquired the Grange in 1774. He built on a new wing with a large kitchen and music-room, and above, bedrooms to house his ten children and various retainers. The rectory continued as a school.

On 12th February 1771, Gilbert White wrote from Fyfield: 'My musical friend [ie his brother] at whose house I am now visiting has tried all the owls that are in his near neighbourhood with a pitch-pipe set at concert-pitch and finds that they all hoot in B flat.'

The rectory and the Grange are now private residences. The manor is now a famous horse racing establishment. It boasts two Grand National winners – *Highland Wedding* in 1969 and *Little Polvier* in 1989.

The village school, now a listed building, was built by a 'philanthropic lady of the village' in 1790 for the local children. The money from its sale in the early 1960s is used as a fund to send boys and girls on Venture holidays and to help to buy tools for their jobs and apprenticeships.

Grateley 🦋

Grateley is situated in the north-west corner of Hampshire, fairly close to the Wiltshire border. The nearest town, Andover, is seven miles away. Grateley gets its name from the great lea or meadow, which lies to the south-west of the church. The church of St Leonard was built mainly in the 13th century, although some parts are said to be Saxon and three courses of bricks in the tower are thought to be Norman. The stained glass in the south window came from Salisbury Cathedral.

Grateley's claim to a place in history lies with the council of AD 925 called by King Athelstan, which was thought to have been held either at Manor Farm or at the Iron Age fort at the top of Quarley Hill, which overlooks the village.

Grateley is a small village split into two parts. One part is made up of houses clustered around the church, Manor Farm and the Plough Inn. The other part is about a mile away and has developed since the railway line was built in the late 19th century, which attracted trades and businesses connected with coal and grain. The road joining the two ends of the village, known as Station Road, was once a private road which connected Grateley House (which belonged to the Boutcher family) to the station. The family did not wish to have a station near to the house, so it was built a mile away. The public house, once known as the Railway Hotel but now called the Shire Horse, was also owned by the Boutcher family until it was sold to the Gibbs Mew brewery.

In the late 19th century the village had 226 people living in just 24 dwellings. Now there are nearly 200 dwellings. A further housing development is being built at the station end of the village, near the council houses which replaced the Nissen huts erected by the army during the Second World War. Most of the houses near the church, and the adjoining land, were once part of the estate of the Marquis of Winchester who owned Amport House in the neighbouring village of Amport.

There are general stores at both ends of the village and there is still a local bus service to Andover. The station no longer has any buildings – it is just a halt now. However mainline express trains between London and Exeter still stop there. Although many people living in Grateley still work in the area, either as part of the farming community or in the coal business, grain trade or construction industry, many residents are now commuters who have been attracted to the village because of its proximity to the railway and to the motorways.

Greatham 🦢

Greatham is a village of approximately 600 people, situated to the north of Petersfield.

The old church, which is now a ruin, was in use in 1290 and Dame Margery Caryll is buried in the chancel. Her family took possession of the village in the 17th century. They were a very wealthy family with many estates in Sussex. The ghost of a lady dressed in grey and a white veil haunts the woods, which are part of the estate of Sir Arundel and Lady Neave, but she remains a mystery for nothing is known about her.

A new church of St John the Baptist was built in 1875. Land was given by William Foster in memory of his parents, who are buried in the family tomb in the old churchyard. His brother was curate-in-charge at Greatham. The family lived in the house known as Le Court, on the site of the ancient manor house of Greatham. Le Court was demolished in the 1950s but the name lives on in the Leonard Cheshire home for the disabled, which was the first of its kind and opened by the Queen Mother in the 1960s.

Life in Victorian days revolved around the church, which was the centre of social activities. Letters exist, written by Rev F. Bryans, relating how stricken he was that a 'second Aldershot' was about to be built on the heathland, now Longmoor Camp. He was convinced the licentious soldiery would do great harm to the villagers, particularly the females! When the military camp was finally established, King George V made an inspection and local legend says that the name of the hill outside the camp, which is known as Apple Pie Hill, was coined by the King when he remarked, 'everything is in apple pie order'.

The old village hall and school were sited near the old church but are now a private residence. A new school was built in 1911 and the new village hall in 1976, of which the villagers are very proud. Greatham used to have a Methodist church, cinema, blacksmith and wheelwright, and local industry was mainly agriculture. Tearooms, a provisions merchant and a cycle agent were also in evidence but they no longer exist. Today there are two public houses, the Queen (very old) and the Silver Birch. There is also a post office/grocery store, although as late as 1923 Longmoor Camp was used as a post office, and a newsagent which is also a provision store.

There are three charities still in existence. The Allotment Charity supplies financial help to those in need who live in *Old* Greatham. Smith's Bread Charity was originally intended to provide bread for the 'labouring poor of Greatham and Hawkley' (the next village). Today vouchers are given to a few people in the two parishes at Christmas. The Coryton Almshouses of West Liss were built by F. Coryton, JP and lord of the manor, to provide accommodation for those locally in need. All are in use at the present time.

Greywell 🐾

Greywell is a small village of 90 houses with a population of around 200, lying in the north-east of the county.

The first Lord Dorchester (first Governor General of Canada) acquired the manor in 1786 and it has remained with the family ever since. It is alleged that the old manor house was on the east side of The Street where there is an extensive unexcavated mound of earth, perhaps the remains of the house.

The recently restored Basingstoke Canal, opened in 1798, ends in a tunnel, three quarters of a mile long, which in 1932 caved in at three places. It is now famous for one of the largest colonies of bats in the United Kingdom. Controversy reigns between the Canal Society, who would like to rebuild the tunnel and make it navigable and the naturalists who wish to preserve the bat colony. The river Whitewater rises and runs through the village and has the unique feature of passing under the canal. One bridge over the Whitewater is known as Tolls Bridge – Tolls being a former owner of the manor. Greywell is rich in wildlife, particularly wild flowers, and 15 acres of The Fen have been purchased by the Hants & Isle of Wight Naturalists' Trust to be managed as a nature reserve.

The church of St Mary the Virgin was built in the 12th century and was linked with Odiham until 1901. On the Norman doorway the marks of the Crusaders' crosses can still be seen. The village hall celebrated its centenary in 1985 and is still in constant use for meetings, sales and playgroups, etc. Displayed in the hall are the stumps used in a cricket match on 8th, 9th and 10th September 1862 when Greywell played the England team – but sadly lost!

In its heyday the old school housed 120 pupils. At the end of the 19th century a replacement building was found further up the village, and this continued in use until 1935. Both buildings are now private houses but the original bell-towers can still be seen.

The village shop has moved several times over the years and eventually was housed by the river Whitewater, with the post office, until its closure in 1971. There is now no shop or post office. The only public house is the

Fox & Goose. The former Royal Oak was closed in the mid 1950s and is now a private house.

During the Civil War the whole area saw much activity and to this day there is a block of cottages known as The Barracks. Few changes have been made to the village, although the ditch along The Street to which housewives would cross the road to throw their slops has been paved over!

Hale 🦢

Few places can claim to have witnessed the 'seizing' of their village green, but such was the ritual performed on a bright Saturday aftenoon in February 1975 in the presence of some 200 villagers.

Hatchett Green, as it is known, is one of the main attractions of the small village of Hale, which lies in the northern corner of Hampshire and close to the boundary with Wiltshire. The picturesque green, surrounded by fields, houses, the village school and the village hall, extends to about 13 acres.

The Hale Cricket Club have used it for many years and some exciting matches have been played on it, much to the delight of local spectators, who sit around the green every Saturday afternoon during the summer months. Hatchett Green has also always served as the playground for the children of the local primary school.

For many years, in the absence of any indication of a legal owner or title to the land, Hale Parish Council had exercised a form of guardianship over the green. This ensured a degree of protection, but not being the owners of the land, the Council were unable to enforce their edicts. They therefore gave formal notice of their intention to 'seize' Hatchett Green and to hold it in perpetuity for the benefit of the inhabitants.

No-one came forward to oppose the 'seizing', but it was considered advisable to enact an ancient ceremony by which a person who had entered into possession of unclaimed land made it clear to his neighbours that he was the legal owner.

So, on 22nd February 1975, the villagers assembled on the green to see the ritual performed. The chairman of the Parish Council cut a sod from the green, held it up at arm's length, replaced it and solemnly proclaimed that the land was now vested in the parish. Registration of the Council's 'possessory title' at the Land Registry followed. An historic day for the village of Hale.

Hamble ✒

Hamble's Satchell Lane derives its name from the estate of Sir Henry Shatershall, a knight of Henry III. This winding road was originally the only thoroughfare into the village – Hamble Lane, now largely built up, does not appear on a map of 1725. The amount of traffic it carries is frightening, for enormous vehicles come in and go out all day, bearing boats for the three marinas and oil and petrol for BP and Shell, which have had an important base here for nearly 70 years.

Hamble boasts three things all proper villages should own: an ancient church, a common and a green.

Hamble's church, consecrated in 1109, is dedicated to St Andrew, patron saint of fishermen, as befits a church within sight of the sea, as it was until modern buildings crowded in.

The 54 acres of Hamble common lead down to Southampton Water and the green looks down on it. Westfield Common, at the western end of the village, is an added bonus.

You come into Hamble by the B3397, which is called Hamble Lane until it passes the church when it becomes the High Street. One stretch of lower High Street is only ten feet wide but it contains three of the village's five pubs: the Bugle dates back to the 13th century and overlooks the quay; the Victory and the King and Queen are only a few yards up the road. Ye Olde Whyte Harte, higher up and next to The Gun House, announces that it was built in 1563 but the Harrier (formerly known as the Coronation – that of George VI) was only built in 1937.

For its size, the peninsula of Hamble has played host to a remarkable collection of notabilities. C.B. Fry, classical scholar as well as famous cricketer for which he is chiefly known, ran the training ship *Mercury* with his wife for 42 years. His memory is perpetuated in a close built in 1970 and the ship is commemorated by the surrounding estate and by an older terrace in Satchell Lane.

Scouting has been a feature of Hamble since 1908 when the first Sea Scouts were established at the *Mercury*, for Sir Robert Baden-Powell was a close friend of C. B. Fry. In 1910 the first Sea Scout troop was registered at the *Mercury* and there has been a troop of Sea Scouts in Hamble ever since, joined over the years by Cubs, Girl Guides (formerly Rangers) and Brownies and, more recently, Venture Scouts.

But it is sailing – yachting, if you will – which comes to mind nowadays when the name of Hamble is mentioned. The first club was the Minima Yacht Club, established a hundred years ago. There are now three clubs: Hamble River Sailing Club, founded in 1919; the Royal Southern Yacht Club, removed from its original home in Southampton in

Ferry Hill, Hamble

1936; and the Royal Air Force Yacht Club, transferred from Calshot in 1951.

Ships, both men-of-war and merchant and fishing vessels, have been built here since time immemorial, while many great ships such as Nelson's flagship, the *Elephant*, have been built on the river. Best known, perhaps, was the *Grace Dieu*, built in the 15th century for Henry V.

Hambledon ❧

Hambledon lies in a dry chalk valley just off the A3 road between Petersfield and Portsmouth. The area has been inhabited from earliest times, as there are traces of Iron Age barrows and worked flints have been found. There are the remains of a Roman villa in the area now occupied by Bury Lodge. A small wood has grown over the site but it was excavated by Sir Thomas Butler in 1910.

In 1644 Sir Richard Norton and his famous troop of Hambledon boys played a large part in the Civil War battle of Cheriton. The first recorded royal visitor came to Hambledon in 1651. After defeat at the battle of Worcester, Prince Charles Stuart escaped. On his way to the coast, Colonel Gunter offered the future Charles II shelter with his sister, Ursula Symons, who lived on the outskirts of the village. It was a risky business as Hambledon was for Parliament. The house still stands and is known as 'King's Rest'.

Probably the great thing that Hambledon has been known for in more recent times is cricket. It was not invented here as some people think, but the rules of the modern game were standardised by the Hambledon Cricket Club. They played on Broadhalfpenny Down with a curved bat and two stumps. Hambledon's finest hour was in 1774 when they beat All England by an innings and 52 runs.

The second recorded murder in the village was in 1782 (the first was in 1376). A stranger got into conversation with a local man at the New Inn and during this conversation cut the top off his walking stick. He followed his victim out of the village and then killed him with the stick. He was convicted on the evidence of the piece of stick which he had unwisely left at the inn. The scene of the murder is marked by the Murderstone.

At the beginning of the 19th century the Hambledon Volunteers were raised to fight Napoleon and colours were made for them by Millicent Palmer and her sister, of Rookwood, daughters of the commanding officer. These colours now hang in the ancient church of St Peter and St Paul.

Before the Normandy landings in June 1944 all the lanes and roads right down to the coast were lined with army vehicles. The whole village was sealed off and no one could get out without a pass. May 22nd saw the second recorded royal visitor when King George VI came to review his troops. It was supposed to be a secret but the whole village turned out to watch.

Since the Second World War a new village hall has been built by public subscription. Money was also raised to buy a green hillside in the middle of the village, which was given to the National Trust. The area has three public footpaths and has been a favourite picnic spot for many years. The village is still flourishing, with two general shops and a post office and stationer's. The vineyard which was started just after the war has recently been enlarged and wine is even exported to France. There is also a soft drinks factory, founded in 1882, four public houses, a school and many social activities.

Hammer 🥀

Though just over the official boundary line, Hammer is included here as its WI belongs to the Hampshire Federation. The village of Hammer nestles between the Bramshott and Lynchmere ridges on the outskirts of Haslemere. It is one of the few areas in the district which once had a substantial industrial base but is now almost entirely residential. The Romans established an encampment by the stream which runs through the village (then known as Pophole) and the noise of hammers resounding between the hills as they forged their weapons and implements, is thought to have given rise to the present day name.

Before the turn of the 18th century there were two main industries. One was birch broom making. The profusion of birch trees and tall heather bushes provided the materials and the 'Broom Dashers' (as they were called) made a very high quality product. A great many of these brooms were transported to London in horse-drawn vehicles, which meant a journey of four days – two up and two to come back, with a regular overnight stop at Kingston to rest the horses. Most of the brooms used in the Royal stables were made in Hammer.

The brick-making works stood alongside the stream, which is part of the river and forms the boundary between Surrey and Sussex. Two clay pits provided the material for the bricks which were hand made in a small yard employing only a few dozen men.

In 1898 a builder friend of Sir Arthur Conan Doyle (one John Grover) travelled from Kent to visit him in Hindhead, which was then an area of only gorse, heather and pine trees. A chance remark that Hindhead was like a 'Little Switzerland' set the builder's fertile brain in motion and he saw the possibility of developing that area as a health resort. Discovering the brick works at Hammer, he acquired the business. While clearing top soil, in order to build new kilns and sheds, a bed of yellow and blue clay was uncovered, giving a fresh source of material – blue clay to make tiles and yellow for bricks.

Thus Hammer Brick Works came into being and soon thousands of machine-made bricks were being manufactured. Many of the first bricks were used to build houses for the extra workers imported from Kent and Staffordshire. Like Mr Grover, the majority were Nonconformist, so the Free church was built for them, the first lay preacher being the works' foreman, Moses Young.

Many thousands of bricks were conveyed to fast growing Hindhead by horse-drawn wagons, Waggoners Wells being their watering place en route.

After the First World War the men came back to the Works, which was busier than ever due to the demand for bricks as the slums of East London were cleared and rebuilt. In 1938 the clay began to run out and the Works was transferred to Hambledon where a vast new clay pit had been found. Now all that remains are the drying sheds.

On the edge of the village in Hammer Vale, stands the Prince of Wales public house. Beside the nearby post box once stood a replica of a Buckingham Palace sentry box where the postman, whose only means of transport was Shanks' Pony, would rest and shelter while awaiting the correct time to empty the box.

Though there have been many changes and the village shop is closed, Hammer is still a pleasantly rural place to live in. Family names provide links with the past and keep alive the memory of the men who made the brooms and the bricks. There is a lively sense of community, people take an interest in each other and no one need be lonely except by choice.

Hannington

Hannington, a North Hampshire Downs village of outstanding natural beauty (with about 280 inhabitants) lies sleepily, sans shops but with one public house, two miles off the A339 between Newbury and Basingstoke. Most people are employed outside the village and since the village school was closed in 1984, the children travel to various schools.

The birthplace of Archbishop Warham, and mentioned in the Domesday Book, Hannington has a beautiful brick and flint-built Norman church of All Saints on the edge of a real village green, with wellhead and bench, as well as a small Methodist chapel. Community life today exists through these and other organisations which tend to meet in the village hall.

The community highlight is the Country Fayre and Barbecue when all village members make enormous efforts for this splendid occasion – people travel from Portsmouth to attend!

There are five thatched cottages in Hannington, the one opposite the village green is authenticated as being 14th century and is called Tyn-y-Bryn. The village green, incidentally, was once a pond.

Hannington Silver Band, formed in 1924, does a great deal of charity work and is the pride of the village.

Farming has always been arable and privately-owned. Few people are employed on the farms from the village today.

Hartley Wintney

Hartley Wintney is a pretty village sitting astride the A30, once a stage coach route. The afternoon coach, the *Telegraph*, ran from the Phoenix Inn to London every day at 1 pm and the *Defiance* left each morning at 8.30. Highwaymen used the same road to hold passengers to ransom for their money and valuables.

Alongside the road is Hatten's Pond, named for Robert Hatten, landlord of the nearby Waggon and Horses pub from 1875 until his death in 1903. His widow, Ann, stayed on as 'landlord' until 1914. In the centre of this pond is a duck-house with a thatched roof, courtesy of the inhabitants of the village, and at Christmastime it is decorated with fairy lights to match the rest of the illuminations.

Trafalgar oaks stretch across the common, planted long ago to provide wood for shipbuilding, and on the green once stood the old lock-up, last used to house the fire engine.

Cricket has been played on the green since 1770 and a new pavilion is being built to replace the former wooden one destroyed during the hurricane of 1987, whilst alongside the pitch stands the Cricketers pub.

Once Hartley Wintney boasted a priory, founded in 1171 (but destroyed during the Reformation), which brought prestige to the village. The remains can be seen at Wintney Moor. The old field names tell their own story: Sheep Down and Hog Moor were grazing lands beyond tilled soil; Flax-field was where flax, with its lovely pale-blue flowers, was grown, and the stems, soaked and combed, provided the fibres for linen to make the villagers' clothes. Furzy Moor was where teazels were employed to tease the cloth and White Field where the spun and woven cloth was laid to bleach in the sun.

In old St Mary's church can be seen medieval wall paintings portraying village dress of several centuries ago, whilst in St John's on the green is a memorial window to young Billy Stoop of Hartley Grange, killed in a car accident in 1936. It depicts Father Christmas under a tree bearing five candles, appropriate, as Billy had been born on Christmas Day.

Toc H are prominent in village life, fielding a hand-bell ringing team who perform at concerts. They also organise the 'Giant Bonfire' on 5th

November. It is traditional for four teams of 'fire-ball swingers' to converge on the bonfire from the four corners of the village, when the bobbing lights through the trees provide a magic spectacle.

At West Green House once lived Lieutenant-General Henry Hawley, a prominent soldier during the Jacobite Rebellion of 1745. After Culloden, when he rivalled Judge Jeffreys for cruelty, he returned to Hartley Wintney, where it's said that on the night of 16th April each year, the anniversary of the battle, the skirl of the pipes and war cries of the Highland clans can be heard in the garden!

Sir Douglas Bader learned to use his two tin legs on the lawns at Hartley Grange whilst staying there in 1932. He then tackled golf, despite constantly falling over on the same lawns, and eventually played at Hartley Wintney golf course. He passed this test with flying colours and went on to become the most famous of the 'First of the Few'.

Headley 🐿️

The history of Headley, which lies in the east of the county, dates back to Saxon times and it is mentioned in the Domesday Book, when it was called Hallege.

The church in the village centre has existed since the 12th century, although the first Headley church in Saxon times was completely made of wood. In 1900 Sir Robert Wright gave the church clock in memory of his son, who died at the age of six. On each corner of the clock are the initials of Sir Robert and his wife, their son and the year. In 1935 a peal of six bells was given in memory of Mr and Mrs Charles McAndrew. They also gave the village hall to the Women's Institute.

The lychgate was erected to commemorate the Queen's Coronation in 1953. The work was carried out entirely by Headley men under the supervision of Mr Johnson-Burt.

In 1601 Queen Elizabeth I granted a charter for a fair to be held annually on the village green. In 1795 the parishes of Headley, Bramshott and Kingsley combined to build a House of Industry, which is now called the Grange. The terrible conditions in the workhouse led to riots and arson. Some of the culprits were transported to Australia and some were hanged. The Grange later became a private house.

A flourishing chestnut tree is a well-known local landmark in the centre of the village. It was planted by the rector, Rev Laverty. A sovereign coin was buried at its roots.

Headley is an ever-growing and flourishing village. Tennis, cricket, football and bowls are all enjoyed in the recreation grounds. Headley

Mill, a famous beauty spot, is still a working mill and its surrounding pond, with the swans and wild fowl, is well worth a visit. Some of the timber in the mill is from the 16th century.

Heckfield & Mattingley

These two villages lie in the north of the county, with Berkshire and Surrey as very close neighbours. Heckfield is the larger of the two villages with its houses and farms quite scattered. It is much involved in the modern world with two of its large houses being adapted as conference centres for international companies. They have not spoilt the beauty of the area in any way and have provided employment for many village people. There is woodland, heathland and some farms, and the soil is of a gravelly and stony nature.

The village hall is a very ancient building and a market has been held in it each month for many years. The church, dedicated to St Michael, stands quite near to the hall. Up to 1863 it was the parish church of both Heckfield and Mattingley. The first part was built in the 13th century and much restoration has been done since then. There is in the church a memorial tablet to Neville Chamberlain, who died in nearby Highfield House.

The churchyard was closed in 1885 and ground for the present cemetery, which lies across the road, was donated by the then lord of the manor. The parents of the novelist Anthony Trollope were married in this church in 1809 and the bride's father, William Milton, the then vicar, was well known for his design of safety apparatus to prevent wheels falling off horse-drawn coaches!

At the north end of the village is the main entrance to Stratfield Saye House, the home of the Dukes of Wellington. Here stands a column and statue of the 1st Duke of Wellington in his Field Marshal's uniform; it is a well-known landmark. Some local farms are owned by the Duke. His country park with its lake and nature trails is enjoyed by many people during the summer months.

Some organisation of the road system in Heckfield has resulted in the lovely village centre being free from all but local traffic, thus making it a delightful place to live.

Mattingley is a smaller village, also rather scattered with many well preserved old houses and cottages. One of the oldest is of Tudor origin and is now known as Bannisters Farm. Some of the older houses are not visible from the roads, being hidden by trees.

There are two commons, one Mattingley Green and the other Hound

Green. Much of the remaining area is heathland and farmland. Two rivers run here, the Whitewater and the Hart.

Visitors come from many places to see the unusual church, which was converted to a chapel of ease from a barn over 600 years ago.

Mattingley is a lovely village, unspoilt by progress, with leafy lanes where a herd of cows on their way to be milked can still halt the modern traffic.

Hedge End 🐝

Hedge End has grown from a small village where everybody knew everybody else, to the sprawling urban area of today. It was first mentioned in 1250 as a piece of land adjoining Botley and bordered by Foord and Butts Road (now Granada) and was known as Botley Common. At that time it consisted of a few mud huts on an enclosed common, used by tenants and squatters. The last mud-walled cottage was demolished in Chapel Path as late as 1934.

In 1786 the Northam Bridge Road Co was formed and a wooden bridge was built across the river at Northam to make a route from Southampton to Botley. To pay for the upkeep, three toll gates were placed along the road, one at Northam, one at Lances Hill and one at Hedge End. The toll was 3d for horse-drawn vehicles, 1d for bicycles. In May 1929 the toll gates were to be freed by the Mayor of Southampton, and there was quite a panic because the one at Hedge End had disappeared in the night. The gate from Lances Hill was rushed ahead of the Mayor to Hedge End to be freed for the second time!

There was a poorhouse in Butts Road and in 1818 a master and mistress were appointed at an annual salary of £15. This was closed in 1835 and the area then came under the jurisdiction of South Stoneham (now Moorgreen Hospital).

There have been and still are many religious denominations in Hedge End. The first was a Baptist chapel in Upper Northam Road, and then in the 1850s a Bible Christian chapel was built at the corner of Chapel Drove. This afterwards became the Methodist chapel and was succeeded by the present one in 1924. The Roman Catholics met for Mass in various places and only quite recently has a Catholic church been established. The Anglicans first met in the day school on Sunday afternoons until 1874 when St John's was built. In 1908 a breakaway from the Methodists built a church known as the Mission Hall on the corner of Northam Road and Wildern Lane. This has been demolished to make way for the shopping precinct and there is now a United Reformed church further up St John's Road.

Hedge End is still growing in all directions with a huge industrial estate and a motorway right on its border. Anyone having been away for a few years would have some difficulty finding their way around today.

Herriard

Herriard and its neighbouring village of Lasham occupy some of the most beautiful countryside in north Hampshire. Lovely beechwoods and parkland, visible from the busy Basingstoke to Alton road, are part of the Herriard Park estate, to which most of the village and surrounding farms belong.

The church of St Mary was probably built by Sir Richard de Hereyard, around 1200. In 1878 it was completely restored by Francis Jervoise, and in 1966 the chancel roof and floor of the family pew were replaced by John Loveys Jervoise.

The original Herriard House was destroyed by fire, and was replaced in 1704 by a Queen Anne mansion. This house in turn was demolished in 1965 to make way for a smaller, more easily run house, designed by Sir Martyn Beckett. The demolition was by controlled fire, and was so carefully managed that the wine cellar and its contents was left undisturbed.

Each successive squire has made his contribution to the village. In 1903 Henry Tristram Jervoise inherited the estate; he was extremely interested in forestry, and planted acres of red oaks in Herriard. His first wife, Mrs Beatrice Anne Louisa Jervoise, was responsible for bringing a piped water supply to the village. She also introduced a flock of Black Welsh Mountain sheep to the estate, a tradition which has been carried on ever since.

Herriard is a long straggling village; the church and the public house are a mile and a half apart. There is no longer a school, shop or post office. At the turn of the century the village had all these, together with a bakery and a station on the Basingstoke to Alton line.

However, the village has not died with the loss of its amenities, nor has it become a 'commuter' village. Villagers still work on the local farms and for the estate, although certainly not in the numbers of former years. There are several small thriving businesses in the village, among them a sawmill, an agricultural and general engineering business, a blacksmith's forge, and a precision engineering firm which has taken over the old school.

It is heartening to see a new 'village centre' growing around Southrope Green, the eight sheltered-housing bungalows built in 1986. This is close to the village hall, known as the Royal British Hall. This is a building that has had a chequered career, having been stables, a blacksmith's forge, and a wood-drying shed in the past. Until just a few years ago you could watch 'Lit' Westbrook, or his father before him, making traditional hurdles at nearby Park Corner.

If you leave Herriard by Bagmore Lane, you may find the Gypsy's Grave, close to the Ellisfield turning. Stories abound regarding this grave, which appeared around 1870, and even now frequently has fresh flowers on it. Anne Pitcher, who is a well-known writer in the Basingstoke area, attributes the grave to Jack Haines, a 'wayfaring journeyman' who hanged himself in 'The Beeches' near the site of the grave.

Another legend of Herriard concerns the enormous pig reared by Tom Bunday of Hale in 1895. This pig weighed 45 score (a score is 20 pounds). It stood three feet ten inches off the ground, was eight feet nine inches from tail to snout, and six feet six inches round its girth. A pigeon shoot was held, with the pig as the prize. Eventually it went to Mr W. T. Wren, the head keeper to Lord Basing.

Highclere

Highclere lies in the northern part of Hampshire. There is real beauty surrounding the place – a fine view from Chericot of Sidown and Beacon hills and a view from 'Heaven's Gate' on Sidown hill looking down on to Highclere Castle, the home for years of the Herbert family, the Earls of Carnarvon and lords of the manor.

The 5th Earl was the great Egyptologist who discovered the tomb of Tutankhamun. Sir Charles Barry, the architect of the Houses of Parliament, and the 3rd Earl of Carnarvon together converted the mansion, which for 800 years had been a home of the Bishops of Winchester, into the present day castle.

There was a prehistoric way across the Downs on the southern boundary and this was a military road. It was once a mere track called Honey Way, and is now the Newbury–Andover road.

When the church was moved from the castle grounds to its present site many of the stones which were left over were used to build three cottages in Penwood for estate workers – known as Bottle Row. Some of the original stones are still to be seen on one wall.

The house now known as the Old Beer House was, over 200 years ago, called 'Little Hit and Miss'. Beer was sold through a small window from the pantry to the front room and there was a skittle alley in the yard at the back.

The Temple in Highclere Park which overlooks the Temple Lake was used many years ago by the gentry, who would eat their shooting lunches there. The first thrift club in the county was called the 'Temple Club', and was the Hants and Dorset Deposit Society. The members all met on Whit Monday after a church service and went in procession with banners to the Temple in the park. The girls wore white dresses and their hats were wreathed in flowers. After a lunch at the Carnarvon Arms it was time to return to the Temple for festivities. The club ceased when insurance societies started.

During the latter half of the 19th century a wood turner in Highclere made wooden false teeth. No doubt, if the weather was cold, they sounded like castanets!

One of the old Highclere industries was brickmaking. The deep excavations can still be seen where Pyke's brickfields and kilns were situated, from the north-east end of Tubbs Lane to Old Kiln Cottage, The Mount. Mr Pyke lived at Pyke's House, on the corner at the junction of The Mount and Andover Road. He supplied bricks for the construction of Highclere Castle.

The many wells to be seen in Highclere are indicative of the fact that they were the only source of water in the area until fairly recently. In fact it was not until 1957 that work commenced to pipe mains water from artesian wells at Kingsclere.

Highclere Street, now a small hamlet, is about one mile from the centre of the present village. It is evident from the centrally placed ancient inn and several medieval and hall-type houses around it, one of which has a 15th century moulded plaster royal coat of arms on it, that this is the original village. The lane to the original church leads from here. The present Highclere has a 19th century church and most of the houses are of the same date. It has virtually no older or ancient buildings.

Hinton Ampner

The village of Hinton Ampner lies on a ridge above the A272 Winchester to Petersfield road. It forms part of the civil parish of Bramdean and although sparsely populated, it is the larger of the two, hence the correct name: 'Hinton Ampner with Bramdean'. Whilst being little more than a hamlet, the existence of a parish church with a road leading to it qualifies it technically as a village.

Until 1984, when it was bequeathed to the National Trust under the will of the late Right Honourable Ralph Stawell Dutton, the 8th Baron Sherborne and the last of his line, the village had changed very little in the previous 40 years.

The village school, now closed, had a romantic history. Mary Stewkely was the third daughter of Sir Hugh Stewkely; he lived at Hinton, dying in

1719 at the age of 81. In his will he bequeathed £5,000 apiece to each of his three young daughters 'if and when they marry with the consent of my wife'. Shortly after her father's death, Mary did marry, presumably with her mother's permission, one William Blake, who had been her father's groom. William is reputed to have been a coal merchant in Weeke, just outside Winchester, where they lived until Mary died three years after her marriage at the age of 37. William died six years later at the age of 49, having left money to erect a monument to his wife and himself in the church at Weeke and also to erect and endow a free school at Hinton Ampner.

The village also has one of the best documented ghost stories of the 18th century. The original Tudor manor house was demolished in 1793 after 20 years of remarkable and unexplained happenings.

Sir Thomas Stewkely had lived there at the end of the 16th century and after his death his descendants, Mary Stewkely, married to Edward Stawell (later Lord Stawell), and her younger unmarried sister Honaria occupied the house. When Mary died in 1740 an affair developed between Lord Stawell and his sister-in-law, who had continued to live at the manor after the death of her sister. There were stories of 'wild happenings' and a baby was supposed to have been born and to have been murdered. In January 1765 the property was let to a Mr and Mrs Ricketts. Mrs Ricketts lived at Hinton with her three children and eight servants during the absence abroad of her husband, who had property in Jamaica.

In August 1771 Mrs Ricketts and her family were compelled to leave the place after years of strange sightings and noises like footsteps, heavy knocks, strange music and curious murmurings and groans. After a short let to a family called Lawrence, who also seemed to have trouble with apparitions, the house was left empty for 20 years and then it was demolished.

A new Hinton Ampner House was built in about 1793 some 50 yards from the site of the old building and this Georgian house forms the central part of the present building. During the demolition of the old manor a small skull was discovered under the floorboards in one of the rooms.

Holybourne cum Neatham

Holybourne takes its name from a spring which is believed to rise under the altar of the church of the Holyrood. It flows under the main road and joins the river Wey at Neatham. The church dates back to the 12th century and stands beside the village duck pond.

Holybourne, situated on the A31 London to Southampton road (now bypassed), could never be described as a quiet little country village. Surprisingly, both Neatham and Holybourne were once greater in size and importance than Alton. Within these boundaries three of the nine mills between Alton and Farnham worked on the river Wey, for grain, fulling and tanning. A row of tanneries still exist on the main road.

Holybourne abounds in old cottages dating back to the 16th century, one of them said to have been visited by Charles II on his way through to Alton.

One of the most outstanding features of the village is the school. Thomas Andrews gave his lovely Georgian house for the use of boys and girls of the village. He also gave a grant of £20 yearly to provide a pair of boots for boys and dresses for the girls of poorer families. Outwardly the house is unchanged and all further developments are discreetly hidden.

The village has altered considerably since the 1940s. Both the cricket and football teams have gone. There is no village Flower Show with its bowling-for-the-pig, brass bands, sports etc. Where there were two pubs, there is now only one, and a post office and general store replace three shops. The forge and wheelwright's is now privately owned, but the traditional chestnut tree and old forge are still in good condition.

The Mill, Holybourne cum Neatham

116

The village has opened its doors to the Florence Treloar College for handicapped children, and another great asset to the village was the building of a theatre in an old Nissen hut used by prisoners of war. It was rebuilt in 1950 and opened by Sir Michael Redgrave. The club presents three plays a year and a grand pantomime at Christmas.

A large farming community surrounds the village – but the old hop gardens have gone. The entire village, including women and children, would turn out to help with the picking. That, sadly, is a thing of the past. With the closure of Courage's and Harp, hops are now imported from Europe by Bass.

The dig on a small Roman settlement caused a great deal of interest. The 'finds' are now in the museum in Alton and the site is now a housing estate called 'Vindomis'.

Neatham is now divided from Holybourne by the railway (1852) and the bypass, but it still maintains its quite lanes and fields, though the noise from the bypass frightened away the swans and the kingfishers.

Hook ✥

The misconception of Hook as a modern village comes because, until 1932, it was not a parish in its own right – it was a hamlet overlapping the parishes of Newnham, Odiham and Nately Scures. Neolithic flints, Bronze Age artefacts, Roman pottery, tiles and coins have come to light showing that there has been occupation in the vicinity since Stone Age times.

The village of today has evolved over the past two centuries. In the late 1700s, Hook was a tiny hamlet with several public houses, a number of ponds and a few cottages – the oldest of which is probably the 14th century 'Forge'.

One of these public houses was the White Hart Hotel. It was a staging post at the crossroads of the London to Exeter and Reading to Gosport turnpikes and therefore it attracted a lot of trade to the area. Nearby was a road-wagon station which repaired stagecoaches. Talking of stage-coaches, one immediately thinks of highwaymen. Thomas Boulter, in 1778, held up three post chaises in Hook, robbed the occupants and then had to make a dash for freedom pursued by a posse of men. He was never caught.

1883 was an important year for Hook because it won its long campaign for a railway station – village life was never quite the same again. The village school, built in 1843 to serve Hook and Newnham, had to be enlarged for the second time in 1896. In 1902 the goods station was added and what had been principally a farming community started

117

to change. Industry arrived in the form of a cornmill, a sawmill and a coal yard. The new railway sidings at Hook also meant that livestock was able to be transported to and from market more easily and Gowers iron foundry was able to move larger items of machinery.

By 1938, Hook needed a new church to serve its growing community and to replace the tin church which had been built in 1886.

At that time there were still the 'big' houses for the gentry. Old Raven House, Hook House and Oaklands are still standing, but Crossways (the home of Thomas Burberry, maker of the famous raincoats), Sheldons, Rookswood, Hartletts, Seton House and Nightingales have sadly been demolished to make way for new housing.

The 1960s saw the start of the building of private housing estates. Growth, which had been gradual, increased considerably with the village doubling in size during the 1980s. In just seven years, Hook changed from a tight-knit village of 1,100 houses and 3,000 people to a commuter-based community with over 2,000 houses and a population of more than 6,000.

Hook, which falls in the Hart District, has tried to keep pace with its dramatic increase in population by investing in a new surgery, a larger primary school and a new community hall.

Hordle ⚜

The original church stood two miles distant from the village, on the cliff, 'in sound of the sea'. In 1830, in response to a petition from the parishioners, the church was dismantled and re-erected on Hordle common. Sad to say, this had again to be rebuilt 40 years later, owing, perhaps, to faulty construction. The third church, an example of mid-Victorian architecture, was consecrated in 1872. Stones from the ancient church can still be found scattered around the parish.

The church of All Saints has always been the hub of village life. This is still evident today. Together with the newly formed Community Association, great efforts are being made to combine the old and the new in the social life of the community.

One or two thatched cottages remain in the village. Building development increased rapidly in the 1960s. Agricultural land was sold and country houses were demolished to make way for housing estates. The pattern of the village inevitably changed. Early census returns give the population numbers in the region of 400. The latest figure is nearly 5,000.

Past inhabitants of Hordle worked mainly on the land. Some do so today as there are still a few farms and some fine horticultural nurseries.

A well known benefactor of the village was John Collett (1798–1856). Known as the poacher's friend, he was opposed to the Game Laws and frequently paid fines imposed on poachers. A large grey monolith erected to his memory, stands in the churchyard.

Mrs Mary Ann Girling was a strange religious figure who claimed to be immortal. She was foundress of the sect 'The Children of God', nicknamed 'The Shakers' from the manner of showing their religious fervour. Mrs Girling (her followers called her 'Mother') arrived with her disciples at New Forest Lodge, Hordle in 1872, and completely changed the lives of about 170 people, it is claimed, by hypnotism. The group suffered much hardship in the 14 years of existence. Due in large measure to their peculiar beliefs, the Shakers were evicted for failure to pay monies in connection with the property they had occupied. Mrs Girling died in 1886. The few remaining followers kept a dawn vigil at her grave awaiting her resurrection. Three said they saw her spirit rise from the grave.

Smugglers once used Hordle Cliff to watch for danger, for it commands an extensive view of the ocean. The treacherous route along the cliff became a nightmare for a Customs Officer one dark night, when his horse mistook the path and hurtled him down 70 feet toward the sea. Lovey Warne passed this way with her contraband silks and lace bound about her person beneath her crinoline.

Horndean ✿

Horndean is a village with a population greater than that of its neighbouring town of Petersfield, yet it has no bank and no parish church, though it has a brewery, which celebrated its centenary in 1988, and it has five pubs, an Indian restaurant and a Chinese takeaway.

It has grown enormously since the Second World War and is now bisected by the A3(M). It was not until the 20th century that it became a village of note. In 1903 the Light Railway, which ran from Cosham to Horndean was opened. The fare was 5d single and 8d return. Trippers would come from Portsmouth for a day's outing in the country. There was a tea room and tea garden at the Good Intent and also at the Ship and Bell. The trams were painted in emerald green and cream, and known popularly as the 'Green Cars'. The Royal Mail was carried by the tram during the life of the Light Railway. It ceased running at the beginning of 1935 due to unprofitability.

Merchistoun Hall, home of the Horndean Community Association, is a listed Grade II building. Not much is known about the Hall before 1800. When Admiral Sir Charles Napier bought it in about 1836 it was called Quallets Grove or, more simply The Grove. He renamed it Merchistoun Hall after his ancestral home in Stirlingshire. He retired there in 1855 and was MP for Southwark until his death in 1860. In his last years he divided his time between experimental farming, becoming an authority on sheep and turnips, and attempting to remedy abuses and discontents in the Navy. He was a well-known figure in the village with his strange dress, ugly gait, strikingly untidy and somewhat repellant appearance and his meddlesome monkey.

When the Hall was sold in 1926, on one of the sale notices a wag chalked, after the various items, '– and one ghost'. People have claimed to have seen the ghost in the day and at night, inside and outside the house, dressed in a grey hooded cloak.

The Red Lion is also reputed to have a ghost, 'a rough lady dressed common in the style of a street tart', who has been heard singing and laughing in the bar. It is thought she may have been murdered in or near the cellar.

In 1978, as a result of a nationwide appeal by the ITV children's programme *Magpie*, Cadlington House was obtained, upgraded and refurbished as a home for severely mentally handicapped children. It is now a home for 28 young people under the auspices of Mencap. The New Blendworth Garden Centre has been more recently set up in grounds which were part of the Cadlington estate and is run for the training in horticulture of 32 mentally handicapped young people. There is a garden shop on site and they have some small livestock. They undertake local contract gardening and also keep the village clean and tidy.

Hurstbourne Tarrant

Anyone sighting the village from the top of Hurstbourne Hill, with the church nestling among the farms and cottages in the valley below, must surely feel the urge to explore. The village, which embraces the hamlet of Ibthorpe, originated as a Saxon settlement and for centuries its people have earned a living from the land. Most of the higher ground around the village was at one time forested and some woodland still exists within the parish, notably Doles Wood to the south and Faccombe Wood to the north. These were at one time part of the extensive King's Forest and in 1226 this crown property was granted to the Cistercian nunnery of Tarrant in Dorset – hence the present name of Hurstbourne Tarrant.

St Peter's church was built at the end of the 12th century. The font dates from the 13th century and 14th century wall paintings still survive faintly on the north wall. One depicts the 'Morality of the three living and the three dead'; the other 'The Seven Deadly Sins'. In the 14th century the vicar and many of his parishioners died of the plague.

Relatively little is known about village life until the beginning of the 19th century when much of the forest land had been cleared and replaced by pasture and arable land. Common lands were also established for the use of farm labourers. We learn much about conditions in the early 19th century from William Cobbett, who often stayed in the village with Farmer Blount at Rookery Farm while gathering material for his *Rural Rides*. 'In no part of England', he wrote 'have I seen the labouring people so badly off as they are here'. Living conditions in the workers' cottages were primitive and families were large. The population reached a maximum by 1871 of 887. However, cheap corn was already coming in from the colonies. Local farmers could not compete and the population soon began to decline. Two other industries allied to farming helped to sustain the villagers – malting and forestry.

The malthouses not only supplied Andover breweries but became brewhouses in their own right supplying the village inns, of which there were six. The Five Alls stood by the tollgate at the top of Hurstbourne Hill and served villagers who used the nearby common land. At the other end of the village was the King's Arms on the Newbury Road. The Coopers' Arms in the centre of the village was destroyed by fire in 1904. It was noted for its Coopers' Club, the members of which held a feast in the inn every Whit Monday after a parade around the village. Close by was the Plough and, at Ibthorpe, the White Hart, now both private residences. The only remaining inn is the George and Dragon with its Georgian frontage, at one time a posting house with stabling.

The surrounding woodlands have always provided work for the villagers. They were the main source of fuel and of timber for wagon making. At one time there were 22 hurdle makers working on the hills.

Over the years the village has had its share of celebrities – resident and visiting. Jane Austen was a frequent visitor to Ibthorpe House and her brother James was married in St Peter's church in 1800.

Hurstbourne Tarrant also seems to have had a particular attraction for artists. Anyone who has visited the Tate Gallery cannot have failed to have seen the well-known painting *Love Locked Out* by Anna Lea Merritt, an artist who was born in America and came to London in 1873, where she set up a studio with her sister. She found a mentor in Henry Merritt, a practical artist and critic and she married him but, within a short time, and already a sick man, he died. Anna was devastated and began to suffer from asthma. In 1891 she decided to move into the country and chose Hurstbourne Tarrant where she lived in a cottage called The Limes at the bottom of Hurstbourne Hill (since destroyed by fire). She continued to paint and used some of her work to illustrate her book *A Hamlet in Old Hampshire.*

The two World Wars had a profound effect on the village. Many families lost sons and husbands. Soon after the Second World War ended, two council house estates were built – Dene Rise with the Crescent, and Dines Close. Families which had been living in somewhat cramped conditions in small cottages with primitive sanitation were only too glad to move to houses with modern conveniences. These old cottages, mainly in pairs or groups, were soon acquired by townspeople anxious to live in the country. The old wells and cesspits were replaced by piped water and mains drainage and the former cottages were converted into single dwellings. Some of the incomers are retired people, others are prepared to commute to work in order to enjoy the quiet and friendliness of village life in their spare time. It is a pattern common in our Hampshire countryside.

Hyde (Winchester) 🌿

Hyde lies to the north of Winchester outside the city walls. In earlier times it was a village in its own right, but now it is very much a part of Winchester. In the 1970s an area between City Road and Victoria Road was excavated before extensive building, and a Roman cemetery was found. The Romans always buried their dead outside city walls, and it is only one of the cemeteries found outside the walls of Winchester. There were grave goods in some of the graves and not in others, suggesting that some people had been converted to Christianity and others not, but it may be that those with grave goods were playing it both ways. After the Romans had left and the Anglo-Saxons were established, Winchester was besieged by the Danes in AD 927. A single combat was suggested by the Danes who had a giant of a man called Colbrand on their side. Guy of Warwick was the Saxon hero who ousted him in Hyde Meads by the river. Whether a true story or a legend the area where they are supposed to have fought was called Danemark after that. A recently amalgamated secondary school for girls was also named Danemark. The New Minster had been founded close by the Old Minster by King Alfred although it was not consecrated until after his death by his son Edward the Elder in AD 903. The New Minster was moved to an area in Hyde in AD 1110 and the bodies of Alfred the Great, Edward the Elder and St Grimbald, who had been the first Abbot, were taken there and buried. Alfred's queen Alswitha was also translated from its original burial place. In AD 1141 Hyde Abbey was very much damaged in the time of the war between Matilda and Stephen and the cross of King Canute, which had been a present to the monks, was melted down in the fire, 'so great was the conflagration'. It was rebuilt in 1196. Later it became very poor and was surrendered to Bishop Edington on account of 'need, indigence and misery'. In 1445 the bell tower was destroyed by fire and Cardinal Beaufort gave £200 for its restoration.

Hyde Abbey became very rich and owned much property. Abbots Barton, just north of Hyde, was one of its farms and supplied the Abbey. Many of the street names bear testimony to the presence of the Abbey – Monks Road, Nuns Road and Hyde Abbey Road; and to the Kings – Arthur Road, Egbert Road, and King Alfred Place. Saxon Road and Danes Road are also to be found in this Edwardian ribbon-developed suburb.

At the Dissolution of the Monasteries by the Crown in 1538, the Abbey was well-nigh demolished and Richard Bethel, a cloth merchant, had the lease for £110. Apparently, the king had the proceeds from the selling of the lead from the roof. In Oliver Cromwell's time more damage was done and stones from Hyde Abbey may be found all over Winchester.

In the 19th century during excavations on the site of Hyde Abbey, bones found close to the site of the high altar and thought to be those of Alfred and his Queen, were moved to the graveyard of St Bartholomew's church nearby, and covered with a plain unmarked rectangular gravestone behind the church. Citizens of Winchester like to think this is the last resting place of Alfred the Great and in 1901, a thousand years after his death, they raised in the Broadway, the splendid statue by Sir Hamo Thornycroft, as a tribute to the greatest of the old English kings. It is claimed that 'More than any other man he was the first maker of England.'

St Bartholomew's church, which had been built at the same time as the Abbey for the use of the people who worked at Hyde Abbey, was allowed to remain as the parish church after the Dissolution and some of the stone from the ruined abbey built the tower. The list of vicars of St Bartholomew's dates from 1310 and life and witness still continues today in the parish (village) of Hyde.

Several large houses were built by rich families. Hyde Abbey House is 17th century but has a Georgian facade. A Dr Richards ran a successful school there and as it grew in size he had to have a large schoolroom, which was designed by Soane, built in Hyde Close. This is a carpet showroom now. Hyde House has 1660s Dutch gables in dark red brick and is now part of the Historic Resources Centre which also includes a group of buildings of the 18th century, once a malthouse known as Hyde Barn. This probably was once owned by the Abbot of Hyde. Part of the entrance to Hyde House is displayed on a wall in Victoria Road.

During the Second World War, a German plane dropped its bombs near a bus stop in Hyde Street, just as people were going to work first thing in the morning. There were several casualties including schoolgirls and the owner of a furniture shop in Jewry Street. These, apparently, were the only bombs dropped on Winchester which can count itself extremely lucky.

Nowadays, Hyde boasts a large recreation and sports centre, a school, a park, a camping site, a church with a church hall where Winchester City WI meets monthly. Most important of all Hyde is the headquarters of Hampshire WI. WI House is located in Hyde Abbey Road.

Lastly, one must mention the odd ghost or two which have been seen by local people. They are always monks or nuns of course.

Hyde & Frogham

Not so much a village as a collection of hamlets, Hyde parish is situated two miles south-east of Fordingbridge, and within the boundary of the New Forest. These hamlets are Hyde, Frogham, Stuckton, Ogdens, Gorley, Blissford, Hungerford and Furzehill. There are about 400 houses and around 1,000 people, served by a church, a chapel and a school at Hyde, and a new sub-post office and garden shop. Many residents have moved here to retire, others commute to Salisbury or Poole, and there are many who were born and bred in the Forest.

Hyde school stands prominently in Hyde; Victorian Gothic and built in 1885, it replaced the mudwalled school located in a nearby thatched cottage. The land for both the school and the church of the Holy Ascension at Hyde (1850s) was given by the Eyre Coote family, large landowners at that time who lived at West Park, Rockbourne. The name of the school, stone-cut on the face of the building, was erased in the Second World War. There are lots of pupils now – a good sign for the village's future.

Thatched cottages are interspersed with more modern houses and bungalows, but the charm of the area, woods and heaths and grazing animals, remains. Some of the old farm cottages used to be rented out on a curious system called 'the rent for three lives' – but by the time the third generation took up residence in them they had often become so dilapidated that they were beyond repair.

Through the parish runs Latchmoor Brook, a latch or laece meaning a boggy stream. The brook's name changes to Hucklesbrook (meaning the brook of little bends) before passing Tuck's Hole. This hidden spot below Gorley Common was a special gypsies' encampment in the past, shielded by four large oak trees and known locally as Squatters' Square. In autumn these trees held the annual rooks' and starlings' chattering 'Parliaments'; they also used to gather in three large elm trees in North Gorley, but these trees have all gone now. The gypsies, however, own a knoll north of the church, and live in up-to-date caravans.

Farming and market gardening have been the main occupations in this area for centuries past, and still are to a certain extent, with the landowning 'Commoners' usually having a second occupation in rearing New Forest ponies. The Romans lived here too, and ancient man – their pottery kilns and tools were found on Gorley Common when gravel was extracted.

Just over 100 years ago it was wise not to cross Hyde Common after dark, as it was on the direct smugglers' route from Poole to Bramshaw Telegraph and so on to London, where they travelled with their illicit liquor from France.

Many properties have Rights of Common attached to them, Common of Pasture gives grazing rights. Mast means pigs can be turned out to eat the crop of acorns in the pannage season. Turbary entitles the Commoner to cut turf for burning in his dwelling, while Common of Fuelwood, also called Estovers, allows the Commoner to collect his allotted cord or cords, ready cut and stacked by the Forestry Commission. Marl is the right to take marl from forest pits, though modern farming methods make this more or less obsolete.

Bartletts Common, the smallest of these open commons, was once owned by Mr Bartlett who had a fairground there. Now, an annual Country Fair takes place on August Bank Holiday weekend, attracting many hundreds of people.

At Frogham crossroads is the hostelry called The Foresters Arms and also the principal meeting place for all the village – the new Hyde War Memorial Parish Hall. The hall was built in 1987 to replace the old sergeants' mess which was brought from Tidworth on Salisbury Plain by horse and cart, and served the village well for 66 years.

During the autumn the owners of ponies on the Forest arrange 'drifts', when mares and foals are rounded up, either for branding or for sale. This tough breed can exist on a very poor diet. The really wild animals are not so obvious, but the roe and fallow deer will come to raid gardens in the winter if they are hungry – they love roses! Foxgloves flower un-nibbled, for they are poisonous; so too is ragwort and it is illegal here to allow it to grow on your land.

Hythe 🖎

Hythe (the name means a landing place) is a large village in the parish of Dibden, on the south-east edge of the New Forest and on the western side of Southampton Water.

Most visitors would visit Southampton by the Hythe Ferry to see all the shipping. In the old days a walk down the 650 metre long pier was a 'must'. It was officially opened in 1881 and an electric train was added in 1922. All the great passenger liners sailed past the pier, and Imperial Airways had a maintenance base at Hythe, so Sunderland flying boats took off from Southampton Water with passengers and mail for far-flung outposts of the Empire. In fact they were called Empire Flying Boats.

To the east side of Hythe Waterside was the British Power Boat Company, where the famous Miss Britain power boat was designed and built by Hubert Scott Paine before the Second World War. During the war the yard was turned to the building of motor torpedo boats for the Navy and high speed launches for the RAF Rescue Sevices.

Hythe Waterside is still provided with many pubs. Most are nautically named, with the exception of the Drummond Arms, named after a Scottish banker who lived on one of the large adjacent estates. These large estates have long since been broken up to provide land for housing estates, the Esso Refinery, and so on.

Today the Waterside is still busy, with a large marina on the west side and another proposed on the site of the old British Power Boat Company. You can still see the majestic *Queen Elizabeth II*, or the *Canberra* when they arrive from their cruises. Container ships which look like large moving hotels can also be seen, not nearly as graceful. of course, as the pre and post-war liners.

Hythe is a busy place with small factories in Shore Road and an American base. A supermarket was built on the site of Knighton's. This was a stately home built over 120 years ago in the Italian style, with spacious grounds and fine views of Southampton Water. Stone busts of poets including Milton, Dryden, Shakespeare and Byron graced the gardens. Knighton's was always called the 'Black Wall' by the locals because it was surrounded by a very high black wall like a fortress.

The road between the hotel and the one time Anchor and Hope public house was referred to by the old folks as 'the bridge'. There was a marsh where the road called The Marsh is, and an underground tunnel ran from near the pier to what is now New Road car park, meeting a stream coming from Hollybank estate. This was a smugglers' run in the old days.

Most of the terraced houses in School Road relied on water from wells. At the bottom of School Road was a pump, opposite the old 'Consumer' supermarket. Next to the pump were two cottages and the village blacksmith. Most of the tradespeople had horses in those days, as had the gentry who lived in large houses in the Hythe area.

There was a roller skating rink at the bottom of South Street behind Gladstone House many years ago. Later this became the Hythe cinema with firstly silent films then the 'talkies'. Everyone went, there was little else to do in Hythe. Prices for admission were 7d, 9d and 1/3d. It was a small place, like a bungalow. When it rained heavily it was difficult to hear the sound track because of the corrugated iron roof!

Itchen Abbas 🦋

Three miles from Alresford, Itchen Abbas lies in the lovely Itchen valley on the B3047. It is a small rural village with church, primary school, police house and country pub – the Plough Inn. The one shop and post office closed a few years ago.

The church of St John the Baptist contains memorials to the Corrie and the Wright families. Of Norman design, it was rebuilt in 1863 on the site of the original church dated 1092. Some of the original stones and part of the chancel arch were used in the rebuilding. In the churchyard a magnificent and stately yew tree, which was possibly a sapling planted when the first church was built, shades the grave of the gypsy John Hughes, the last man hanged in Winchester in 1825 for horse stealing. He was buried in consecrated ground due to the Christian spirit of the rector, Rev Robert Wright.

There are several old houses in the village. Bignall's Cottage at the top of the hill was the home long ago of Peter Bignall, the village carpenter and wheelwright. He is reputed to have seen the village ghost, a white lady who walked up and down on moonlit nights without her head. The Elms, built in 1843, is still to be seen on the east side of Rectory Lane and was the home of the Corrie family and the Rev Robert Wright.

Charles Kingsley often visited Itchen Abbas. He stayed at the old Plough Inn, the predecessor of the present Plough, and immortalised the village in *The Water Babies*. On his visits here he used to fish what he described as 'the loveliest of vale rivers' and in *Hereward the Wake* he described the waters of the Itchen, so clear 'that none could see where water ended and where air began'. Robert Browning also loved Itchen Abbas and wrote his well-known verse *The year's at the spring* as part of his poetic drama *Pippa Passes*.

The village primary school became quite famous in recent times for its discovery of Saxon remains.

Itchen Stoke ✣

The village of Itchen Stoke lies east of Itchen Abbas, on the B3047 road to the nearby town of Alresford. There are delightful thatched cottages and later ones built of flint and brick. The old school and schoolhouse built of undressed flint is now a private house and lies at the top of ancient Water Lane, which leads downhill to a once very important ford over the river Itchen. A footpath along the riverbank is much used by people walking to the village of Ovington about a mile away.

On the opposite side of the road is the church of St Mary the Virgin, which lies in the centre of the village. The present church was built in 1866, the design based on that of La Sainte Chapelle in Paris. It is worthy of a visit – there is an ancient font of stone standing on four pillars which was found in pieces in the present churchyard hedge and reassembled by a recent vicar, and the rose windows are beautiful. The pulpit is unusual and can be entered only from the vestry. Although no longer used for regular worship it remains consecrated and is now in the care of the Redundant Churches Fund.

Kempshott ✣

A long barrow or burial chamber was located on land now developed near Pack Lane. Neolithic tools, scrapers, arrow-heads and other flint tools have been found in further evidence of those early times of settlement. A Bronze Age round barrow was discovered at a private residence in Kempshott Lane. During the course of extensive developments many more such burial grounds must have been ploughed in.

The original Roman road ran from Silchester in the north through Kempshott to Winchester in the south and parts of this still exist and are traversed.

The major part of land developed at Kempshott was originally known as Basingstoke Down. Sheep fairs were held on Basingstoke Down until the 1786 enclosures, and there was also a racecourse.

Kempshott House (which no longer exists) was a mansion which in about 1788 was rented by the then Prince of Wales as a hunting lodge. In 1795 he married Caroline of Brunswick and spent his honeymoon there.

Down Grange House was another mansion, the grounds of which ran alongside the main A30 road. Here Jane Austen danced the night away. She had many associations with this part of Hampshire.

There were extensive farms and grazing lands all around Kempshott and district, and after the First World War people began to build and settle there. In 1960 when businesses were moving from the London area and elsewhere to Basingstoke, Kempshott and its rolling acres were further developed and many people bought new homes here.

Kempshott is now the size of a small town and it is now in its own parish. Its newly erected church of St Mark was opened in 1987. Hitherto there was no church in Kempshott, and in earlier days would-be worshippers went on foot to Worting church some five miles away.

Kilmeston

The main industry of Kilmeston was and still is agriculture but, with the mechanisation of the farms, only one or two villagers now work on the land.

The shop and post office in the centre of the village closed over 25 years ago, and is now a private house. A second shop and petrol station is still operating on the outskirts of the village.

The church is dedicated to St Andrew and was built in 1772 on the foundations of what the Domesday survey noted as a chapel annexed to Cheriton, thought to be of Saxon or Norman origin.

Thomas Ridge, squire of Kilmeston from 1736 to 1801, was a typical country squire of the 18th century. The eldest son of George Ridge, a brewer of Portsmouth, Thomas inherited Kilmeston manor in 1736, married his cousin Mary Ridge at Portsea in 1767 and was blessed with 18 children. He took over the Kilmeston Hunt from his father, maintaining it at his own expense until eventually accepting subscriptions toward the cost. In 1784 it became known as the Hampshire Hunt, and still exists with stables and kennels at Ropley.

George III and his son, the Prince Regent are said to have stayed at the manor for the hunting, and on a pane of glass in the kitchen window can be seen the King's initials etched with his own diamond ring. Thomas Ridge was buried in Kilmeston churchyard on 10th February 1801.

In 1701 a Dame Mary Sadler bequeathed £100 toward the establishment of a village school. The school was closed in 1920, and the interest was then used for the Sunday school. The school building is now used as a village hall. Dame Mary also bequeathed College Farm toward the foundation of 16 lectureships on algebra within the University of Cambridge; the lectures commenced in 1710.

Kimpton 🪴

Kimpton village is situated about six miles west of Andover, close to Thruxton racing circuit. It is a small, pretty, rural village, in the centre of which stands the church and several thatched cottages – even the bus shelter is thatched! The village is in two parts; the main part clusters around the village green, while the other end of the village had the village school, now demolished, and accommodates the village hall.

The church of St Peter and St Paul stands behind Kimpton Manor and is reached via a grass path. It was originally a plain rectangular building, although it is possible that the nave may retain the walling of an earlier church which had a narrow chancel. The chancel dates from about 1220, as does the original north door, now blocked up. In the Shoddesden chapel, on the north side of the church, there is a panel with brasses taken from the tomb of Robert Thornburgh and his wife and their children. Robert Thornburgh was the lord of Shoddesden manor and died in 1552. The altar in Shoddesden chapel is the village war memorial.

Kimpton Cottage was once a post house and later became Kimpton's police house. The police house subsequently moved to Ringwood Cottage and is now situated in Deacon Road at the other end of the village. Kimpton once boasted an off-licence and two shops – one at each end of the village. Today, however, all three have reverted to private houses.

During the drought of 1921, water was available for five shillings a barrel. The only records of purchase were by the Rev Brady Moore who paid a total of £6 10s. Rev Moore was the only person who owned a bath in the area!

In 1922, the murder of Beatrice Emily Wordsell and suicide of Horace Hyde in Kimpton was reported in the *Daily Mirror*. Beatrice broke off her engagement to Horace and returned home to Kimpton from Cobham where she worked. Horace pursued her and they were seen walking together through the village on a Sunday afternoon. A scream was heard and Beatrice was found lying in the road with her throat cut. Horace was found dead further along the road with a knife lying beside him.

In 1966, a Kimpton farmer, Mr William Flambert, was walking his farm and noticed an area of excessive stones and fragments of pottery thrown up by the tractor. He contacted Max Dacre, a local archaeologist, and the local archaeological organisation. Within hours they were in Kimpton to investigate and their enthusiasm was infectious. The farmer left the field alone for four years whilst a dig was carried out. They found 108 burials, up to 3,500 years old, ranging from the time of Stonehenge until 800 BC. Also found were 150 urns and calcified human remains. The importance of this dig was testified by a request from the British

Museum that all finds from this Bronze Age burial ground be kept under their control, thus enabling the nation to enjoy the finds – Mr William Flambert agreed.

Kimpton remains a rural village with the annual village fete bringing many members of the village together to raise money for local funds. The highlight of the day is the enjoyable but fiercely-fought Dog Race!

Kingsclere 🐾

Watership Down, a name familiar to millions, is part of the downland surrounding Kingsclere, made famous by Richard Adams' novel and now better known than Kingsclere itself. The downs provide an undulating green backdrop to the village. An excellent spot for flying kites and model aeroplanes, a venue for archery and horse riding events and the Wayfarer's Walk attracts ramblers. Tourists who seek the background to the story are likely to be confronted by racehorses on training gallops, flocks of sheep, exhaltations of skylarks, but rabbits are fairly rare, for, in the words of a local inhabitant, 'Inadvertently it seems, Mr Adams has started a hare.'

A village that is steeped in history, named Kings Clere at the beginning of the 13th century, it has received royal patronage since Saxon times. The 12th century parish church has a unique weather-vane, traditionally identified as a bed bug, ordered to be exhibited by King John after a bad night at the local inn! It is more likely to be a stylized tortoise or dragon. However, the symbol is used on church publications and at least one local business makes use of the logo.

The fast pace of modern life has changed the face of Kingsclere. In some respects it is cleaner as a bypass has channelled the traffic away from the centre of the village. Oak-beamed 16th century houses, no longer fretted by dust and fumes, have been renovated and colourwashed and are interspersed with new houses and courtyards built in traditional style. While new housing estates on the outer perimeters owe nothing to rustic design, the heart of the village retains its character.

This great surge of building and renovation has resulted in more houses and fewer shops, although the remaining shops are open longer hours and some seven days a week. During the 19th century there were ten public houses, a number now reduced to three. The Swan, once the haunt of the local stable lads, has been upgraded to an hotel. The dartboards and bar billiards have gone, but restoration work uncovered the 15th century roof with beams coated with soot from over a century of fires that burned in the centre of the floor. This fine example of medieval

Kingsclere church, 'bed bug' weathervane and Victorian lamp standard

craftsmanship, with its double set of wind bracing and carved central brace, has been renovated and now canopies the hotel dining room.

A golf course and a small industrial estate are recent additions to the village and provide some local employment. Most people work in nearby towns or commute to London. The village was once almost self-sufficient, with a diversity of employment in agriculture, brewing, rope-making, tanning, milling and building.

A steady influx of new residents eager to enjoy country life has generated a spirit of appreciation and conservation. The ramblers have cleared and reopened footpaths and the council delay mowing part of the recreation ground in order to preserve the wildflowers, including two types of orchid. The clear chalk stream that runs through the village supports a variety of wild and domestic ducks and geese. A new footpath makes it possible to enjoy the quiet beauty of the stream in the very centre of the village.

132

Seats and flowerbeds have been set out in the village square and the magnificent Victorian lamp standard removed in 1969 in favour of a modern one, has been restored and returned to grace the square once more.

Kings Somborne 🌿

The Sombornes lie in the low hills on the edge of the beautiful Test valley. Up Somborne is a ribbon of houses some three miles from the main village, and Little Somborne is scattered round an enchanting small chapel of Saxon origin.

Kings Somborne, known to walkers as it lies on the intersection of the Test and Clarendon Ways, has a population of about 1,200. It has probably never been so pretty, as affluence and paint have brightened its buildings. Barely 30 years ago the impression was tumbledown and shabby. The shortsighted policy then was to destroy unfit buildings rather than repair them, so some character has gone from the village. There is still one pub and a few shops, and the ecclesiastical parish is

Cruck Cottage, Kings Somborne

unusual in that it is joined only with nearby Ashley. The church of St Peter and St Paul, basically Norman, was regrettably rebuilt in 1885. It and the pub stand pleasantly on a mini-green, complete with war memorial.

The 'Kings' of the village name were Saxon. Somborne was a royal manor before the Norman Conquest, and the remains of a stone-built palace, comparable to that at Clarendon in Wiltshire, lie below the ground near the village hall. In medieval times Somborne was the centre of its Hundred and Deanery; since then there has been a relative decline as the manor and Hundred courts have been superseded and the centre of the Deanery shifted to Romsey. It remained a royal possession until sold by Charles II. The boundary of John of Gaunt's deer park is still marked in places by a bank and yew trees, but the fishing pool known as John of Gaunt's which lies within its boundaries was only made in the 1930s.

The village achieved fame in the midst of the agricultural depression that beset rural Hampshire in the mid 19th century. In 1837 Richard Dawes, blocked by his liberal views from an academic career, was appointed to the living of Kings Somborne. He found a parish run down and demoralised, so in the belief that education would improve social and moral conditions he organised a school, which opened in October 1842. He believed that the school should be self-supporting and that teaching should be practical and interesting and of evident benefit to everyone – views much ahead of his time. By 1847 the school was one of the best-known in the country, and it was visited by the Prime Minister, Matthew Arnold and Florence Nightingale. Dawes became Dean of Hereford in 1850. The school continues in the same buildings today.

Langley & Lepe

Today, Langley and Blackfield are virtually indistinguishable but Langley used to be a village in its own right, centred around the area of the present day Langley Tavern. Langley was mentioned in the Domesday Book, the name deriving from Long Wood.

Langley Lodge was the childhood home of T.E. Lawrence (Lawrence of Arabia), but the house is no more and is the site of a modern estate, Langley Lodge Gardens. Old fields and orchards are now built on, many of the houses having forest rights though few exercise them.

A Roman road through Dibden Purlieu passes through Langley (through present day St Francis Close/Chalewood Road) and it is believed that this road went on to Lepe and linked up with a causeway to the Isle of Wight. Legend has it the causeway had a gap in the middle which it was possible for a man to 'leap', hence the name!

The modern road leaving Langley continues through farmland. The visitor on occasions may be amazed to see the superstructure of shipping, mirage-like, sailing through trees and fields. However, the way drops down suddenly to the shore of the Solent and you arrive at Lepe beach, at this point only three miles from the Isle of Wight.

Lepe now consists of a row of old slate-hung coastguard cottages and the Boat or Watch House, once the home of a fast cutter on the alert for smugglers. Lepe House, with its panoramic view across the Solent to the Isle of Wight and as far west as Hurst Castle is now hidden from the road and the curious eye of the passing visitor. Early this century is was 'The Ship Inn' and before that was known as 'The Launch' and was notorious during the 18th and 19th centuries.

Lepe saw much shipping during the 18th century when Henry Adams was building ships of the line at Bucklers Hard. Men-of-war were floated down the Beaulieu river to be fitted out in the boatyards at Lepe. No evidence of these activities remains but a walk along Lepe beach in the direction of Calshot brings you to an area of concrete fortifications. Here during the Second World War troops and tanks, landing craft and Mulberry Harbours were gathered together in preparation for the D-Day landings.

The Hampshire Recreation Department administer the Lepe Country Park, which attracts many visitors for a day by the sea and the yachting activities in the Solent. Here is grandstand viewing for watching Cowes Week or the line-up of entries for the Admiral's Cup of the Fastnet Race. It is also a turning point for the aircraft taking part in the recently revived Schneider Trophy Race.

Moments of history in the 1980s include the return from the Falklands war of the *QE II*, to be met off Lepe by the Royal Yacht *Britannia* with some members of the royal family on board, and that incredible moment when the liner *Canberra* emerged from the mist, battled-stained but victorious, to be escorted through Southampton Water by a thousand small boats.

The North Solent National Nature Reserve is a recent designation, preserving part of the area for the benefit of wildlife. The shore and salt marshes along this coastline have abundant wildlife and are an important winter feeding area for many birds.

Langrish 🌿

Langrish is only a small village, on the A272 Winchester to Petersfield road. It also leads to the Meon valley, with lovely views of Butser Hill and the surrounding countryside, and there are many footpaths through the surrounding fields, lanes and woods.

There is no village shop, pub or post office, but Portsmouth, Southampton and Winchester can be reached by bus or train.

There is a small church, St John the Evangelist's, and the community life of the village is mostly centred on its village fete, held each year and always very well supported. Once a fortnight the mobile library calls at the village green.

The main employment used to be in agriculture but now there are only two local dairy farms and most of the villagers go off each day to their place of employment. A tapestry shop and business has opened in the centre of the village.

There is also an engineering factory (Tooling Products), which was started by Mr Talbot-Ponsonby at the beginning of the Second World War, though most of its employees now come from outside the village. Langrish House Hotel used to be the home of the Talbot-Ponsonbys. There are many plaques in the church in memory of the family, whose ancestors had the church built.

Lasham 🐝

The tiny village of Lasham adjoins Herriard, and for about 200 years was part of the Herriard Park estate. Until recent reorganisation, Herriard and Lasham shared a vicar, with the rectory being in Lasham. Now it is part of the benefice of Shalden, Bentworth and Lasham. The church of St Mary was built in 1866 on the site of a Saxon building.

During the First World War Mrs Beatrice Jervoise managed Church Farm at Lasham. She was so concerned by the shortage of water that she brought in a dowser. His findings were so successful that Major and Mrs Jervoise were able to found the Herriard and Lasham Water Company, with reservoirs in Lasham Wood. This enabled water to be piped to Lasham, Herriard, Shalden, Bentworth, Wield, Tunworth, Weston Corbett, Ellisfield, Medstead, Bradley and Preston Candover. This remarkable feat is recorded on Mrs Jervoise's tomb in Herriard churchyard.

Although such a small village, Lasham is known throughout the country for its gliding club, the National Gliding Championships often being held at Lasham Airfield.

The airfield was built during the Second World War, when the beautiful beech avenue planted by George Jervoise in 1809 was sacrificed to make way for it. The old road between Herriard and Lasham was closed, and gangs of Irish labourers and Italian prisoners of war were brought in to make the 'concrete road' which is now part of the A339.

Since houses and farms have been sold by the Herriard Park estate many of them have been modernised and extended. The Old Post Office is one of these, and so is Pear Tree Cottage, which was once the home of the blacksmith. In the grounds is the 18th century building which was the forge and blacksmith's shop.

Church Farm is being developed into a modern housing complex. The farmhouse, dating from the 17th century, has been completely modernised inside, without altering the exterior. Farm buildings are being converted into small houses surrounding an open space, and a very ancient barn is being repaired, again without altering its original exterior. It is hoped to use this for village functions, as there is no village hall at present.

The villagers are justly proud of their pretty pond, which is fed from local springs. It is regularly cleaned out, and is the home of mallard and moorhens, as well as large numbers of goldfish.

We know from the records of Herriard and other villages how the name has changed over the centuries. In Lasham it is happening in our lifetime, not so much in the spelling, but in the pronunciation. Until about 20 years ago it was called 'Lassum', but more and more it is called 'Lash-am'. No doubt in another 20 years 'Lassum' will have passed into the history books.

Laverstoke & Freefolk

The parish of Laverstoke and Freefolk was united in 1872, when, on the closure of St Mary's in Laverstoke Park, the tiny 13th century church of St Nicholas became the parish church. St Mary's in the Park then became the vaults of the Portal family. In 1896 a new church named St Mary the Virgin was built, dominating the village of Freefolk, situated next to the school which dates back to 1850.

Portal's Mills originated in 1712, when Henri de Portal, a French refugee, landed with others at Southampton. He was eventually offered an apprenticeship at Stoneham, and on completion he became naturalised. He then acquired the lease of Bere Mill, where he perfected papermaking. As he progressed he needed to expand, so he applied for Laverstoke Mill, and built a new mill on the site in 1718. In 1724 the Bank of England requested him to submit samples for use as banknote paper. It was approved and the contract still exists, amid strict security. The production takes place at Overton Mill, two miles to the east, which one of Henri's successors, Sir William Portal, built in 1922. A great deal of its success is derived from the river Test, which rises at Ashe a mile upstream. After use and recycling the water then flows on through Laverstoke, Freefolk and on to Southampton Water. This river is also famed for its trout, for which fishing is private.

Laverstoke Mill

Lord Portal, who died in 1949, was Head of the Olympic Games when it was held in Germany in 1936, and as a mark of respect for his services to the Games, Hitler awarded him the Iron Cross. In 1948 the Olympic Committee honoured Lord Portal by allowing the Olympic Flame to be carried by a runner through the Park.

Lord Portal had 18 thatched cottages built in memory of his father Sir William Portal, for the use of employees in Freefolk. A white house in Laverstoke bears a plaque indicating that it was the residence of the Bank Officer, 1785, built by Joseph Portal.

In the past, all houses in the area were Portal's company houses, but many have been sold, including the vicarage and schoolhouse. This is a popular area, as it has easy access to the railway and major towns, and the M3 runs five miles to the south.

Agriculture is still very evident, but on a wider scale, mostly arable. Portal's employ a Farms Manager, where once there were about eight tenant farmers. Contractors do seasonal work, and grazing is 'let'.

The public house previously nicknamed 'The Jerry' by labourers working on the railway, has been renamed 'Watership Down' with the popularity of Richard Adams' book, dedicated to this area.

An annual event, which took place until the school closure in 1989, was the picking of snowdrops by the schoolchildren and teachers, in Laverstoke Park. These were then taken to the church room, where ex-employees bunched and packed them. They were then distributed to sick employees and clients of Portal's.

Leckford ✤

Until 1928 Leckford's village population consisted of farmworkers, game and water keepers, gardeners, a carpenter, a thatcher and a bricklayer, all employed locally. Leckford Abbas, the 'big house', with its estate and cottages, was home to the Ansdell family. In that year, John Spedan Lewis, having sold his two London stores to trustees, who would run them on behalf of all employees, bought Leckford Abbas estate, together with other cottages in the village.

He at once laid on running water to every dwelling and provided a central bathhouse. Gradually, as they became available, he bought every single building in Leckford, except the parish church of St Nicholas. He laid out a cricket field in the Abbas grounds and a nine hole golf course on the estate. These, together with the seven miles of fishable banks on the river Test, are still there for the benefit of all John Lewis Partnership employees, including those in Waitrose supermarkets. All employees are called 'Partners'. Every dwelling in Leckford is now occupied either by an active Partner or a pensioner Partner and all the buildings are carefully maintained.

Many of the cottages are thatched and date from the 1600s. The old village school is now a well-used clubhouse, community centre and village hall. The 4,000 acre Leckford estate (about half of which is over the Test in Longstock) is run from offices in the old vicarage. Just beyond the village on the Winchester Road lie apple orchards and refrigerated apple stores. The latest innovation is a thriving mushroom farm.

The central bathhouse is now the Ecological Centre and every step taken on the estate by the Partnership is looked at by scientists to ensure that it is ecologically desirable before it is acted upon. Mr Lewis having been a keen naturalist, the Ecological Centre has been studying all aspects of the local valley and downs for 50 years, long before the development of popular interest in conservation.

St Nicholas' church, which dates from the 12th century, has a Norman font and altar. The latter was found buried in the churchyard, where, it is presumed, it had been hidden at the time of the Commonwealth, to save its destruction.

Lindford ✤

Lindford began as a riverside hamlet on the edge of Woolmer Forest and slowly grew into a small village until, with the development of the surrounding green field sites with new housing estates, it has become a very large village with a density of population rivalling nearby towns.

From the 16th to 19th centuries Lindford remained a hamlet of cottagers, smallholders and farmers. Quite a number of Lindford folk had commoners' rights to use nearby Broxhead common (Brock's Head – the home of badgers even today) to graze their goats, sheep and geese; indeed, the owner of Watermeadow Farm, a charming 16th century farmhouse, exercised his rights to gather fallen timber after the 1987 Great Storm. The common also supported turf and peat cutters. The population in 1773 was 64 in twelve dwellings. Census returns for the mid 1800s include the occupations of carpenter, miller, cordwainer, farm labourer and wheelwright, and a cottage industry thrived with housewives making paper bags, perhaps as outworkers for the paper mill at nearby Passfield.

A period of growth at the turn of the 20th century coincided with the development of nearby Bordon and Longmoor into an army camp, beginning an association which continues today. Lindford contractors dealt with many aspects of the camp's life from laundry and milk delivery to waste disposal and providing a horse-drawn taxi service to Bordon station. Older residents recall hearing troops marching and riding into Bordon accompanied by their regimental bands.

By the end of the First World War Lindford was still mainly a farming community, plus the necessary associated jobs of blacksmith, wheelwright and veterinary, and a hirer of steam engines for farm work such as threshing. A number of houses had been built along the High Road, now Liphook Road, together with the Royal Exchange public house, two general stores, a bakery and a butcher's, which succeeded the small 'front room' shops which had previously supplied the villagers' needs. There were two cricket fields in the village, the one next to the Royal Exchange being used for Sunday matches.

Many people came to Lindford as evacuees during the Second World War and some stayed on afterwards. Then, a steady increase in the size of Bordon military camp resulted in great demand for housing locally and the village really started to grow. The now unused cricket ground by the pub was developed and a parade of shops built. During the 1980s the growth of Lindford has gone on, estate after estate, until all but four of the 200 acres of the parish have been built on.

Although the development of Lindford has destroyed its small village atmosphere and appearance, it remains a friendly and lively community to those who use its facilities, and there is still much beautiful countryside all around to enjoy.

Liphook 🐾

Rural life in Liphook has changed since the arrival of the motor car. Once, carriages carrying royalty passed through the village and the occupants would often stay overnight at the Royal Anchor Hotel.

At the present time, community life in Liphook could possibly be stronger than it was in the 1800s. There is a thriving, caring attitude amongst most of the residents and the new community school helps to provide recreational facilities and further education for adults and children alike.

Six roads converge on the Square and in the early days of the 20th century there were hardly any houses along them. Now there are blocks of flats tucked into every conceivable corner.

On the northern boundary the river Wey winds through water meadows, which in olden days were flooded regularly in order to provide a second cereal crop. This area has now been restored to parkland, which serves as a much needed recreational facility for the residents of the village.

Sadly a connection with the Navy was lost when the King George's Sanatorium for Sailors closed down. The building served the community for many years as a local hospital and was renowned for its yearly Fete.

The village carnival, which takes place in October each year, started life as an 'Old Boys' Bonfire Club', which celebrated the anniversary of the Gunpowder Plot. In the beginning it was simply a bonfire made from wood cut and collected by 'the boys' of the community, but it evolved into pranks being played upon other residents and gradually the Carnival came into being. When a chimney sweep by the name of Stacy entered a float depicting a model of his cottage, which sported an advertisement and had a brush sticking out of the chimney, the character of the procession changed. Today the event attracts floats from all sections of the community.

Sanitation has changed only during the past 50 years and the earth closet has gone, but so too has the fresh well water. This water had an icy coldness and a taste completely different to the tap water of today.

Unfortunately many of the picturesque cottages which had their own wells have now disappeared but the Square, which is dominated by the Royal Anchor Hotel, is a designated conservation area and some of the old houses and shops are still there, even if the smithy is not. People who need to have their horses shod rely on travelling blacksmiths, who set up their equipment wherever it is required, usually in the open fields.

Liphook boasts of having Flora Thompson, the authoress of *Lark Rise to Candleford*, as one of its celebrities. She used to be the local postmistress. The post office was once housed in a building completely on its own. It is now only a counter in a local supermarket. What would Flora have said?

Liss 🌿

The village of Liss, previously spelt Lys or Lyss, lies in the north-east corner of the county and could well be the largest parish, of some 3,567 acres of semi-rural countryside.

In AD 900 King Alfred the Great granted a manor in the parish of Liss to St Mary's Abbey in Winchester, which was dissolved by King Henry VIII. Remains of a chapel and a Tudor wall can still be seen, and rumour has it that the ghostly figure of a monk still haunts the place.

Despite the ultra-modern steel and glass station which greets the traveller as he alights at Liss, the village still contains some Victorian buildings. In fact, nowadays it is a mix of old, modern and very new – from its typical village hall donated in 1897 by the Money-Coutts family, to the block of recently built flats with a variety of shops below them.

Barn Place was built in the 17th century. Plestor House, built about 1720, in West Liss, is opposite the Spread Eagle Inn, where troops were recruited during the Holy Wars. On the green, close to the Plestor, stands an ancient oak tree under which the village stocks once stood. The Old Rectory was built on an old bakehouse which was destroyed by Cromwell. The Blue Bell Inn, also in West Liss is noted for its old fireplace, which dates back to 1752. On the eastern side of Liss is Pophole Farm, a picturesque 16th century farmhouse which has a lovely ornamental lake in its grounds. Yet another old house is Palmers, noted because it gave shelter to destitute pilgrims on their way to Canterbury.

There are two old churches in the village. St Peter's is mostly 15th or 16th century, but the tower and doorway are 13th century. It is thought that once a wooden church stood on the spot, as there is evidence of a much earlier burial ground. St Peter's has six bells, whilst St Mary's which is the parish church boasts eight bells, which are still rung. St Mary's was built in 1892, and schoolchildren were asked to take 1d a week to school to help towards its cost. This sum must have been quite a hardship where there were large families.

Running through the centre of the village, the railway goes from Waterloo in the north to Portsmouth on the south coast, and being only one hour from the capital, Liss has its fair share of commuters who gladly face the journey to and from work in order to live in this semi-rural area.

A few yards west of the railway finds the little river Rother meandering on its journey to join the Arun on its way to the Channel. Small boys armed with fishing nets and jam jars can still be seen ankle deep in its water catching tiddlers, and mallards and swans float majestically on its surface or sun themselves on the grassy banks. Occasionally they halt the traffic whilst shepherding their young from one side of the road to the other.

The old railway which used to run from Longmoor camp to Liss was closed in 1972. It had been used by soldiers from the camp during the First and Second World Wars. This line is now a pleasant walk, joining an ancient footpath from Palmers to St Peter's.

Littleton 🦡

Littleton lies north of Winchester, signposted off the A272 Stockbridge road, and today has a population of 3,728.

The name Littleton ('the little town') is Saxon, and there is Saxon work in the church of St Catherine. The village is not mentioned in the Domesday Book (1086) but it is likely that the manor belonged to St Swithun's priory in Winchester both before and after 1086. The nearby Harestock estate also comes within the civil parish boundary. The name suggests some connection with hares, so that its local hostelry was called the March Hare, but this is misleading. In early times, Harestock was a place mentioned in a Saxon charter as 'the head stakes'. Apparently after the heads of criminals had been cut off they were displayed here, fixed on the top of posts, as a warning to others.

Hampshire is remarkable for its variety of medieval buildings including hall houses, five of which have been found in Littleton, namely Littleton Manor, Monks Rest, The Red House, The White House and St Swithun's Cottage. The design of hall houses varied considerably, but the essential component was the hall itself, open from floor to rafters so that smoke from the fire in the hearth could rise unhindered to blacken the rafters before escaping through a louvre in the roof. The houses were occupied by men and women from the middle rank of society, yeoman farmers, village priests, and moderately well-to-do craftsmen.

A more recent development of note is the fine Sir John Moore Barracks built on Flowerdown (which was previously a Naval wireless receiving station). It is now the home of the Light Division.

Walking into Littleton at the turn of the century you would have found a row of large houses just outside the Winchester boundary at Harestock, and you would have had to walk another mile before coming to the public house and on to the cluster of houses around the church. The land between these points – which represents most of the village today – has

143

been gradually filled in since 1908, so that now the village comprises the old portion around the church, the later development in between, the older houses at Harestock and the latest addition, Harestock Estate.

Farming still plays a part in village life and the Running Horse Inn is a reminder of the times when horses were trained in Littleton Stables for the Winchester races. Race horses are still trained there today, in addition to which Littleton Stud still raises famous horses as it did in the days when Lord Astor kept his breeding mares here.

Littleton still has a good village shop and post office (recently rebuilt), which includes an off licence and newsagency – a good meeting place for a friendly chat. Another advantage is the much looked forward to fortnightly visit of the County Library van which again brings villagers together and is a friendly meeting place for exchange of news and information.

The seasons of the year bring with them the well loved customs of church and village life including walking the bounds, church fund raising events for various causes including Overseas Aid, etc, Harvest Supper and sale.

Perhaps one of the best loved happenings which brings the year to a close is the 'Eve of The Eve' held in the Memorial Hall, which is transformed to create a Christmas atmosphere with stockings hanging from the large mantelpiece over a fireplace bedecked with holly. The glow of candles and Christmas tree create all the warmth and expectancy of the season.

St Catherine's church, Littleton

144

Lockerley ✒

As a human settlement the Lockerley area is older than Stonehenge. Five thousand years ago the south Hampshire Ridgeway, along Dean Hill and Tote Hill on to Newtown, carried travellers across the Test near Kimbridge. By 1000 BC a settlement existed at Canefield Farm, where pottery of the Bronze Age has been identified.

The outside world intruded on the peaceful village only relatively recently when the Southampton to Salisbury Canal was excavated through Lockerley and Dean. Fifty years later the London & South Western Railway was built across Butts Field, Church Close and Lockerley Green on its way to Salisbury.

At one time the two churches of Lockerley stood together. The old medieval church was pulled down in 1891, just after the present church of St John was built.

Lockerley school opened in 1871 by the generosity of two Lockerley gentlemen, Sir Francis Goldsmid and Mr F. G. Dalgety. The school was supported financially by the Sarah Rolle Charity and each November the children showed the Governors the garments the parents had been helped to purchase. The charity still exists today.

Lockerley was proud to have a VC awarded to Mr Frank Luke in 1914. He was decorated in France by the King and when he arrived at Romsey station, amid cheers, he was presented with a gold watch by the Honourable Mr Dalgety. Mr Luke lived at Lockerley Green.

The Lockerley children were the fortunate recipients of treats from the Dalgety family. In the summer the waggons used to fetch the children to go up to Lockerley Hall for tea and games, and at Christmas a tree and tea was given at the school and later in the Hall. The children in those days came to Lockerley school from Newtown and Carters Clay. The strawberries at Newtown and Carters Clay were picked by the local women, to be carted to Dunbridge station to catch the strawberry trains.

There were three chapels in Lockerley: at Newtown, at Lockerley Green and at Lockerley Hole ('The Ebenezer'). The latter was pulled down in the 1960s, but when in existence people were baptised in a large tank in the floor.

During the Second World War Butts Green had a sawmill, mostly run by prisoners. Most of Lockerley was owned by two families, the Aylwards and Dalgetys. The village had a blacksmith's shop, owned by Mr Gilbert.

The Pritchard family started Lockerley Silver Band in 1880, all the family being good musicians. The Pritchard, Moody and Webber families provided most of the musicians. Another prominent family after the First World War were the Collins. They were a farming family, who took sheep to market in Salisbury and Wilton in horse-drawn waggons.

Locks Heath 🌿

One hundred and fifty years ago the village of Locks Heath did not exist. Not for us the manor houses and abbeys of other Hampshire villages or a nestled hamlet on the springy sheep-nibbled turf of Hampshire downland. Locks Heath began with a wedge-shaped piece of almost empty heathland covering 1,000 acres owned by the manor of Titchfield. On Titchfield Common, as it was known, stood a farmhouse of Tudor origin owned by a yeoman farmer named Lock and it is probably safe to assume that the village name derived from that part of the common known as Lock's Heath.

The common was used for cattle grazing by the people of the surrounding villages of Warsash, Sarisbury and Titchfield until the Enclosure Act in 1866. During the next ten years the common was divided into plots of land and either sold to outsiders or apportioned to local landowners with adjoining properties, or those who had seceded rights to the common. Roads were built following the old trackways and slowly people began to rent or buy plots of land alongside the newly built roads, planting hedges to surround their two or three acre smallholdings. The solid, square, red-bricked villas so typical of Locks Heath were built about this time and it was not long before several smallholders discovered that the heathland soil was highly suitable for soft fruits, especially strawberries. So successful was this venture that strawberry growing became the main occupation in the village.

Carts travelled daily during the season to Botley and Portsmouth taking gallon baskets of fruit to load on trains for the London markets, until the acreage under cultivation grew to such proportions that the Southern Railway exended the line through Swanwick. Old photographs show horse-drawn carts piled high with wicker baskets of fruit, queuing at Swanwick station during the short, lucrative season. The entire family, including children, would work in the fields, planting, pegging shoots, layering with straw, picking and later burning the fields. As crops intensified the shortage of labour was overcome by the annual influx of gypsies attending the Horse Fair at Wickham. They would camp in their colourful caravans in the corner of the strawberry fields or build their 'benders' on unclaimed land. The women, when not working in the fields, would go from door to door with a baby slung in a shawl around their neck, selling pegs and lace. Many of these travellers returned year after year and eventually settled in the village, increasing the population until the provision of a schoolroom became essential.

In 1886 the Tea and Concert Committee of the St John's Mission raised the amazing sum of £150 to build a combined schoolroom and church on the corner of Abshot Road. The building opened later that year with 30 pupils during the day and classes in Horticulture, English and Arithmetic for adults in the evening. Both children and adults paid a few pence for the lessons.

Near the school stood the Jam Factory, built to can the residue of the strawberry crop. The St John's Mission held an anniversary tea and concert in the Jam Factory on 28th December 1887. It was so popular at sixpence a ticket that tea was served in two sittings. Mr Lynn, the owner of the building and several hundred acres in the village, spoke of the moral improvement of the common since the opening of the Mission church! This is hardly surprising since the pub had been the only venue for socialising before this time.

The Sir Joseph Paxton (originally two cottages) was named after the man who had been Head Gardener at Chatsworth and had designed the Crystal Palace. His claim to local fame was not due to his international renown but to the strain of strawberry he perfected and named which grew extremely well in the soft soil of Locks Heath.

As the Enclosure of the Common Act in 1866 began the village of Locks Heath, so the Western Wards Action Area Plan of 1975 ended it. The plan proposed the building of thousands of houses in the area to accommodate the overspill from Southampton and Portsmouth. It was strenuously opposed by the residents, especially Charlie Peckham who lived at Course Park Farm and was already engaged in a continuous running battle with Fareham Borough Council who objected to his roadside fruit and vegetable stall. This indomitable man sat through every session of the four month long Western Wards Inquiry and was later presented with a scroll by Hampshire County Council for his 'courage and fortitude'.

Alas, despite the efforts of Charlie and many others the planners proceeded and the developers moved in. Locks Heath now lies under a sea of roofs, with ring roads and through roads all choked with traffic at peak times.

The village that was rooted in the land has become in one generation a commuter and dormitory suburb. It is rare now, in May or June to find a punnet of local strawberries for sale by the roadside. Yet gardens on the new estates are full of trees and shrubs and Locks Heath is once more becoming green. Who knows, people might even begin to grow a few strawberries again!

Longparish 🌿

Towards the end of the 10th century the area known as Longparish was in fact the manor of Middleton (or Middletune). The manor was in the possession of the Benedictine nunnery of Wherwell, which was founded in AD 986 by Elfrida, widow of King Edgar, who was indirectly responsible for the murder of her step-son King Edward at Corfe. Lower Mill House was originally a cloth mill known as 'Middletune Mill' and belonged to the abbess of Wherwell. Middletune Mill is mentioned in the Domesday Book.

The name Longparish first appears in the middle of the 16th century, at about the time of the Dissolution of the Monasteries, when it was said to consist of East Aston, Longparish, Middleton and Forton and the greater part of Harewood Forest.

In Harewood Forest there is a monument known as Deadman's Plack. In the year AD 963, King Edgar, called the Peaceable, sent for the Earl Athelwold to meet him in the forest to hunt, but instead he slew him with his own hand. Athelwold had betrayed Edgar and had married his intended bride, Elfrida, daughter of the Earl of Devonshire.

The church of St Nicholas was built between 1100 and 1200. The tower was added during the 16th century.

The Church school was opened as a National Society school in 1837. In 1957 a new school was built and the old one pulled down.

There are stocks by the church and an old grindstone by the roadside for the village people which is still used. Just along the road is the wishing well or Ash Burn Rest, bearing the inscription 'O ye wells, Bless ye the Lord, Praise Him and magnify Him for ever.' The well was first erected in 1868 and has been restored twice.

Cricket at Longparish has a long and checkered history, stretching from the first memorable match in 1878. In 1980 Longparish reached the final of the Whitbread Village Cricket Championship, and on 24th August they went to play their opponents Marchwiel from North Wales on the hallowed ground of Lords, but sadly they lost. However, on Monday 31st August 1987 Longparish played in the final again, against Treeton Welfare from Yorkshire. Longparish won by 76 runs and returned home with the cup to the celebrations of the village.

Longstock 🌿

Longstock is well named. Stoke or stock means a place with stakes or wooden piles, often a place with a timber bridge – and the village is about three miles long. It was recorded in the 1086 Domesday Book as Stoches.

The list of known vicars begins in 1315, although there was a church here before that. The present church of St Mary, however, dates from 1880. Nowadays the rector of Stockbridge is also vicar of Longstock and of Leckford.

In the 19th century most of the inhabitants worked on the many local farms: Upper Manor, Lower Manor, Charity, Church, Waters Down, Westover, Windover and Hazeldown. Over 40 day-labourers would wait at the sharp bend near Corner Cottage and hope to get a day's employment. In 1865 the village had two blacksmiths, two builders, two beer retailers, two landlords, a horse-trainer, a baker and grocer, a shoemaker, a maltster, a wheelwright, a postmaster, a miller, a bricklayer, a shopkeeper and a schoolmistress. There was also an unusual cottage industry – the making of baskets and mats from the sedge grass growing on the banks of the river Test. Children were set to plait the prepared sedge and the women formed the plaits into rush mats and light baskets. By the end of the century this had died out but the craft was successfully revived between 1919 and 1949 on a smaller scale.

Most of the houses, many thatched and timbered, are now occupied by retired people, with a few younger commuters. There are only about half a dozen of the old village families left. There are some 20 modern houses and a considerable number of council houses. Of the latter, the first four were built in 1919 and the most recent in 1950. The latter are up Salisbury Hill and are largely occupied by Stockbridge families.

From the middle to the end of the 19th century, Stockbridge racecourse, which lay in Longstock parish under Danebury Hill, was, with Ascot and Goodwood, a very fashionable affair. The then Prince of Wales, later King Edward VII, regularly rented Hermit Lodge, a Regency house just down Houghton Road, at Longstock's southern end. Miss Lillie Langtry, a well-known actress of the period, also rented a house in Stockbridge for the race weeks. The gardens lie on opposite banks of the Test and are still joined by a private footbridge. The racecourse was closed when it was inherited by a lady who did not approve of gambling, but the derelict grandstand can still be seen.

At the northern end of Longstock is Longstock House and park. The family who sold it to Mr John Spedan Lewis, together with a considerable amount of farmland, was named Beddington. They built a watergarden near the Test, opposite the house. This has been enlarged and

The Peat Spade inn, Longstock

improved and is now open to the public six times a year between April and September, in aid of different local charities. Also in Longstock Park is a commercial nursery and many of the gardening and horticultural staff live in company houses nearby.

Long Sutton & Well 🦋

To the south of the parish of Odiham, and the helicopter base of RAF Odiham, lies the village of Long Sutton, known as early as AD 979 as Sheep Sutton. The name is an indication of the mainstay of its farming for many centuries. Set in a fertile valley, the scene is of an ancient and attractive village surrounded mainly by arable fields.

The Harrow Way, one of the oldest roads in England, runs through Long Sutton. The present church, dedicated to All Saints and dating back to the 13th century, may have been a refreshment stop for pilgrims on their way to Canterbury on this branch of the Pilgrims' Way. The building, of flint and rubble, with chalk quoin stones, replaced the earlier timber building. The south chapel was added in the 14th century and was used for many years as a vestry, but was restored in 1961 as a memorial to the dead of two World Wars. It contains an interesting medieval oak vestment chest.

Near the church is the pond. Here the smithy used to stand, where now there are two seats erected in 1979 to the memory of Madge Stratton, for many years the lady of the manor. Horses used to be watered here, but now the only occupants are ducks and moorhens.

Opposite the church is the village shop, a 17th century building which has sold sweets and groceries since the turn of the century, and which has also been the post office since the latter half of the 19th century. It is still a focal point of village life, as is the village hall next door.

Several of the old village houses have wells going down deep into the chalk sub-soil. Of these houses, Hydegate, built soon after 1570 by Stephen Terry, is probably the oldest, and much of the Tudor house remains. The Terry family continued to live here until 1738 and it is now lovingly looked after and enhanced by the present occupants. Another interesting house is Chapel Cottage, which used to belong to a Methodist group called the Countess of Huntingdon's Connexion. Services were discontinued in about 1909 and the chapel became a reading room, in fact the first village hall.

Between Long Sutton and the hamlet of Well lies the Four Horseshoes Inn, and from its verandah on a clear day, one has a magnificent view across open country to Basingstoke with its high-rise buildings. Adjacent are the main gates of Lord Wandsworth College. These were built in the 1920s at the same time as the main college buildings, and are said to be based on a design for one of the memorial gates erected in Belgium to commemorate the men and women who fell in the First World War. The college was founded for the education of orphan boys of agricultural workers and is now a public school of about 400 scholars. It is situated in an estate of 1,200 acres of arable land.

The road between Long Sutton and Well is known as White Hill because of the chalk dust once raised by carriage wheels and horses. At the top of the hill is the Chequers Inn, and across the road is the ancient well, the canopy of which was erected to commemorate Queen Victoria's Silver Jubilee.

Lovedean ✺

History records it as a 'parcel of land given to Thomas Loveden by a relative, in the 16th century.' No mansion, church or school, therefore is it a village? Hardly even a hamlet then, just land with possibly a few dwellings, bounded by what is now known as Horndean, Cowplain and Denmead.

This small area changed little until the First World War, when city people began to buy parcels of land and erect temporary wooden and iron chalet-type accommodation to provide a place to spend their summer leisure days. Some even cultivated their small plots. The slow increase in habitation and cultivation took place, along with a few more permanent dwellings. During the 1930s the real changes took place with the coming of mains water. The sunken water pits that had gathered rainwater became obsolete. Electricity followed and the sanitation was improved (no longer the early morning or late night trip with 'the bucket' to the ditch at the end of the garden prepared earlier in the day).

Lovedean was by 1935 becoming known for the number of older folk who moved to the area in peaceful retirement. The war years of 1939 to 1945 altered life for everyone. The Portsmouth city residents made nightly journeys to 'the country', Lovedean included, in order to shelter from the air raids. The growth of Lovedean really began. The huts that had been summer retreats were replaced by more permanent houses. The green fields became housing estates during the 1960s and 1970s and building continued.

Frogmore Lane, once lined with high hedges and lit by a solitary gaslight, marked the boundary of Victory Avenue. On the right was Matheron poultry farm, as far as Yeolls Lane, which led to Yeolls Farm. The rest of the lane was just a track into Lovedean Lane. Returning to Frogmore Lane, most of the dwellings on the right are post First World War. On the left were a few of the chalet-type structures. Most of the land was taken up by the cricket pavilion. Gypsy Lane was so overgrown by trees (mostly maple) that it was only just possible to ride a bicycle through. Gypsy Lane today has seven bungalows and no streetlights, either gas or electric.

A local celebrity was Mr John Baggs. He was born in 1884 and lived in Lovedean Lane. He appeared in the *Guinness Book of Records* as the longest serving milkman. He was on his round for 80 years and still serving customers at 91 with the help of his son, John junior, aged 64. He cycled the village on an old delivery bike with 24 bottles in the front carrier, returning many times to the dairy to replenish his load.

Lyndhurst 🌿

The village of Lyndhurst is known as the capital of the New Forest. Written as Linhest in 1086, its name is derived from the linden or lime tree, 'hurst' being a wooded hillock. Perhaps of Jutish origin, the village was ancient when Canute demonstrated at nearby Southampton that even a king could not rule the waves. A few years later another king, William of Normandy (the Conquerer) visited Lyndhurst whilst enjoying his hunting.

Only a few really old buildings are now extant, the best known being the Queen's House, parts of which are several hundred years old. This handsome brick building is now occupied by the Forestry Commission. Attached to the Queen's House is the Verderers' Court with a history going back hundreds of years. The present court, as now constituted, dates from 1949, but it still has the power to deny Lyndhurst its urgently needed bypass. The heavy commercial and commuter traffic passing through the High Street is the only blight on the village.

The offices of the New Forest District Council are situated in Lyndhurst. At Foxlease the Girl Guides Association Centre entertains Guides from all over the world. The Hampshire Police Force are represented by a large modern police station. Crime must be infrequent here, the station is closed at night!

There is an active and well run community centre, situated by the large free car park. Another social centre complex in the village contains a small theatre, a bowls green and tennis courts.

The village also boasts a splendid little hospital; attached to it is a day centre partly run by volunteer helpers.

Churches supply the needs of three denominations. The largest, St Michael's, an imposing brick building, contains a famous fresco by Lord Leighton and windows by Burne-Jones and William Morris. In the churchyard is the grave of Alice Hargreaves, for whom, when a little girl, *Alice in Wonderland* was written.

There is a golf course and a very old cricket ground. The beautiful little mound known as 'Boltons Bench' hill, makes a perfect grandstand for cricket spectators and attracts skiers and tobogganists in winter. The opposite end of the village to Boltons Bench is Swan Green, world famous for its picturesque thatched cottages, often depicted on picture postcards.

Marchwood ✣

Marchwood was a thriving village on the edge of the New Forest near Southampton Water before its links with the Forces began in 1813. Due to its position a depot for storing ammunition and powder was built and a jetty for unloading powder from barges. In 1891 it passed to the Admiralty and was in operation until 1959. This, and Husbands Shipyard which had opened up at Cracknore Hard, employed many local people.

The church of St John was built and endowed by H. F. K. Holloway of Marchwood Park in 1843 but prior to this services were held at the Magazine. The school was also built by Mr Holloway in 1854 and as the population was then about 800, was large enough. The influx of soldiers and their families added to this and made it necessary to build further classrooms.

The Fawley branch railway line opened in 1925, ceased to carry passengers in 1966 and now carries only oil and military supplies.

There were about eight farms in and around the village. The Solent was dredged during the 1920s, resulting in beautiful fertile reclaimed land in the marshes at Cracknore Hard – later to be taken over by the Army.

There were four large houses with live-in servants but the Second World War changed this way of life. Marchwood Park became a rehabilitation centre for airmen, Woodside House was bombed and Byams House was taken over by the Air Force and later by the Army. Byams House is now the Officers' Mess. Only Green Farm remains as a private house.

During the Second World War, Marchwood was very vulnerable when bombers attacked the docks. Barrage balloons began to appear, anti-aircraft gunsites were set up and searchlights were to be seen nightly scanning the skies. Army and air force personnel were stationed in the village in Nissen huts or under canvas and some were billeted in private homes. The worst raid was on 19th June 1940 and lasted six hours. The Magazine was hit, Tavells Farmhouse and Woodside House were destroyed by fire but the other bombs landed mostly in fields.

The land on which the military port is situated was originally acquired by the government in 1943, but since 1948 it has been the home of the 17th Port Training Regiment – now the Royal Corps of Transport. It is now the only military port in the British Isles.

Many changes have taken place in Marchwood in recent years. The power station was officially opened by Princess Margaret in 1957 and was closed in 1983. A sewage plant was opened at Slowhill Copse in 1971 and an incinerator in 1975. Where a new distributor road, feeding the military port and the shipyard, opened up fields, large housing estates have been built. A new junior school has been built and several new shops in the village centre. Over 200 army married quarters have been built with their own NAAFI shop and community centre.

Martin & Damerham ❧

Martin and Damerham are tucked away in the 'Martin Peninsula' in the far west of the county, surrounded on three sides by Wiltshire and Dorset.

It is an area of outstanding beauty and steeped in history, with many burial mounds, Roman remains and roads, ancient earthworks and the famous Bockerley Ditch, built about 1,600 years ago.

Martin (Mertone in the 10th century) is a linear village with grass banks and some fine thatched cottages. It is the 'Winterbourne Bishop' of W. H. Hudson's book *A Shepherd's Life*, the story of a Victorian countryman.

All Saints' church, set behind the village, dates back to the 12th century. There is also a Methodist Chapel but no public house. There is a club though, a post office and a village hall.

Damerham is set on the Allen river, more a stream, which rises above Martin. After many meanderings and change of name, it flows into the Avon at Fordingbridge.

St George's church, on a hill on the edge of the village, was built around the time of the Norman Conquest. This is just one of four churches which are in the Western Downland benefice, the other three being Martin, Rockbourne and Whitsbury. The rector lives in a new rectory which can be seen from the church across the water meadows. There are two other places of worship in the village, namely the Methodist chapel and the Baptist church.

The thriving village school is one half of the only Federated School in Hampshire. The other half is in the village of Rockbourne two miles away. Children from both sites meet together regularly.

The village pub, the Compasses, is a popular meeting place for villagers and visitors to the area. They used to brew their own beer as well.

Parkfield Stores is the thriving village shop selling everything from fresh bread to paint-stripper. Further along the road is a family-run garage, formerly the blacksmith's, with the post office attached.

With a population of approximately 450 there are many occupations followed. A few are still employed on the land, many commute to the surrounding cities and towns, some are retired and there are several small businesses run from the village.

A good community spirit exists in both villages, which thankfully have remained relatively small because of county planning regulations.

Medstead ✀

Medstead lies near the Pass of Alton on the old royal highway from Winchester to London. This pass was notorious for bandits and at one time the woods were ordered to be cleared for the flight of an arrow (200 ft) on either side in a bid to stop the king's wine and goods being stolen.

Lack of water has always been a problem on this high chalkland some

600 ft above sea-level and there have been very few wells sunk. The one at Southtown Farm is 270 ft deep and in the past horses were used in a treadmill to raise the water. Many older properties still have their 'catchtanks', which were hollowed out of the chalk and rendered and which then had all the rain water gutterings led into them.

When William Cobbett passed through Medstead on one of his rural rides in the early 1800s, he noted 'the excellent spring turf' and 'probably the best beech wood in all England'.

One old custom on Shrove Tuesday was the annual parading by the village children singing:

'Knick knock, pans hot
Eggs and lard and flour are dear,
But we're come to Shroven here,
Piece of bread and piece of cheese
And piece of pancake if you please'.

The village has a charity left in a will of 1874 by a Mr Mulcock for the benefit of the poor, which until recent years took the form of a joint of beef and a sack of coal at Christmas.

The village now boasts a fine modern village hall and, opened in 1989, a thriving tennis club to add to the Gardeners' Club, Medstead Players and Women's Institute which was formed in 1918.

Meonstoke, Exton & Corhampton

When the Danes invaded southern England they came up the now much smaller river Meon in their longboats, looting and fighting. One battle against the local farming Saxons took place in Meonstoke, the evidence of which was discovered during the construction of the Meon Valley Railway line in 1900. Some Danes subsequently settled in Meonstoke and there was friction for hundreds of years with the peaceful farmers across the river in Exton and Corhampton.

Corhampton church was built in about 1020 and is one of the very few small Saxon churches which has always functioned as an active church. Its dedication is unknown but part of the frescoes remaining in the chancel depict St Swithun restoring the dropped eggs to the widow's basket.

Mr William Collins lived in Corhampton at the end of the 17th century and left money for annual education awards to boys in the parish. Recently the Chalfryth Tithe, a tithe payable by a nearby estate, was bought out and added to the charity to help chldren in all three parishes and Droxford. Sadly the east end of the little church fell down in Victorian times and was not very sympathetically rebuilt, but the 1,000 year old yew tree still stands, protecting some unusual vaulted brick graves and shadowing the old sundial on the church wall, which is divided into eight tides, not twelve hours.

As the people 'across the water' did not speak to each other, each village had its own footpath to Bishop's Waltham. The bridge into Exton was not built until 1805. The white house beside it was the village shop until 1963, complete with village bakery and oven for cottagers' occasional joints. Where the present pub, the Shoe, now stands was the wheelwright's workshop. The old Shoe was a tiny pub in the garden opposite next to the river, which sometimes flooded in spite of the sluice and mill 50 yards upstream. Corhampton and Meonstoke also had their mills, as each village had to be quite self-contained.

Manor Farm, Exton was renowned for its cheddar cheeses, which were exported by the weekly carrier's cart all the way to Fareham and further. One of the indoor dairymaids, Rose Davis, was born in Meonstoke in 1885 and went to school there, then took the unprecedented step on leaving school aged twelve to cross the water. Her work as indoor dairymaid at Manor Farm lasted until her retirement. She sat behind the rector in Exton church choirstalls every Sunday for around 70 years, wearing a navy felt hat in winter, and navy straw in summer – knee high to a buttercup, she looked rather like Mrs Tiggywinkle.

The north outlet from Exton onto the A32 is known as The Grinch, but whether the word has any bearing on the fact that a gibbet was sited there is not known. Very close by a Roman villa was recently excavated; some of it lies under the A32 but one wall that fell flat the other way is well preserved and shows an upper storey of round-topped windows. In 1989 it was laboriously undermined and lifted on to a trailer and transported to the British Museum, where after restoration it is hoped to have it on display. Also in the same field Saxon bones were found, and in one lucky dig a complete warrior lying straight, with his sword by his side and his circular shield boss on his chest, in a shallow grave in the solid chalk.

Some of the mysterious flattened circles in standing corn have been found in Corhampton, not far from the golf course. This nine hole course was started in 1885. One of the dozen oldest in England, it shared its ground with sheep and local cricketers. In the early 1970s it was enlarged to 18 holes, had a new clubhouse built and is now a flourishing concern with membership of 450.

The South Downs Way comes through Exton as a footpath, hopefully never as a bridle path which would make it unfit for many ramblers and others who walk it, and also the Wayfarers Walk comes through Droxford and the back of Corhampton and Exton on its way from Emsworth to Inkpen Beacon. There are several other footpaths and pleasant walks around the villages up to Beacon Hill to the west and Old Winchester Hill, an Iron Age fort, to the east, both commanding extensive views.

Micheldever

Motorists from Popham, driving along the A30, feel that they have some knowledge of Micheldever, a mere scattering of buildings, whilst those on the A33 from the same point are under the same impression. Travellers by train stopping at Micheldever station are even more deceived, especially as they are aware of the oil terminal and can see a pleasant early Victorian building on one of the platforms, while an elegant Georgian building stands outside the station yard. It is therefore a revelation to some who venture a few miles off these routes to discover the lovely and interesting village of Micheldever itself. Over half the dwellings are over a hundred years old, many of them thatched, while the newer ones, with well-kept gardens, fit snugly into the overall pattern of well-loved homes.

The village, together with East Stratton, has been fortunate with its benefactors. Lady Rachel Vaughan who lived at East Stratton House, presented the church of St Mary the Virgin with a silver chalice, still in its possession. Later benefactors have been the Barings, and more recently, Lord Rank, who farmed in this area and resided at Sutton Scotney. Many villagers were employed by him and some reside as his pensioners.

The river flowing through, formerly the North Brook, is now the Dever, the water being augmented by artesian boreholes at the watercress beds. Sedge used to be collected and worked extensively, but no longer. There was once a mill and a fishery which supplied Hyde Abbey with fish.

It is hard to imagine a period of disorder in this pleasant village, but in 1830 farm workers began to riot, demanding twelve instead of eight shillings a week. A member of the Baring family was manhandled at Northington, the result being the trial for attempted murder of Henry Cook, aged 19, of Micheldever. He was hanged at Winchester and buried in the churchyard.

The council houses in the village are attractive and are interspersed by well-planned bungalows for the elderly. Behind these dwellings can be found beautifully kept allotments, so well tended as to give the impression of a park.

The village still boasts a smith, though no horses are shod there now. It is pleasant to see the glow of the fire, the smoke rising from the chimney, and to hear the hammer clanking on metal. It is pleasant, too, to hear the church bells pealing, for Mr Harry Symes, owner of the forge, is also master of the bells. The bell tower was recently restored. It was built in the 16th century, the stones coming from the dismantled Hyde Abbey.

Micheldever is also fortunate to have a post office-cum-stores, where shoes can be taken for repair and clothes for cleaning, and a butcher's shop which serves a wide area. The kind owners deliver when requried. A pleasing row of thatched cottages nearby needs no history – their name is Waterloo Cottages. Northbrook is exactly that – the flat water meadows keeping it a little apart from the rest of the village.

There are several farms in the vicinity, so some people work on the land and with animals, some at the watercress beds and others commute to Winchester, Basingstoke and London. In early summer, the village is alive with tractors pulling loaded wagons of peas for the pea processor at Cowdown near the A33, while later on they draw the grain to and from the dryer.

Refreshment is obtainable in Micheldever at the Half Moon and Spread Eagle, a fine Georgian building standing on a piece of rising ground on Gin Hill. East Stratton boasts the Plough, attractively rural and used gratefully by walkers among others. The Dove at the station is popular for its cuisine and is quite well known outside the village.

Michelmersh ✣

Michelmersh is a scattered village, spread out on the slope of the hill above the road from Romsey to Stockbridge.

The original village grew up around the church, but over the past 100 years or so has spread considerably as agriculture was joined by sand extraction and the making of bricks by hand as the principal employment in the locality. The South Hants Waterworks (Southampton Corporation Waterworks) and the Southern Railway were also local employers. Nowadays, many locals go further afield to Romsey and beyond to their daily job. The brickworks is still flourishing and provides much needed employment together with its traditional occupations.

The village celebrated the millenium of the charter of the parish in 1985. The charter was granted by Ethelred the Unready and the original parish included Braishfield and Awbridge. The church, dedicated to 'Our Lady', but known as St Mary's, was built in the 13th century on Saxon foundations. The square wooden tower was added later in the 15th century.

Sir William Ogle, a staunch Royalist, and a former Governor of Winchester Castle, became linked with the village in the 17th century through his second wife Sarah, who owned Manor Farm. He moved from Manor Farm to the Dower House, now known as the Old House, and legend has it that it is his ghostly carriage which can be heard moving along the lane at night.

Michelmersh is proud of its prize winning Silver Band, formed in 1886 as a Temperance Band; a number of its present members are direct descendants of founder members. The band still tours the village and surrounding areas on Christmas Eve and Boxing Day and can be heard regularly practising in their band hut.

Fairs used to be held by the Bear and Ragged Staff, the local 17th century inn on the main Romsey to Stockbridge road. Today the Pumpkin Club meets there regularly and holds its annual competition which draws people from far afield.

From the days when the school flourished and the village had its own baker's shop with its own bakery on the premises where villagers regularly took their cakes to be baked, to the present day when most people have cars and travel to Romsey three miles away for their shopping and the daily school bus picks up the children and returns them at tea-time, life in the village has changed considerably. Happily, members of village families are still prominent in village life.

Church of Our Lady, Michelmersh

Milford-on-Sea 🎐

Today Milford is popular with visitors with its beautiful views over to the Isle of Wight. It still retains the atmosphere of a village with its central village green and Norman Church. The church has eight bells which were hung in 1928: faith, hope, love, peace, joy, liberty, patience and victory.

The double lamp standard in the village centre has an interesting history. The original lamp standard was erected to commemorate the coronation of King George V and Queen Mary in 1911. When it was demolished by a lorry and replaced by a mundane bollard, there was such an outcry locally that a replica of the old lamp standard was made and erected. It is still known as 'George & Mary'.

Life at the beginning of the 20th century was very different here. Then children could gather primroses in Barnes Lane and Lymore Copse. Pageants and fetes were held at Newlands Manor, before the break up of the estate. The village then seemed to have a lot of 'characters' including 'Old Rodeo'. He visited here every year with his dogs and donkey, and dressed his animals in coloured crepe paper on the village green. When he was too old for travelling he settled in Milford and grew the biggest pumpkins ever seen here.

Monk Sherborne & Ramsdell 🎐

Monk Sherborne is a small village situated in the north of Hampshire. The name probably originated from a word meaning a bright and clear stream. In the 12th century a Benedictine priory was founded near a stream in the locality, hence Monk Sherborne. The village was mentioned in the Domesday Book.

Unlike many villages in this part of Hampshire which have grown tremendously since the Second World War the population of Monk Sherborne has remained fairly static. The village has retained its rural character but, in common with its neighbours Ramsdell, Charter Alley and Pamber, it now has no village store and the only one of the four villages to retain its post office is Ramsdell.

Village life has of course greatly changed since the Second World War. Gone are the shoemaker, potter, rakemaker, blacksmith and so on and in their place is a marble works, a new chalk pit and a rose grower, among others.

Sheep and cattle are still to be seen in the area, though the main crops are arable. One pleasant aspect of the diversification of farming is the large acreage now given over to growing bulbs. This creates wonderful areas of colour in the spring. The bulbs are mostly grown for propagation, though some flowers are harvested and sold. The disappearance of many of the hedgerows is regrettable, but as a result fine views have been opened up.

With the change in agricultural methods the need for farm cottages has diminished and many of these have now been sold, modernised and enlarged. Queen's College, Oxford is one large property owner, which still owns a considerable amount of farmland, woodland, a number of cottages and the Priory church at Pamber.

All Saints' church at Monk Sherborne is 12th century, with Queen's College as its patron. In Ramsdell there is a much newer church of the 19th century and a reading room, also a Methodist chapel in Charter Alley.

The area retains three pubs, the Queen's College Arms at Pamber, the White Hart at Charter Alley and the Mole at Monk Sherborne, which is built on the site of the old village green.

In Ramdsell today there is a group of light industrial units on the site of an old clay pit and brick kiln where hand-made bricks were produced for many years. The old marl-pit in Monk Sherborne, commonly known as 'The Dell', is used now by RAF helicopters for low flying manoeuvres.

Although nobody of great fame has lived in the village, there have been many colourful characters. One of these must surely have been Mr George Ruxton, who was a top breeder of Arab horses. Long after most people had taken to motorised transport, 'Ruckie' could be seen driving his coach and four or tandem. He also rode his stallion into Basingstoke to do his shopping.

Netley ✑

Adjoining Hamble is the parish of Hound which incorporates three villages: Netley Abbey, Old Netley and Butlocks Heath.

The abbey itself, a 13th century Cistercian house, was laid in ruins at the time of the Dissolution of the Monasteries but is well kept and sometimes forms a background for religious or artistic gatherings. Turner painted a number of local views.

Netley's other claim to fame is the Royal Victoria Hospital, built in the middle of the 19th century as a military hospital. Now only the chapel remains, the grounds having been converted into an attractive country park overlooking Southampton Water where many local shows are held.

New Alresford 🪶

New Alresford is an attractive small market town in the heart of Hampshire, which draws thousands of visitors each year.

There are three main streets, Broad Street, East Street and West Street and they are laid out very much as they were when plans were made by Bishop Godfrey de Lucy in about 1200. It takes its name from the river Arle which flows between Old and New Alresford. Near the parish boundary the Arle is joined by the Candover and Tichborne streams, the three forming the river Itchen which flows on to Winchester.

In the year 1294 New Alresford became a borough and had two Members of Parliament. The right to hold fairs and markets can be traced back some 400 years. The centre has been troubled by a number of disastrous fires over the centuries, but rebuilding has not altered the layout in any way, with its very wide Broad Street, justly famous as one of the most beautiful streets in Hampshire. It is planted with lime trees and lighting is from old-style lamps which have been refurbished.

Mary Russell Mitford, the authoress of *Our Village*, lived in Broad Street when she was a child and another house bears a plaque proclaiming that the 47th Infantry Regiment of the United States Army made their headquarters there during the Second World War in the run up to D-Day. The American servicemen had to leave behind their faithful mascot *Hambone Jr*, who had been run over and killed, and the dog's grave can be found on the river walk leading from the Dean.

The building of a by-pass some years ago has made life much easier for visitors. The Watercress Steam Railway draws thousands of visitors each year, eager to travel on the line from Alresford through Ropley and Medstead to Alton.

A favourite haunt for visitors to Alresford is the river walk which takes them past the charming old Fulling Mill. Another popular walk is out past Town Mill and the watercress beds to Old Alresford, walking along the Little Weir and returning along the Great Weir alongside Alresford Pond, a natural breeding ground for wildfowl and of great interest to naturalists.

Alresford's shops alone make it well worth a visit. There are a number of specialist shops, amongst them an antiquarian bookseller's, jewellers, shops selling leather goods, tapestry work and embroidery and needlework supplies, china, quality furnishings and antiques.

There are many old tombstones in the churchyard of St John's, which serves as the local burial ground, but four in particular are worthy of note. They are the graves of French prisoners of war. From 1808 to 1814, during the Napoleonic Wars, there were something like 200 prisoners on parole in Alresford. A number of them died here and were buried in the churchyard, and their gravestones are still cared for. Look up at the church tower and you see an interesting old Saxon cross set in the stonework. Unfortunately a number of the trees in the churchyard were lost in the storms of 1988 and 1990.

There is a small market each Thursday as well as the flourishing WI Market which is in the community centre. A street fair in October is a 'must' for all residents and another day out for resident and farmer is the annual Alresford Show which is held at Tichborne park on the first Saturday in September.

Newtown 🎐

Newtown is in some respects attached to Burghclere but it has always had a distinct character and life of its own. It lies on the south side of the little river Enborne, with a common at its back. On one side is a busy main road and on the other the Greenham air base, not unknown to the press.

Sandleford, which is historically part of Newtown, lies on the Berkshire side of the river. In the 13th century monks who occupied the new priory there, ran a farm and a weaving workshop. In the 18th century Sandleford was largely rebuilt and acquired a social and literary popularity. After being a war-time hospital, it is now a girls school.

The crossing of the river by the great north–south road, now the A34, led to Newtown becoming a market and a centre for travellers. A fall in the river led to a mill being built for grinding barley and processing wool, the two chief local products. Minor products of the area were beer, rake handles, hops and guns. House names still recall some of these activities. The Swan, beside the river bridge, was once a coaching inn with a tollgate. It is still a thriving place of refreshment.

The church of St Mary & St John the Baptist, built in 1865, is the centre of a lively, active community which runs its own hall and a number of social activities, including a good church fete each year. Retired and independent people enjoy their own homes and gardens and working people mostly commute to the nearby towns.

North Baddesley 🎐

The original name of 'Bedeslei' is thought to be a derivation of Baeddes Leah, 'Baeddi's Wood' or clearing. There are signs of Roman and Saxon settlements within the area.

In medieval times, the centre of the village was the parish church of St John the Baptist (still its most cherished possession), and the manor house, which was a Preceptory for the Knights Hospitallers of St John of Jerusalem from around 1167. Now these stand apart on the hill overlooking the 20th century village, half a mile away.

There are two gravestones in the churchyard which have an interesting history. In 1822 Robert Snelgrove, an assistant keeper on the Broadlands estate belonging to Lord Palmerston, found two men poaching at Toothill. One of the men, Charles Smith, fired when the keeper was close at hand and wounded him seriously in the thigh. Both men got away but many months later Smith was caught and condemned to death at Winchester Assizes. This was at a time when the Game Laws were very severe and punishment likewise. Palmerston did his utmost to get the sentence reduced to one of imprisonment but failed and Smith was duly hanged.

The first gravestone was erected by William Cobbett, a writer and social reformer of the time, who felt that Smith had been a victim of oppression. The second gravestone appeared many years after Lord Palmerston's death and was erected by his grandson, Evelyn Ashley, in an attempt to absolve the family from any blame.

In the early 20th century many 'temporary' Nissen hut homes were erected in the village, usually on large plots of land. In their stead now stand grand four-bedroomed homes towering over the few remaining bungalows built after the Second World War. Since the war, many of the surrounding fields have disappeared to developers. Whilst North Baddesley is still referred to as a village, sadly this word does not accurately reflect the situation, as the current population is 7,500.

Since the post office, housed in a supermarket, is situated on the A27 at the only traffic-light-controlled crossroads, maybe this should be considered the village centre. Certainly on the opposite corner is one of the two public houses, the Baddesley Arms, first opened as an inn in 1924. The other cluster of shops is in the area of the second public house, the Bedes Lea, flanked by a private housing estate.

Street names in the village have generally been adopted from the families who owned the manor of Baddesley: Seymour Parade after the famous Tudor family; Mortimer Drive commemorates the Earls of March who held the manor in the reign of Richard II; Chamberlayne Court after the last recent owners; and Tottehale Close and Launcelyn Close are taken from the Preceptors of the Knights Hospitallers.

The village has nine footpaths, varying from rough tracks through wet, marshy hassock grass to more well-trodden paths, with interesting views of open countryside. At the moment there are two allotment areas.

North Hayling

Hayling Island is situated just south of the village of Langstone. This is reached by turning off the main A27 road between Portsmouth and Chichester, at Havant. The Island is connected with the mainland by a bridge, which was built in 1956. This replaced an old 'railway sleeper' bridge that had lasted for about 100 years, and which in turn took the place of a causeway, which could only be used at low tide.

Hayling consists of two old parishes, St Mary's in the south and St Peter's in the north, and the newer parish of St Andrew which was formed right at the south-eastern tip of the island.

North Hayling is now the 'country' part of the Island, being mainly residential and with a few areas of farmland. There are a couple of very small industrial units, and about a dozen only of council houses, which were built in about 1927. There are no schools and only one public house, the Yew Tree, which is right on the boundary line between North and South. In the same area are a saddler's, ironmonger's, post office, fish and chip shop and a general grocer cum wine store. There is also one petrol station with a shop about a mile towards the bridge, and another small grocer right next door.

The church of St Peter was built in about 1104 and has one of the oldest sets of three bells in the country. They are on half shafts and ring only once. One of the bells tolled when the Armada came up the Channel in 1588.

Right at the tip of the Island as one goes off the bridge there are two hotels, but they are only a few years old. North Hayling had the first of the Warner Holiday Camps. Captain Harry Warner started the camp in about 1934. He was the handyman/gardener and his wife was cook and cleaner. After a year or so he bought some land from the farmer next door, and as most people know, went on to have many camps both in England and abroad.

Hayling is situated between the Langstone and Chichester harbours and quite a lot of fishing goes on. The local oyster beds were the original reason for the building of a railway from Havant, across the bridge, to the south end of the Island. There is also good cockling and winkling; once only the locals went out for a few for themselves, but now almost all holidaymakers go as well, and the shellfish are becoming scarce. There is a considerable amount of surf-boarding and hundreds of small boats round the Island and indeed many competitions are now held here.

The two caravan sites between them hold about 2,000 people. Some have been coming for over 35 years, and many have become old friends and even bought houses here.

There is a Roman settlement at the north end of the Island.

The Pycroft family, two brothers George and Albert, came to Hayling in 1901 from Milton in Portsmouth. They built two houses next to one another and originally went in for market gardening. However, after two years of bad harvesting, they returned to brickmaking and have continued the business ever since. Indeed, some of the bricks for special occasions and buildings are still handmade.

Before the Second World War, believe it or not, there was a small airfield, with one aeroplane operating from it, which took people for sight-seeing rides round the Island and as far as the Isle of Wight. This has now mostly been built on.

Northington & Swarraton 🌿

The two villages of Northington and Swarraton are divided by the Candover brook, but otherwise are a complete entity, sharing the church (in Northington) and the village hall (in Swarraton). The villages, consisting of about 100 houses and four farms, cover a wide area about four miles north-west of Alresford.

Until the middle of the 16th century the land was mainly in the possession of three religious orders, but since then village life has revolved around the magnificent mansion known as the Grange. Between 1809 and 1816 William Wilkins transformed it externally to make it one of the first Greek revival buildings in the country, modelled on the Temple of Theseus in Athens. In 1816 it was sold to Alexander Baring, the 1st Lord Ashburton.

In 1830 a Mr George Harding gained unenviable notoriety as the principal witness against a man named Cooke, who in the Agricultural Riots was sentenced and hanged. However, on his death in 1875, Mr Harding left a trust of £200 for the poor of the two parishes. This trust is still in existence.

The 4th Lord Ashburton was the man who probably did most for the two villages. As well as improving the houses, cottages and other buildings on the estate, he was also responsible for building the imposing church which dominates the valley.

It was in about the 12th century that the small church of St Andrew was built in Swarraton, but in 1849, when the two villages were combined for ecclesiastical purposes, it was pulled down.

The earliest church at Northington was pulled down in about 1830. Its oldest portions dated back to about 1150. A new church was erected by the 1st Lord Ashburton and opened in 1832. This was, however, demolished in 1888 and the present church was started. It was said that

167

Lord Northbrook had built a fine new church in the neighbouring village of East Stratton and, not to be outdone, Lord Ashburton determined to build a bigger and better one at Northington. It remains as an example of Victorian-Gothic ecclesiastical art. Novel techniques were used in its construction, and it is one of the earlier churches using flints in concrete. It has a fine tower (which was originally going to be a spire), unusual gargoyles and a unique churchyard wall.

The Baring family sold the house in 1934 to Mr Lewis Wallach, who bought it specifically to house his collection of paintings and *objets d'art*. During the later 1930s he repeatedly tried to present the Grange and its contents to the Nation, but it was not until after the Second World War that it was taken over by the Department of the Environment, who spent an enormous sum on restoring the exterior. It is now on view to the public, where many people come to enjoy the beautiful surroundings.

Under the Baring ownership of the Grange estate, there was much building – lodges, game larders, gasworks, school, sawmill, houses for the butler and chef etc – all of which are now private houses.

The villages themselves have changed from a mainly agricultural community with the majority of houses being occupied by workers of the Grange estate, to one where most of the houses have been modernised and are owner-occupied by people who work elsewhere.

The population has perforce diminished. Once, 150 children attended the village school. Now, a mere 40 travel elsewhere for their education. Along with the school, the village shop and post office have closed and, with an almost non-existent bus service, a car is a necessity. Lack of low-cost housing causes problems, too, for young and old. However, the community, though small, is thriving. The Woolpack Inn in the neighbouring hamlet of Totford, serves Northington and Swarraton, and a flourishing social life is centred on the village hall. This was a reading room which was bought by public subscription when the Grange estate was sold in 1934.

North Waltham 🌿

The village today, with its cottages clustered around the village green, prosperous appearance and a plaque proclaiming that it was a winner in the Best Kept Village Competition, contrasts sharply with the North Waltham of the past. The cottages which once housed farm labourers are now the homes of 'professional' folk and the village pond, for centuries the source of drinking water for cattle, a picturesque venue for a handful of ducks. The residents who live and work within the parish boundary, if counted, would not reach double figures yet, until the Second World

Pond View Cottages, North Waltham

War, nearly everyone worked on the land or in providing some sort of service to the community. Although the changes since then have been dramatic, happily the community bonds, whilst different, remain strong.

North Waltham is situated about a mile from the A30 – once the Roman road from Winchester to Silchester – and six miles from Basingstoke. The soil is mostly chalky with flints, and grain is grown in the surrounding fields. A network of underground streams reached by deep wells ensured a pure and plentiful water supply but only a few are still accessible.

About 40 houses remain which were built prior to 1900, but the majority are modern and were erected in the 1970s, causing the population to almost double in size to about 900. The oldest surviving cottage, Rose Cottage, was built in the 15th century and is of cruck construction under a thatched roof. Several of the earlier properties are thatched, whilst later ones have slate or tile roofs. The walls are mostly brick but a few, such as Chalk Cottage, are built of chalk and flint. Flint is sometimes used as decoration in brickwork on both houses and gardens walls – a most attractive feature, and Hook and Hatchet Cottage is perhaps the best example of this. Some cottages, including Yew Tree Cottage, Blake Cottage and Mary Lane Cottage, are dated, but it is uncertain whether these indicate the time of building or of major renovation.

The church of St Michael, an attractive building, dates from Norman times, but major restoration work was carried out in the 1860s and little of the original remains. The shingle roof required constant attention and 'shingles and nayles' make regular appearances in the Churchwardens' Accounts!

The village has three pubs – the Sun and the Wheatsheaf on the A30 and the Fox in Popham Lane. The Old Barn Stores and two mobile shops provide daily requirements and the travelling library is popular. Cuckoo Meadow was donated to the village by a local benefactor in the 1950s and provides a recreation area, a hard tennis court and a new village hall administered by the Village Trust.

No one of fame has lived here and there were no momentous happenings, but this is a village with its roots firmly in the past. Axe heads and Roman remains in the form of tiles and pottery have been found, and although there is no specific mention in the Domesday survey, there are two references to the village called 'Wealtham', prior to that date.

Old documents reveal much about the lives of our predecessors. The Churchwardens' Accounts record the whippings carried out in 1598 and 1600 because the poor victims were in contravention of the Vagrancy Act. The burial register states that James Troops was murdered in Trinleys Copse in 1694 and also mentions the tragic deaths of nine children from scarlatina in 1855. Two charities still exist, one of which was set up in the 17th century and although eroded by inflation, annual payments are still made under the combined trusteeship of the Church and the Parish Council.

Oakley

The village has changed greatly from its description in the Domesday Book of being seven villagers and seven smallholders with three ploughs, four slaves and a church. During the 1940s Oakley had a population of 350, which expanded rapidly during the 1960s when a great amount of new housing was built. Despite its increase in size, Oakley has retained its friendly village atmosphere and there is a real community spirit. Several charity fund-raising events take place in the village during the year.

The village is very proud of its two village ponds which boast thriving colonies of ducks. Each spring the new ducklings are eagerly awaited and, despite the hazard of busy roads surrounding the ponds, they seem to manage to survive. There is an active pond preservation committee which oversees the planting and upkeep of the ponds. Each Christmas the larger pond has a Christmas tree erected on its bank under which people gather to sing Christmas carols. Until the early 1930s the village did not have a piped water supply and the pond was used for watering horses and other farm stock. The pond was also a source of water for the nearby forge until its demise in 1950.

Several thatched cottages and a thatched barn add charm to the village and are among some of the older buildings to be found in the village. Another is Turnpike Cottage, which was built as a turnpike in 1640. The parish church of St Leonard is even older. The site dates back to the time of the Domesday Book. It is believed that Oakley Hall, which is now a school, contained both the original oak from which Oakley gets its name and the original source of the river Test. The village pub, the Barley Mow, has a name which suggests the origins of the village as a farming community. Although the farms are no longer the employers of the residents they are still an important feature of the village. Surrounding the village, as they do, they provide pleasant country walks along their footpaths.

Oakley boasts connections with two famous figures from the past. Jane Austen lived in the nearby village of Steventon and often walked to Oakley Hall, which was occupied by her friends, the Bramsons. William Warham, who was Lord Chancellor and Archbishop of Canterbury in the time of Henry VII and who crowned Henry VIII, was born in the village. He rebuilt the church and his arms are to be seen carved in stone over the Tudor doorway.

There are also several stories associated with the village. It is said that an outhouse in the grounds of the old rectory was used by a highwayman operating on the Basingstoke to Winchester road. There is a local legend that at the time of the Napoleonic wars all the able-bodied men and women in the village were marched to Southampton, dressed in soldiers' scarlet uniforms, and made to line the coast, in order to give the impression that it was strongly fortified. Oakley is also said to have a local ghost. She is a distraught woman who runs up anxiously to any rider and peers into their face and then turns away. She must be extremely busy as there are an increasing number of horseriders to be seen around the village!

Old Alresford

The village of Old Alresford, on the ancient route from Winchester to London, is three quarters of a mile north of New Alresford, on the B3046. Archaeological surveys have revealed the existence of long, circular and bowl barrows, pointing to settlements here long before the important Roman villa, sited north of Pinglestone Farm.

A great fire in 1160 destroyed the original village. This was rebuilt by Bishop De Lucy who also made the causeway connecting it with his new town of New Market, now known as New Alresford. This causeway, commonly known as the Great Weir, is the greatest medieval construction in England still serving its original purpose as both a road and a dam. It forms the Alresford Pond, some 13 hectares in extent, which drained New Alresford and provided fish for the bishop's palace nearby. Today the pond is badly silted but visited by wildlife all the year round.

Nearby at Abbotstone are the visible remains of a deserted village. The community was affected by the Black Death in 1349 to 1350, but it started to finally decline in the 18th century when large numbers of agricultural workers deserted the countryside for the towns. Godsfield Chapel, north of Old Alresford, was built in the Middle Ages by the Knights Hospitallers who served the pilgrims on their way to Canterbury or Winchester.

Old Alresford Place, now a Diocesan Retreat Centre, was occupied at the time of the Civil War by the rector, Dr Heylyn, a fervent Royalist. He was driven from his rectory and his famous library was burnt by his neighbour, the Cromwellian Colonel Norton, but he eventually returned as rector to the delight of his parishioners. Oliver Cromwell often stayed with Colonel Norton, whose local knowledge was an important factor in the victory over the Royalists, fighting over unknown territory, in the decisive battle of Cheriton.

Alresford House was built by Admiral Rodney with his naval prize money obtained during the wars of the Austrian Succession. Four small French cannon still stand on gun carriages facing the park. Rodney also bought the pond to preserve the wildlife and sold the reeds for thatch. The house remained in the family for three generations and was then sold to William Bullpit.

In St Mary's church, rebuilt in 1753 on the site of a Saxon church, is a beautiful memorial to Jane, the first Lady Rodney, who died in childbirth. A rector of note was George Sumner who later became Suffragan Bishop of Guildford. His wife Mary, also remembered in the church, founded the Mothers Union in 1875, now a world-wide organisation. The original meetings were held in the drawing room of the then rectory, now Old Alresford Place. The church has a peal of six bells and a clock presented by the Bullpit family.

At the north end of the village is the National Childrens Home, built about 1838 by the Onslow family for the domestic training of village girls.

Alresford House, Old Alresford

The watercress industry plays a major part in the local economy due to the clear running Hampshire chalk streams and the constant water temperature. The industry has expanded rapidly in recent years. Container lorries collect the cress for export to Europe.

The attractive village green is now registered as common land and kept mown by the Parish Council. Before 1967 the centre of the village was a marshy piece of glebe land full of nettles and docks along the side of the brook. A generous resident bought the land for the village and with other volunteer residents built underground brick drainage chambers from which the spring water is piped into the brook. The surface was levelled with chalk, given a covering of topsoil and sown with grass. All this at no cost to the village. Since 1969 on the third Saturday in June an Olde Worlde Village Fayre has been held on the green and a bonfire with fireworks on 5th November.

The Cricket Club is over 100 years old and for 80 years has played on the lovely ground on Bighton Lane by courtesy of the owner of Upton Park. Matches have been played against the Imperial Defence College and Hampshire Hogs.

Old Portsmouth & Spice Island

Spice Island is a small piece of land jutting out into the harbour entrance at Old Portsmouth. Spice Island – what exotic fantasies the name conjures up, spices and herbs from the Far East, tea from India, gold and ivory from darkest Africa, rare silks and rice from China, plus of course coal from Newcastle – the Coal Exchange pub still stands at the harbour mouth today. But these are not fantasies, they are memories of the huge trading ships which eased their way into the Camber to unload their wares. Some of them still steam up the Solent with the same wares today, the difference being that most are ordered before they leave their home country.

Many centuries ago Spice Island was a thriving community, pretty spicy in another way, with pubs and brothels dominating the scene, the sailors and soldiers rushing off duty to savour its dubious delights! Later it became a fishing village, separated from Portsmouth by a city wall and a moat. The fishing village atmosphere still exists on the Camber. Sit outside the Bridge Tavern today and watch the fishing boats gently bobbing under the protective gaze of the cathedral and you can easily imagine yourself back in time.

Whereas at one time Spice Island was outside the jurisdiction of Portsmouth itself, nowadays it is considered a very desirable place to live. A tight-knit community spirit reigns with a Residents Association that makes sure it is not spoilt in any way.

New houses have replaced the old Vosper Thornycroft buildings, but these have enhanced rather than detracted from the whole atmosphere of peace and beauty. There are quaint character properties, such as an original bank complete with vault standing on the corner of Grand Parade, and the Captain's House with its Swiss tower where William Wiley painted the famous *Battle of Trafalgar* scene with the help of his daughter, who only died in 1988 in her nineties. It was to the Bath house in Bath Square that the ladies and gentlemen travelled by stage coach down what is now the A3 from London to bathe in the cubicles underneath. All these properties are now privately owned, but still intact. Some of them are owned by descendants of John Pounds, a poor shoemaker and tailor who started a school for poor children in the High Street. John Pounds' memorial church is built close to where he used to live.

Along the High Street itself, once flanked by shops, sharp eyes can still spot the feet of the shop canopies in the pavement outside the cathedral. It is now a smart road with the cathedral one side and good class pubs on the other side, plus many pleasant private houses of individual design and the grammar school at the top.

The meeting point of the High Street is the newsagent's and general shop where everyone knows everyone else and the village atmosphere is strongest.

Nelson stayed at the George, now George Court retirement flats where the residents keep well involved with the community. The Duke of Buckingham was murdered in a nearby house in 1628; the plaque can be seen on the wall.

The garrison church still stands, as this used to be an army town whereas now it is naval. This roofless church, bombed in the Second World War, stands as a proud monument. Services are still held within its walls. Nearby is the museum, built in the style of a French chateau.

Governor's Green, where the free mart fair used to be held, is now used for all local events. Most battles on the green nowadays are tugs of war and other competitive sporting activities. There is certainly still a village atmosphere here in this little corner of a big city.

Otterbourne ✒

The village of Otterbourne, or Otreburne as it was called in the Domesday survey of 1086, derives its name from the Otter Bourne stream. This stream rises just above the bridge carrying the main road from Winchester to Southampton and flows down to join the river Itchen near Brambridge House. The Roman road from Winchester (Venta Belgarum) passed over the river bridge and forked to provide a road to Bitterne (Clausentum) to the left and Nursling, or Nutshalling, which was a Roman port, to the right.

The most famous person to live in the village was Miss Charlotte Yonge, the Victorian authoress, who lived in Elderfield opposite the church. This house is now owned by the Langley House Trust as a home for discharged prisoners and at the moment is being run as a market garden.

At one time the village blacksmith was a lady by the name of Betty Comely who kept up the custom of 'Firing the Anvil' on St Clement's Day, 23rd November. Another old custom was that of making rough music outside a house where a husband was accused of beating his wife. The villagers would gather outside and proceed to bang together pots, pans and buckets with the idea of showing him up in front of his neighbours. On May Day each year the village children made posies of spring flowers and paraded them around the village.

The present church, dedicated to St Matthew, was consecrated in July 1839, replacing the old one in Kiln Lane, which was too small and inconvenient for the village. The newly constructed railway also made it very noisy. The nave of the church was demolished in 1842 and the chancel in 1970. When this was done several wall paintings were discovered, but unfortunately they were in such a poor state that they could not be preserved. A 13th century piscina was also discovered bricked up in one of the walls, probably since the time of the Reformation, and this was carefully dismantled and stored.

One of the earliest canals in the country, the Itchen Navigation runs through the parish, but the last barge to use it arrived in Winchester in June 1869. The opening of the railway between Winchester and Southampton brought about its demise.

An important building in the village is the Southern Water Authority Works and more recently a large new block of offices. Water is pumped from deep wells and up to 10 million gallons a day is taken from the river Itchen. This is treated and pumped up to the reservoirs on Otterbourne Hill and from there it supplies Southampton. The water used in the village comes from the Yew Hill reservoir at Compton.

A number of Roman coins were found recently in an area off Poles Lane near the incinerator. A Roman medallion was found there in 1744 by two men digging sand in the pit, the site of which is now occupied by the incinerator.

The oldest building in the village is the manor house, which was originally moated and dates from the late 17th century. The original building was probably constructed in the 13th century. The court of the manor was held there until the late 19th century by the President of Magdalen College, Oxford. The house and adjacent farm passed into private ownership in about 1925. Otterbourne Common was the manorial waste for the manor and certain householders had rights on the common, which included gathering wood for fuel, furze for bedding and brushes, and gravel for paths and roads. These rights have all now lapsed.

Two large houses in the village, formerly in private ownership, are the Grange, now a nursing home for the elderly, and the Old Parsonage, with additional units built in the grounds, which is owned by the Brendon Care Association and used as housing for the retired. The village school built in 1963 to replace the original Victorian building was the first in Hampshire of the 'Scola' system and has since been enlarged twice and now takes some 200 children up to 11 years. A recent development adjacent to the main road contains a new village hall, opened in 1987.

Overton ❧

Overton lies either side of the famous trout river, the Test, on the B3400 between Basingstoke and Andover.

Overton was a 'church' manor from at least the time of King Alfred and is mentioned in the Domesday Book. The original settlement was on the north bank of the river and the church building dates back to the late Norman period. The White Hart Inn at the main crossroads in the village was a coaching inn on the old stage coach route from London to Exeter. In the 19th century, sheep fairs were held annually in the wide thoroughfare called Winchester Street and this is still the site today for Overton's summer carnival activities.

Since 1920 Overton has been the home of Portals Limited – a company which produces banknote and security paper for world markets. The mill today is a vast purpose-built complex but no longer does everyone in the village have connections with it as in past times. People who live in Overton work here or in nearby towns, and increasing numbers commute to London. The population has increased and new housing areas have arisen. Shops in the High Street and Winchester Street are numerous and varied. The doctors have a surgery and there are restaurants, pubs and clubs for evening entertainment.

Overton has its own primary school and playschool but it is the abundance and variety of leisure organisations which thrive here that promotes the friendly and caring atmosphere of the village and welcomes newcomers. There are Cubs, Scouts and Guides, clubs for local history, dramatics, photography, senior citizens, the Women's Institute and evening classes at the school, to mention just a few. The recreation centre – built on an area of drained marsh in front of the church – caters for almost every sport from rugby and golf to netball and archery. Some of the Overton Harriers have taken part in championships at county and national level.

Ovington ❧

The village of Ovington, about seven miles from Winchester, lies to the south of Itchen Stoke and south-east of Itchen Abbas. It is of Saxon origin and was one of a chain of settlements along the valley of the river Itchen. The Domesday Book (1086) records land in Ovington held by the Abbess of St Mary of Winchester; the first document confirming the existence of a church dates from 1284.

The original church building was destroyed by fire and only the entrance arch, recently restored, can now be seen. The present church was built in 1866 for the sum of £3,500 by Mrs Hewson of Ovington House – today over £26,000 is needed just for the repair and maintenance of the roof. The church of St Peter in 'the United Benefice of St John the Baptist, New Alresford with St Peter, Ovington and Itchen Stoke with Abbotstone' – surely a history lesson in itself – has one service each Sunday, taken by the rector or by retired clergy living in the district. There are one or two baptisms annually and the occasional funeral – very different from the period over the turn of the century when there was a steady stream of christenings, many of illegitimate children and frankly shown as such in the church records. Occupations were then given as farm worker, carter, welder, gamekeeper and river bailiff; today the corresponding entries are bank manager, company director and insurance broker.

There are about 20 houses making up the village with a population of a little more than 100, including children. Apart from church activities village life is limited. At one time the village could boast a village hall, a rectory and a post office/shop. These are all now private houses and the facilities they offered for meeting and social intercourse have been lost.

Only about 20 per cent of the population are now associated with farming. One farm, around the village centre and hitherto almost entirely arable, has recently been substantially converted to intensive pig-rearing but this does not intrude into everyday life. Across the main Alresford–Winchester road are two outlying mixed farms. Visit one and you will be surprised to find not only an aviary of colourful birds but also zebras and llamas happily grazing with the home-bred Shetland ponies.

The hub of the village is undoubtedly the Bush Inn. Built in the 17th century when a bush of twigs indicated the availability to wayfarers of food and drink, the Bush must be one of the oldest and busiest inns in Hampshire. In the bar can be seen a copy of a poem written in 1782 urging people to 'walk along the river bank and partake of a goodly dinner'. Today little urging is needed. The Bush occupies a spectacularly attractive site on the river Itchen and draws its customers from a wide area and from many countries. The public comes not merely to patronise the Bush but to wander over the wooden bridge and along the river bank, hoping to spot the famous Itchen trout in the clear chalk water and to watch the wildlife of this peaceful part of the Itchen valley.

Owslebury

Owslebury is a scattered village picturesquely situated among hilly downs and woodlands some five miles south-east of Winchester. Set on a windswept chalk ridge 350 ft above sea level, Owslebury is the second highest village in Hampshire and commands views of the Portsdown Hills and the Isle of Wight. In contrast some of the lower parts of the parish have wet and poorly drained clay soil.

The civil parish is made up of Owslebury, Morestead, Baybridge, Marwell and Hensting which together cover 5,434 acres with a total population of 817 at the time of the 1981 census.

An archaeological excavation in the 1960s uncovered evidence of an Iron Age settlement in Owslebury dating from 2,500 years ago, though it was more formally recognised in AD 964 when 'Oselbyng' was granted by King Edward the Peaceful to the Bishop of Winchester as part of the manor of Twyford and Marwell.

In the Domesday survey Owslebury was recorded by the name of Marwell and it was from the monastery there that priests came to take services at Owslebury church, built in the 13th century (the Domesday Book records a church at Morestead 200 years earlier). Nearby Marwell Hall (now a zoological park) was once the home of Sir Henry Seymour, whose sister Jane was the third wife of Henry VIII.

The Ship inn, Owslebury

The Owslebury riots of 1830 caused a considerable stir when a mob broke threshing and other farm machinery and robbed Lord Northesk's steward. John Boyes, a local farmer, took round a petition which demanded higher wages for farm labourers, and for his part in the riots was convicted and transported to Australia.

The interesting features of village life in the latter half of the 19th century were the windmill and the windpump, built to take advantage of the high position. The former was the last working corn windmill in Hampshire, and although there is no longer any sign of their existence, some of the bricks from the windmill were incorporated into the building of Old Mill Stores.

In the Second World War Owslebury had its own invasion (though thankfully not an enemy one) when American troops were billeted at Longwood and an airfield established at Marwell. Its proximity to the ports made it an obvious mustering point for the men and equipment preparing for the D-Day invasion.

Pamber Heath

The village of Pamber Heath is situated in north Hampshire close to the Berkshire border. It is six miles from Basingstoke and, with Pamber End and Pamber Green, is part of the parish of Pamber. St Luke's church forms the centre of the village along with a post office, store and pub. There is also a large village hall, opened in the late 1970s and paid for by fund raising from the local people.

The village has developed greatly over recent years, although some of the older houses still remain, as do many of the old families who have lived in the area all their lives. They would have seen many changes. At one time there were many more shops, and the post office was once a bakery with a reputation for the best Lardy cake around. There was also a forge where all manner of welding jobs took place. Cricket was played on the village green where houses now stand. Before the turn of the century, local children attended school in the church rooms until this became too small and they then went to the next village of Silchester to join the school there.

With a country background, besom broom making was well established in the area and continued until recently. Jobs were to be found with the industries which had come to Basingstoke in the 1950s. The growth of the Atomic Weapons site in nearby Aldermaston also gave jobs to many local people.

The name Pamber, originally spent Pambeare, goes back to Norman times, the addition of 'Heath' coming in later centuries.

Henry de Port founded Pamber Priory in the 12th century, and its remains stand today as a reminder of the time when this was one of the most important monastic establishments in Hampshire.

The three Pambers are surrounded by open lands: Silchester common, Tadley common and the extensive Pamber Forest, an ancient woodland.

Pamber Forest is a nature reserve of some 478 acres with a warden and a management committee to look after its needs. The forest forms a Site of Special Scientific Interest. Hazel, chestnut and oak have been coppiced for many years, and the structure of the woodland varies from dry open heathland through to dense hazel, to streams lined with alders and willows. The forest is home to many species of butterfly, some 30 species have been recorded. Bat boxes can be seen high up on some trees, to provide a home for the bats that choose to live in the forest. Flora, insects, small mammals and birds all make the forest their home, as do roe deer and fallow deer. Snakes, especially adders, are in abundance and can often be seen basking in the warm sunshine.

Passfield ✺

Anyone looking for the 'village' of Passfield would be somewhat confused. There is a piece of common grassland, on one side of which is a post office and useful village store; opposite is a public house, the Passfield Oak, and a row of large cottages look across the green towards it. The majority of the remaining houses in Passfield are scattered around this central point.

Originally most of the area was owned by Ludshott manor. The lord of the manor, Sir Archibald Macdonald, in 1896 gave a plot on Passfield Common as a village recreation ground. The Commoners, who still grazed a few cattle on the common, turned out in force and threw down the banks round the ground. The dispute was not finally settled until 1923. In 1911 some 200 acres of Passfield Common and neighbouring Conford were bequeathed to the National Trust by the lord of the manor, Dr Lyndon.

The river Wey was once a focal point of the village and was the site of a mill. Originally a corn mill, in late Elizabethan days it became a 'hammer' mill which beat out the pig-iron into a form which smiths could use. Charcoal for heating the iron may well have come locally from Gentle's copse, of which the millers were long-term tenants. In the 1680s the mill was converted into a paper mill.

In the 19th century the mill was owned by the Warren family who were earnest Bible Christians and did much for their workers. In 1851 they employed 40 women sorting rags for paper-making and 29 men in

181

the production of it. The Warrens built employees' houses, founded a Thrift Club and, in 1870 took their staff to a fete at the Crystal Palace. In the early 1900s paper was produced for Postal Orders and Old Age Pension books, such work ceasing in 1924. At the present day it is used for manufacturing plastic-wire products.

Passfield had a forge which although now a private dwelling, still boasts a Sun Insurance wall-plaque dated 1603. Grandfather clocks were made at the forge of which three or four still exist, and it was also possible for paupers to have teeth removed. The owners probably lived in the house next door, the building eventually becoming the Cricketers public house. One of the earliest landlords was Benjamin Fitt, famous for his home-made toffee. In 1902 the licence was transferred to the newly-built Passfield Oak.

At nearby Conford, edge-tools were made and were famous all over southern England for keeping their sharpness – some are still in use today. The local school for Passfield was at Conford from 1871 to 1964, when it was closed. The village bakery which had continued to use the traditional oven method ceased trading, much lamented, in 1989.

There is no church in Passfield and a group of early Quakers refused to pay tithes to the parish church at Bramshott: this led to trouble. In 1658 'a fat cow worth £4' was seized (by the rector it was said) and again in 1660 other cattle were taken in compensation for non-payments. Elizabeth Streeter was in gaol in Winchester for 21 weeks for 'what she said to a priest on the highway'. Henry Streeter died in the same gaol in 1661, and was buried in the Friends' burial ground at Bramshott.

Queen Victoria took a picnic lunch near Passfield and is remembered by a plaque, formerly on the tree which shaded her but now in Liphook village hall.

Edward I is reputed to have had a royal house on the site of the former Lynchborough Lodge and there is a legend that his wife, Eleanor, planted the snowdrops which appear in the surrounding woods each spring.

Sidney and Beatrice Webb – great Fabian thinkers – came, in about 1923 to live at 'Passfield Corner'. In 1926 a large Labour demonstration was held there, at which the first Labour Prime Minister, Ramsay MacDonald spoke. On being granted a baronetcy Sidney was known as Lord Passfield, but Beatrice stubbornly refused to use her title. Their request that they should be buried in the grounds of 'Passfield Corner' was carried out but a Labour Government in the 1940s had their bodies removed and they now rest in Westminster Abbey.

The present inhabitants of Passfield are largely commuters to London, Alton, Liphook and other neighbouring towns. In addition to the Auriol Plastic works there is a small industrial estate in the Hollywater road which provides some employment.

Pennington 🖎

Pennington is situated on the south coast of Hampshire, opposite the Isle of Wight and one mile west of the historic town of Lymington. The parish of St Mark, Pennington is divided into three parts – Upper, Centre and Lower Pennington.

In Upper Pennington is to be found the common which gave the village the nickname of 'Donkey Town', as large numbers of donkeys used to graze there. Nowadays a few goats are to be seen, but the common's use now is recreational, and each year the village is visited by a circus and a fair. Washing used to be dried on the common, but no more and the blackberries are less abundant than in the past.

The church, which is a brass rubbing centre, the schools, business premises, post office and two pubs, the Sportsman's Arms and the Musketeer, are situated in the centre. The original schools, which are listed buildings, are at present woodstripping and antique restoration businesses. The present schools are situated on Priestlands Fields, after which they are named. The fields are the only green space left separating the village from Lymington.

The village is fairly well off for shops, which include a post office and stores, fishmonger, fish and chip shop, newsagent, chemist and bank. Further south at the area known as Fox Pond, are a butcher, hairdresser and others. Nowadays most employment is found outside the village. Local employment can be found, though, in farming, horticulture, light industry, boat building and fishing. In past times most employment was in farming, fishing, the saltworks, and skills such as baker, blacksmith and thatcher.

The salterns have existed on the marshes at Lower Pennington from early times. At one time there were 13 saltworks, but now only paddling pools for children remain. The marshes are now a haven for birdlife, birdwatchers and walkers. It is possible to walk from Pennington to Lymington or Keyhaven along the sea wall – a defence against flooding. Commander Peter Ouvry, who lived at the 'Salterns', was the first person to dismantle a magnetic mine in the Second World War, which enabled the Allies to find a defence against it. The first Rocket Post was launched from the marshes to the Isle of Wight, and can be seen in the National Science Museum.

Pennington House can be found at the edge of the marshes and is occupied by Lord Lurgan, who opens the grounds to the public approximately twice a year. The house was built 250 years ago as a farmhouse, and the present owners added a new wing in 1923. The most interesting farmhouse is Sadliers Farm in Lower Pennington Lane. Built in the time of Charles I, it takes its name from the Sadliers who came over from France in about 1790.

In the centre of the village is Jubilee Cottage in Wainsford Road. Built in 1897 by the lord of the manor to commemorate Queen Victoria's Diamond Jubilee, it was originally the soup kitchen, but was converted to a dwelling in the 1930s. Yarrell Cottage in Ramley Road, overlooks the common. It is a very old building, and was at one time an inn called the Cricketers Arms. King's Huts at Upper Pennington were built by Mrs Powell King of Wainsford in 1908. These are six cottages in the shape of a horseshoe. The unusual interior design was Mrs Powell King's own idea, on the advice of Sir Edward Lutyens. Yaldhurst Lodge, which is found at the end of a private road off Ramley Road, was mentioned in the Domesday Book. Until recently it was a local crafts centre, but has now reverted to a family home again. Sir Thomas Beecham, conductor, lived at the lovely Ramley House, in Ramley Road, for many years. It has now been converted into a rest home for the elderly.

Penton Mewsey & Penton Grafton

Penton is not one village, but two, but why the parish boundary between Mewsey and Grafton winds amongst its houses is a thousand year old mystery.

'Penitons' means 'the farm at a penny rent' and indicates likely Saxon origins, although the site is much older, as the Roman farms in the area testify. There is also a possible long barrow in the meadow to the south of St Benedict's convent, though some say it is merely a Victorian folly.

Mewsey derives from the Meysey family, related to the Earls of Gloucester, who were lords of the manor from shortly after the Conquest until 1316, and who probably came from Maisy on the Normandy coast.

Grafton owes its name to the Abbey of Grestain, also in Normandy and to which William the Conqueror granted the revenues of the parish, which continued to be paid until 1348. Shortly afterwards the manor passed to the De La Poles, who became Dukes of Suffolk. In 1437 Duchess Alice by her will founded the Charity of the Two Chaplains and Thirteen Poor Men of the House of God of Ewelme in Oxfordshire, and gave the manor of Rambridge within the present day parish to it. Parts of Penton Grafton and much of the land to the west belong to it to this day. Vine Cottage and Grafton Farmhouse opposite both owe their construction to Ewelme money in the 18th century.

The church of Holy Trinity is mentioned in the Domesday Book. The present building, though much restored by the Victorians, probably dates from 1367 shortly after the Black Death and the inheritance of Edmund de Stonore. The Stonor's wealth was in sheep and wool and both played a large part in Penton's history until recent times.

The rich and famous have largely passed Penton by, but notable residents at the Convent (formerly Penton Lodge) have included George Nesbit Thompson, a memorial to whose children will be found in the church and who was secretary to Warren Hastings of British East India Company fame, and several MPs including William Cubitt, co-founder with his brother of the civil engineering firm of that name and who built the present building in 1842.

Portchester ✣

Situated at the northern end of Portsmouth Harbour, the district of Portchester has developed from being a close-knit community into its present semi-urban form.

Most of its inhabitants at one time lived within the vicinity of its ancient castle, located right at the water's edge, but since then Portchester has grown well beyond the original boundaries. Northward from the railway, which now runs through the locality the ground rises steeply to Portsdown Hill, from where there are outstanding panoramic views of virtually the whole Solent area. It attracts residents and visitors alike, and at night the multitude of lights which illuminate the whole scene present a rare and unforgettable sight.

It was after the Second World War that a significant growth in its population occurred, increasing by as much as 60 per cent in a short period of 20 years.

In conjunction with the expansion of the residential area, a limited amount of business and industrial development has also occurred. At one time, local industry was confined to agriculture and the making of clay pipes for smokers, the latter activity thriving for about 100 years.

Not surprisingly, shipbuilding and ship repair have also provided employment, and today Vospers, from a moderately sized shipyard, remains the largest employer in the locality.

It is in Castle Street that a number of 18th century houses still reflect the character and tranquillity of a past era, but the real glory of Portchester is its Roman castle.

Set on a spit of land, the castle is lapped on two sides by the sea. It was in the 3rd century that the Romans built a fort on the site, which covers nine acres. It is bounded by a sturdy stone wall and includes 14 of the original bastions. During the late 12th century, Henry I added the keep, and the whole edifice stands as a fine example of Roman and medieval engineering. It is considered to be probably the best preserved Roman castle in northern Europe.

Standing in one corner of the castle grounds is the parish church of Portchester. St Mary's is a fine example of Norman architecture.

In its time the castle, with its church, was popular with the English Monarchy, and it is hard to believe that Portsmouth was once governed from Portchester. It was a Royal Borough when Portsmouth was a small fishing village. However, with the growth of the Navy, Portsmouth gradually established itself as one of our key sea-faring ports, and the importance of Portchester slowly declined.

Nevertheless, in various ways it has retained an affinity with the Royal Navy. One such reminder stands on the border of the district where the first Nelson's Column was erected in 1808, three years after Trafalgar. The edifice, placed to give it a vista of the Naval dockyard, also looks appropriately towards HMS *Victory*, now lying in dry dock.

Another Admiral, Sir William James, although not so well known as Lord Nelson, achieved some distinction while a child at Portchester. He was the little boy made famous by the artist Millais, who painted him for the portrait *Bubbles*, later used by Pears Soap to advertise their product. There is little doubt that it was painted at Turret House, which once stood in West Street. On the site now stands a new library and health centre in the recently built shopping complex.

Like so many other places, Portchester has lost its quaint and old fashioned shops, its bakery, the blacksmith and other similar family businesses. Hence, to the people of Portchester, the castle and its surroundings remain as their treasured and prized reminder of bygone ages.

Purbrook 🦢

In the 19th century Purbrook was a quiet sleepy village, where a daily horse bus ran down to Portsmouth. In dry weather the water-cart sprayed the main street, which then comprised a few cottages and houses, shops and inns and the smithy where Mr Miles the blacksmith was kept busy at his anvil. Among the Miles family were other tradesmen, with Chris Miles being a chimney sweep and Francis Miles a carpenter and builder.

The village was well served with builders, as there were also Josiah and Reuben Clear, who were responsible for the building of St John the Baptist's church, which was commenced in 1843 but was not consecrated until 1858. The delay was caused by feuding between Sir John Deverell and the then rector of Farlington, whose church Purbrook people had formerly attended.

In the early 18th century a toll road was built to run through the village, tollgates being erected at Cosham and Horndean.

Purbrook Park House is now a school. In 1837 the Deverell family bought about 600 acres of the original estate and the new squire, Sir John Deverell, had a new Purbrook Park House built. This was erected in classical style and there were three carriageways leading to the house from diverse directions.

Sir John Deverell was Purbrook's benefactor. In 1869 he had built an industrial school housing 60 and later 120 boys. Sir John also had Christ church built, dedicated in 1874.

In 1859 there were three inns in Purbrook: the Leopard, an old coaching inn, the White Hart and the Woodman, then listed as a beerhouse. The White Hart inn had a horse trough in the front and stables at the side and there are stories that cockfighting took place there as late as the early 1900s. Next to the Leopard inn a train depot opened in 1907, the fare from Cosham to Purbrook then being 2d.

Sir Charles Napier, hero of the Peninsular and India Wars, lived in 'Oaklands' in Stakes Road. This has been greatly enlarged and is now a well-known Roman Catholic school that boasts a fine concert hall and has become a mecca for devotees of serious music.

The hamlet of Stakes, now part of Purbrook, was named after the De Stakes family who were the local lords in the 13th century. Originally it was known as Friendstaple, whose name has now been introduced as that of a housing estate.

There are still old buildings in Purbrook. Cottages in Old Van Diemans Road were built by Dutch prisoners of war, who were held in Portchester Castle. Adjacent to the cottages stands April Cottage, a house built in 1844. At the Widley end of Purbrook is the Portsdown petrol filling station, which in the early years of this century looked like a film set in a developing Texan township. Petrol was then hand-cranked into glass containers at the top of lighthouse-like dispensers and delivered by gravity into consumers' cars!

In 1903 the Portsmouth & Horndean Light Railway ran from Cosham to Horndean through Purbrook. The cars were coloured cream and emerald green, had curtains at the windows and an open top deck.

The Purbrook Park estate was sold in 1919. It was broken up and copious building took place. Park Avenue, once a carriageway, is now a busy road along which buses run. In the 1930s the population of Purbrook was 2,000, in 1963 it was over 6,000. In 1925 the whole area from Waterlooville to Portsdown was largely open land, which would suggest that the main occupation was agriculture. Today there are fewer open spaces, though fortunately Purbrook Heath still survives.

Quarley

Quarley lies north of Grateley, and is a neighbouring parish. Whereas Grateley derives its name from the 'great lea', Quarley derives its name from a quarter of the lea. It has a manor house and a church which are mentioned in the Domesday Book. A feature of St Michael's is that three church bells are housed in a frame, with a roof over it, in the churchyard.

The village hall was built and opened in 1987, due mainly to fund raising efforts by the villagers. The school, which was built in 1817 for 36 pupils, is now a private house and the children of the village go to Amport school.

The village used to have a public house, but this was destroyed by fire in the late 1920s. The Marquis of Winchester, who then owned virtually the whole village, gave the villagers a choice of a new pub or a water supply for the village. The villagers chose the water supply, and an artesian well was dug, with a water tower. Hence the villagers who wanted something stronger walked across the fields to the Plough Inn at Grateley.

Quarley is still a small village, although a few new houses have been built over the last few years, but it remains fairly quiet and unspoiled, with a great community spirit.

Quarley church bells

Ramsdean ✿

The small hamlet of Ramsdean is part of the parish of Langrish. A place that has not changed very much, it is still a farming village, with no shops. It is a peaceful place with a lovely view of Butser Hill.

The farms have been handed down from father to son, which means that some old families are still living here. There have been a few changes, the chapel has been converted to a house, and the pond, which was in the centre of the village, is now a village green. The house known as Cartridges is now a nursing home for the elderly called Ramsdean End.

The Pond Cottages are still as they were, with the same flight of steps leading up to them. The little thatched cottage by the chapel house is still there, and is now the only thatched cottage in Ramsdean. One new house has been built and one new barn has replaced a lovely old barn which was damaged beyond repair during the hurricane of 1987.

Romsey ✿

Most people associate Romsey with Lord and Lady Mountbatten and the Broadlands Estate, but this small market town has all the attributes usually associated with village life and has retained the feeling of a close-knit rural community.

Stand on the central area and look around at the old buildings which surround the market place. With a bit of imagination you are transported back to the turn of the century and can visualize the horses pulling drays and carriages.

The Town Hall is not as imposing as some but it has an air of belonging about it with an imposing wrought iron lamp bracket fashioned by a craftsman of bygone days. Past the Town Hall towards the Abbey United Reformed Church you may pause a moment to admire the arch which allows cars to pass through singly, a relic of a more leisurely period. If you take the road to your left, Abbey Water will lead you to a small garden on the left which is no larger than 15 feet square, with two strategically placed seats where one can sit a while and admire the houses along Abbey Water.

After your rest, take a good look at the first house; it was obviously on the corner of two thoroughfares as its angled front suggests. One road has now been replaced by a car park for use by council officials using the Town Hall. Follow the angle upward and read the sign which is still visible on the side of the house, proclaiming:

THOS. ELY and SONS

Whitesmiths   Gasfitters

Tinsmiths and Glaziers

Proceed along Abbey Water with its picturesque houses on your left; opposite, beyond the railing, is a pond with the Abbey United Reformed Church providing an idyllic backdrop with shrubs and vines rampant on the bank. This quiet backwater leads to Narrow Lane which wanders away to the left. Turn right and proceed through another arch for five yards before turning left once again. Continue along this road; if you wish to visit the Abbey turn right, but if you can spare the time, continue straight along the road to the bridge which spans the river Test.

In front of you is Rivermead House, now used as business premises. Note the chair cut from the stump of a tree which had stood on the pavement in front of the house – someone had been inspired when they were disposing of the tree! The seat is quite comfortable and allows a few moments contemplation before entering the Memorial Gardens, a tranquil spot with some very comfortable benches with a view of carefully tended colourfully planted areas.

Retrace your steps to the Abbey and continue along the paved walk, admiring the magnificent doors as you pass, and go on towards the market place. Turn left and proceed along the north side until you reach The White Horse, an old coaching inn which retains much of its original structure when viewed from the market place. One can wander through the doorway which was used by the coach and horses down into what was the original stable yard.

When next you visit Romsey, and can spare some time to wander down the out-of-the-way side roads and lanes, you may be pleasantly surprised and delighted.

Rotherwick

Rotherwick is an attractive village in the east of the county. The name is believed to be of Saxon origin and means 'a cattle enclosure'.

There is no mention of the village before 1200 but it is assumed to have been a part of the Hundred of Odiham. By 1302 it had become a part of the manor of Greywell and eventually the title of lord of the manor passed to the owner of Tylney Hall. This estate dates back at least to the 16th century and the house has been rebuilt three times. The present house dates from the end of the 19th century, and for generations provided work for the village people. It is now an hotel.

The church, dated from the 13th century, has no dedication or patron saint. The tower was built in 1730, but one of the six bells is 14th century. The church was restored at the end of the 19th century and the Tylney chapel was added, the fabric having got into a poor state of repair.

The village school was founded in 1713 when Frederick Tylney built a school room for ten boys and ten girls. In September 1983 when it became necessary for Rotherwick school to amalgamate with Heckfield, the combined school became the Whitewater School.

The magnificent village hall was presented in 1932 by Mr Henry de Forest, an American millionaire who rented Tylney Hall for the shooting. It was given in memory of his son who had left Harvard to go on a world tour and died in Italy.

For many years a plantation of hazel trees was grown for the manufacture of eye drops.

Rowlands Castle ◊

Nestling at the end of a beautiful valley by Charlton Down, running from Buriton, Rowlands Castle village is indeed set in a perfect spot between the ancient Forest of Bere and the entrance to Stansted Park on the edge of the Hampshire-Sussex border.

Upon entering the village from either the railway arches or Redhill Road, the eye is immediately drawn to the attractive variety of houses, cottages and shops surrounding the well cared for expanse of grass called 'the green'.

Records show that in the 1750s local people were granted leave to build near the green and smallholdings and cottages began to appear.

A booklet of around 1865 tells one to visit 'the handsome Almshouses on the Green at Rowlands Castle and see the small Inn', presumably the Fountain. The almshouses, called Stansted College, were built in 1850 to house six 'distressed gentlemen' and are now an attractive estate of some eight mews-style houses, not 'on the green' as we know it today.

The arrival of the railway line in 1858, and the building of the two arches to support it, changed the whole look of the village. Considered then to be ugly by many locals, the arches were built where the White Hart alehouse stood. This inn, the scene of the infamous murder of two Customs men in 1748, was knocked down about 1853, rebuilt on its present site and named 'The Castle Inn'.

The embankment holding the railway line runs over the site of the castle and nothing remains of its walls except two large fragments which fell into a deep chalk pit. Sad to say we are unable today to even see the

191

View of Rowlands Castle

remains of the grassy mounds that once used to form the motte and bailey castle that existed here. The ancient castle was supposed to have occupied the site of a Roman or Saxon entrenchment. It is said in one legend to have been built by a giant or 'forest free-booter' called Rowland.

Since 1973 there has been a Children's Fair each summer and the green comes alive for a day to the delight of local children. The village Flower, Fruit and Vegetable show is held at the same time in the parish hall and many activities and shows are staged.

Cycle races regularly start and finish here and ramblers and walkers meet to commence their walks to local beauty spots, finishing their day in one of the four old public houses or having tea in the garden of the Coffee Pot.

Tennis courts, football and cricket facilities as well as a children's play area are catered for up on the recreation ground adjacent to the green.

The golf course was built in 1902 with only nine holes and was extended later to 18 holes and then again to championship length in 1969. At least two big events have been held there.

It is still possible to live here and not require a car; both buses and trains serve the village and one can buy everything from the local shops. Today the green is nearly surrounded by houses and the population of the parish is around 2,500.

St Mary Bourne

St Mary Bourne is in the Hampshire Highlands, the highest points of the southern range of the South Downs running a little distance away to the north of the parallel Bourne valley. The Bourne, from which three villages on its bank take part of their name, is an intermittent, typical chalk-country stream. The volume of water has undoubtedly lessened over the centuries. Some are inclined to attribute this to springs tapped for watercress beds, which have much increased in the 20th century.

The original church of St Peter was probably a Norman building without aisles. Of this, the only parts now remaining are the chancel arch and the responds of the tower, which are of the late Norman period. The church contains several items of considerable historic interest, including what is undoubtedly one of Hampshire's greatest antique treasures – a massive font, carved eight centuries ago from black Tournai marble. An ancient part of the church has a recumbent effigy in stone of an armoured knight, whose crossed legs indicate that he had been a Crusader. The walls of the church are in the characteristic flint work of the area. Many of the village houses and farm buildings carried on the tradition till the 20th century, when brick, and then cement blocks, being quicker and easier, generally took the place of flints, to the detriment of local flavour.

In the centre of the village is the Summerhaugh, used for festivities such as May Day, when it was decorated with hawthorn in flower, and dances took place round a maypole. The name Summerhaugh probably comes from a place by the stream where the cattle were brought down from the hill slopes in summer into an enclosure surrounded by a hedge, 'haga'.

One of the oldest houses in the Bourne valley is Butlers, a mellow brick and beam building in Gangbridge Lane. In alterations made there recently a beam dated 1590 was discovered. Another thatched cottage of interest is Mundays, which used to be the home of a rope maker. There are certainly other houses in the village dating from the early 17th century.

Life in all villages several centuries ago was self-contained and isolated. The men cultivated their allotted strips of land. The exercise of any Common rights for cattle, poultry and wood-gathering supplemented a hard-earned living. Numbers of sheep were kept and spinning at home was an occupation for the women, with wool from local sheep, or with coarse linen thread, and loom silk, perhaps for Whitchurch silk mills.

Selborne 🌿

This small Hampshire village is known internationally as the birthplace of Gilbert White, the great and famous naturalist. His book, *The Natural History and Antiquities of Selborne*, is recognised as a classic of natural science and English writing. A celebration to mark the bicentenary of the publication of this book was held in 1989.

Gilbert White was born here, in his grandfather's vicarage in 1720. He was ordained as a priest after graduating from Oriel College, Oxford, but was never inducted as vicar of Selborne as the living then was held by Magdalen College. During his lifetime in Selborne, as well as studying and writing about the natural world, he took a great interest in the village school which had been started by his grandfather.

Life then, of course, was vastly different from what it is today. The population then numbered about 700 and was made up mostly of agricultural workers, wheelwrights, harness makers, carpenters, builders, bootmakers and many other trades.

Although there have been many changes in the village over the years, much of Gilbert White's Selborne is still recognisable today – Selborne Hanger, the Common, the Plestor (the old name for the village green), the hollow lanes and the two streams. For the enjoyment of future generations much of Gilbert White's countryside is now owned and cared for by the National Trust.

The school, too, has changed over the years and the number of pupils has fluctuated greatly. One villager who was at school here in the 1920s remembers what school life was like in those days. For instance, there were three classes, each with more than 30 children. There was a general exodus from school during hop picking time, as whole families went to the fields to gather the crop. Later, school holidays were varied according to the hop season, so that the children's education was not interrupted. Another reason for school closure was the chapel and church Sunday school treats. The whole village would shut down for this and coach loads would be taken to either Bognor or Littlehampton.

The main road through the village is very busy and like many other villages, Selborne has suffered greatly with the noise and heavy lorries passing through. Such was the concern that it was necessary to have a 'lorry watch'. This was a check on all lorries passing through the village and was carried out by members of the community being on duty throughout the day. Eventually the Department of Environment banned lorries over 7.5 tonnes from using this road. This was just one example of all pulling together in a common cause.

Selborne has two thriving pubs, three equally thriving shops, one with a post office, a good village hall, sports pavilion and ground, all managed and maintained by voluntary committees. The village hall has recently been renovated, thousands of pounds being raised by various fund-raising activities for this purpose. The sports pavilion too was built by funds raised by an enthusiastic body of local inhabitants.

Shalden 🍂

Although there was a Roman settlement in Shalden, and it is mentioned in the Domesday Book, existing records only go back to the 17th century when this was a farming community and almost all the residents worked on the land. One can imagine the farming life of those days, and on Tuesday mornings the preparations to get stock to the market in Alton, which is some three miles away. Alton has not had a livestock market for several years now, but some residents well remember driving sheep or cows to town for the weekly market. It was also an opportunity to get horses shod when the forge in Shalden closed, probably in the early part of the 20th century.

The church was built in 1865 by the generosity of the then Squire of the village. It is small but adequate and seats about 150 persons. It was built to replace a Late Norman thatched church which stood a few yards to the south of the existing building. The old font has been retained and is still in use, also a silver chalice and paten cover dated 1628. An underground passage used to run between the nave of the old church and the cellar of the Old Cottage about 100 yards away. When the old church was demolished the entrance to the passage was exposed, and has now been blocked in for the sake of safety. Until 1939 Shalden had its own rector, but on one cold winter's afternoon the rectory caught fire and was burned almost to the ground, destroying many church records.

A novelty in the early 1930s was a silver fox farm in Southwood Road. It was a thriving establishment, with a tall wooden tower for the owner to observe the mating habits of the foxes.

One of the most interesting village characters of those years was Willy Oliver. He was a small kindly man who was very lame, but his work load was prodigious. Willy was a gardener at the manor house, and Ernest Wood the squire saw to it that he did not have too much spare time. However, he was also verger at the church, dug the graves, mended shoes and cut villagers' hair, truly a most versatile fellow, and there is a plaque in the church in his memory.

Of course Shalden has changed. Whereas most of the residents at one time worked on the land, and long summer evenings were spent stooking corn or carrying to the rick, times have moved on, and the principal landowner no longer lives in the village.

There are no haystacks or corn ricks now, and cows are no longer driven through the village lanes on their way to milking. Village hall parties are not as popular as they used to be, though the annual flower shows and bonfire parties are always well attended. Large cars sweep through the village where once horses and traps served as transport, and sheep have replaced cows in the meadows. Vast combines trundle through Shalden, but as we move aside for them to pass, we know that once again it is harvest time in this still beautiful village.

Shedfield ✿

Shedfield parish is made up of three villages, Shedfield, Shirrell Heath and Waltham Chase. Twenty-seven Roman kilns of the 1st century AD were found in a meadow in Sandy Lane in May 1989.

Eilert Ekwall in *The Oxford Dictionary of English Place Names* attributes the original name of the parish to the Anglo-Saxon 'seida falda', meaning a plank of wood split thin, possibly in the sense of a footbridge. This seems appropriate as there are streams at most entrances to the parish, although these now pass under roads. Through many changes these words gradually became Schidefeld and then Shidfield, which by the dawn of the 20th century had become Shedfield.

The former village centre was along the Botley Road between the entrances to Sandy Lane and Old Shidfield Lane, as St Ann's Lane was then styled. There stood Shidfield House, a 17th century farmhouse, bounded on one side by Sandy Lane, and there were cottages, a village green and a pond with ducks and geese on it. Shidfield Lodge fronted Old Shidfield Lane, about 250 yards from the Botley Road.

In 1832 one James George Crabb had retired from the East India Naval Service and married. He had been given Shidfield Lodge as a wedding present. In 1834 Mr Crabb gave the village its first school, a school for boys and, when in 1861 plans were made for a mixed school, his wife gave the land on which it was built. In 1837 the family name was changed to Boucher when James George became the beneficiary of a will.

In 1867 his daughter Elizabeth founded a cottage hospital at Hill House, Shirrell Heath. She rented the house and installed a nurse and a few beds, later establishing a dispensary. The hospital was a success so the number of beds was doubled and it was agreed that a new hospital should be built as soon as the money was available. Mr Frederick Townsend, then of Shidfield Lodge, provided the money to buy land for it in what became Hospital Road in 1875.

A red-brick chapel of ease was built on common land in 1829 and was generally welcomed by the community. It became redundant after 51 years, however, when the present church of St John was consecrated. The architect was John Colson and the building is reckoned to be one of his best. Mr Colson, however, had planned for a spire, for which there was insufficient money and eventually Mrs Franklyn, who by that time lived at Shidfield Lodge, gave the tower in 1887. After the building of the new church and school the village centre gradually moved to the new Church Road.

Sheet 🌿

A picture postcard view of a sloping village green with a magnificent chestnut tree towering over it; a four square village pub in the background; a lane lined on one side by a terrace of old cottages and a high grey stone wall on the other, and above all a village church behind its border of bright flowers, white flagstaff and newly painted blue notice board. This is the village of Sheet as seen in a flash by motorists negotiating the A325 as it bends sharply round the green at Sheet, a mile or so north of Petersfield. Behind this rapidly appreciated scene lie hundreds of years of village history.

Sheet grew up near the ancient ford over the river Rother used by cattle drovers – their route still traceable along the deep Sandy Lane which climbs up the river near the bridge on the A3 to the Midhurst Road. There was plenty of water in the Rother and its tributary the Ashford stream to provide power to turn the three mills mentioned in the Domesday Book. Ironstone was found in the district and this led to the making of tools and weapons with the forest trees providing wood for smelting and the river water power for hammering the iron.

Records show that in 1327 Sheet was a hamlet with twelve taxpayers. Wool was 'fulled' (whitened) in the ancient mill on the Rother by Pulens (possibly Fuller's) Lane. This mill was rebuilt in 1742 and has one of the now rare Sun Insurance plaques on its wall. The miller's house, a short distance away on the other side of Pulens Lane, dates from the 16th century and is full of interesting detail.

Sheet Bridge Mill in Old Mill Lane, was built where the Ashford stream joined the Rother, thus increasing the power flow of the water. The mill operated from AD 900 until the 20th century but is now derelict. The mill house dates from the 15th or 16th century. Most of the oldest cottages and larger houses in the village are grouped round the village green or the sites of the mills. Some of the cottages in Village Street are 15th or 16th century. The village smithy stood next to the old post office on the village green and was in use until a few years ago.

In 1711 the Sheet-to-Portsea Turnpike Act was passed to keep the high road maintained for the transport of arms and men. In 1859 the London to Portsmouth Railway was opened. Some forty years later the villagers draped the hedges along the line where it passes through the village with laurel wreaths in mourning for Queen Victoria, whose coffin was carried past on its journey from Osborne House to London.

Sheet school has a long history. In 1674 John Locke gave a tithing of Sheet, consisting of a yearly rent of 50 shillings, to maintain a school-teacher. Later on Mount Pleasant, a house standing back above the green, was the village school and the large eight-light window which can still be seen, was the original schoolroom window. In 1897 John Bonham-Carter, who lived at Adhurst and whose family were great benefactors to Sheet, gave the present school to commemorate Queen Victoria's Diamond Jubilee. In the same year he planted the chestnut tree on the green. A framed photograph of the tree as a sapling hangs in the church vestry. The village hall by the green was also built to celebrate the Diamond Jubilee.

The large grey gabled house of Adhurst St Mary which stands in a wood overlooking Sheet on the far side of the river Rother, and was the home of the Bonham-Carter family for many years, was used as a hospital in the First World War and in 1940 Portsmouth High School for Girls was evacuated there.

St Mary Magdalen's church forms part of the parish of Petersfield with Sheet and is served by a priest-in-charge who lives at the Parsonage in Pulens Lane. It has a large congregation and is noted for its music. There are two stained glass windows in memory of members of the Bonham-Carter family. A large flag belonging to Admiral Algernon Willis which had hung in the Chapel of the Order of the Bath in Westminister Abbey, was hung in Sheet church after his death.

Sherborne St John

Though Sherborne St John lies only three miles from Basingstoke, it still has the true feel of a village.

The name Sherborne probably means 'clear stream' and certainly there is a stream running through, and no less than three duckponds. There has been a settlement here for a very long time as Roman remains have been found in many places.

It must have been larger too, as at one time there were seven alehouses. Now there is only one, the Swan, which is over 500 years old and is still thatched. Interestingly, the piece of ground on which the village hall now stands was once the allotment of the Swan.

Just round the corner from the Swan stands the Haye. This has one of Lutyens' earliest extensions and it is said that you can tell it is Lutyens' work because you can't see out of the windows! It was once a Quaker meeting house and some of their graves have been found not only in the garden and under the kitchen floor but in the grounds of the school next door. The Haye also has a resident poltergeist.

At Numbers 6 and 8 West End is a rare example of a Wealden house, of the kind which is usually found in Kent and Sussex. It is thought to be unique in Hampshire and dates back to 1450. It also has a magnificent kingfisher living on the stream in the back garden.

Next door to this is Cleeves, which used to be the village brewhouse but which is now a pleasant home. Legend has it that hidden in a well in the garden is the treasure of Vasco da Gama, though what he could have been doing here is difficult to imagine!

On the opposite side of the road are Gable Cottages. These are built of solid chalk with walls up to 18 inches thick and their roof is made of swept tiling.

The beautiful village church of St Andrew dates back in part to 1150. After the siege of Basing House, Cromwell is supposed to have given two of Basing's bells to Sherborne St John. Whether this is true or not is unknown, but it is a fact that Sherborne has two pre-Reformation bells and Basing has none. There is also a chained *Foxe's Book of Martyrs* which is rare in a village church.

The churchyard is worth a visit too. There is a stone to the memory of Henry Raymond Biggs, who was a pioneer of jet aviation. The most entertaining stone stands by the church porch and is to the memory of George Hickson who:-

'. . . . had lived above 20 years in the service of William Chute Esq. as whipper in and huntsman and continued after he died in the family as coachman. . . .'

He may not really have been a phantom coachman but there is a ghostly coach and horses which was last seen on the Kingsclere road in 1944. There is also Smith Grindle who returns from time to time to search for his treasure in Smith's Green, not to mention the exorcism which was performed in 1923 to stop the rattling of chains in Church Path.

At the turn of the century the village employment was in agriculture or brickmaking, but the brick kiln was closed in the 1950s and anyone who wants to work on the land nowadays has to leave the village.

But fallow deer still come warily to the edge of Sherborne and there are fish and freshwater clams in the ponds and dragonflies and herons fly overhead. In their season partridges, snipe, woodpeckers, goldfinches and redstarts make their appearance. There are bats in the church roof and the occasional squirrel comes in. Hares and rabbits abound in the fields.

Sherfield English

Sherfield English, a small parish of some 542 souls, lies mainly in the valley to the north of the A27, on the borders of Wiltshire.

It was named originally Sirefelle and became Shirefelde in the 13th century. Later 'English' was added to the title after the d'Engleys family took the manor.

The 20th century has seen the loss of the mill (1940s), and the bakery (stopped actual baking in the 1940s and stopped the bread round in 1965, when the delivery man reached the age of 80 years old). The cricket pitch and its pavilion went from Glebe Farm in 1957, Melchet Orchard went in 1977, the Sunday school in the church hall is gone, the garage with its attendant snack bar went in the 1980s, the smithy is gone and the old rectory is now a private dwelling.

The years have also seen the break-up of the old estates. Sherfield English estate was sold in 1921, Melchet Court was sold in 1936. The Wellow Wood school became a private house, now called the Lyon House, with lion decorations originally from the old manor house. Ellingham Hall and Broxmore House with its deer park have also gone. On that estate, caves were used to house ammunition during the Second World War. The explosives became unstable due to damp and, because of the inability to move them, they were exploded in situ (about 1943). After the war, Broxmore House fell into disrepair and had finally to be demolished. Several newer properties have now been built on the land.

Watercress has been grown at the source of the Sherfield English brook for many years and can still be obtained in the local shops in Romsey (before the war bunches were sent up to Covent Garden and sold for 1d a bunch). The watercress is still supplied to London hotels.

The village is fortunate in still having two shops, one being the sub-post office, taking in shoe repairs, dry cleaning, laundry, films for development as well as delivering milk and newspapers; the other shop sells most items of everyday necessity, sweets, vegetables etc. A third shop did exist, but finally closed its doors in 1971 when the currency changed. This shop, the old bakery, was renowned in its day for its excellence in old fashioned lardy cakes.

The third church to be built in Sherfield English was given to the village by Lady Ashburton, in memory of her only daughter, Mary Florence, Marchioness of Northampton who died in 1902. St Leonard's dominates the skyline and has an impressive peal of eight bells, which are regularly rung.

Sand extraction is a great source of aggravation in the village today.

There have been sand pits in the area for very many years, but the infilling as well as the extraction fuels the fires of exasperation, changing a normally quiet village into a pocket of rebellion.

Sherfield-on-Loddon ❧

The parish of Sherfield-on-Loddon covers over 2,000 acres of north-eastern Hampshire. It is part of the Rural District of Basingstoke and has twice been judged Hampshire's Best Kept Village.

It is encompassed by the river Loddon to the east, Bow brook to the north and Petty's brook to the south. Only the Basingstoke to Reading branch of what was once the Great Western Railway breaks this pattern.

A mystery surrounds the parish church of St Leonard. Today strangers are puzzled by its position, seemingly on the outskirts of the village. Probably responsible was the coming of the Black Death via Southampton in the 14th century. Whole villages were wiped out, or their terrified inhabitants fled. Whatever the reason, those early Sherfield folk retreated towards the common land of Sherfield Green, a mile away. The original site is called Church End.

The Green supported a thriving community of cows, goats, horses, pigs, donkeys and geese. Within living memory, animals were still grazed there. Alfie Bailey minded cattle, but had difficulty in controlling a heifer belonging to Mr Brown of Rose Cottage. It bellowed constantly and was known as 'Bugler Brown'.

Nowhere has the changing pattern of village life been more evident than on the Green. It fell into neglect in the 1920s as the rural economy declined. The magnet of industrial employment at Basingstoke and elsewhere drew people away from the land. The Green became unkempt.

What saved the situation eventually was the fact that the lord of the manor lived elsewhere. This spurred on the Parish Council to seek and obtain permission to manage the Green. In 1972 the Green Committee set out to restore the common land for the common good, in 20th century terms.

The Green was gradually transformed. It became a mixture of grassland and trees, cricket ground, football ground, play area for little children, tennis courts, children's log-encampment, and cycle track. Sports pavilions were tucked away unobtrusively. Daffodils and crocuses were planted. To save the duck population as they crossed the road between their two ponds, special notices warned drivers.

The village hall, originally five Victorian cottages, was donated by the Barker family in 1909. It caught fire in 1939 during a football match between Sherfield and Old Basing, when the latter were leading 5–1.

Both teams sprinted for the hall, where Old Basing had left their clothes. Others had already put out the blaze but the clothes were totally destroyed. Old Basing returned home very briefly dressed.

Once an old lady distilled 'dillwater' and sold it to the public to aid digestion. She, the shoemaker, the saddler, the candlemaker, the wheelwright and the blacksmith have all gone. There is, however, a comprehensive range of occupations besides farming. The post office and the general stores thrive. The latter manages to compete with a giant Tesco three miles away. It provides a lifeline for the elderly and is usually crowded. Village news travels fast there.

Strange noises have been heard at night in Longbridge Mill. Some blame the Longbridge ghost as it rattles downstairs in chains and slams the front door; others blame shifting timbers.

Only two pubs, the White Hart and the Four Horseshoes remain, although Billy Wicks, who ran the old Jolly Farmer, is remembered as having one of the reddest noses ever seen. The White Hart, an old coaching inn, still has the wooden post rack.

Most villagers wish to remain here. Some who do move out, move back. Many reach a great age. There's an old saying: 'You live as long as you wish in Sherfield-on-Loddon'.

Shipton Bellinger

Shipton Bellinger is not, like some of the Hampshire villages around and about, a pretty 'chocolate box' village. It has a church of St Peter dating back to the 14th century, a pub, a butcher's shop, a village store cum post office, and a smattering of thatched cottages in the main high street, but mainly it is a village that is simply home for, and loved by, many. Therein lies its beauty for the community spirit is, for many, second to none.

Its history goes back a long way, there being evidence of a settlement as far back as the Bronze Age. There would appear to be fairly strong evidence of a Romano-British settlement on the site, as various Roman artefacts have been excavated over the years. It was during Saxon times (about AD 500) that Shipton Bellinger's rather unusual name started taking shape. It was at this time that it was named 'Sceap Tun', which is Saxon for sheep farm, thus giving a clue to its main occupation.

The village is recorded in the Domesday Book of 1086 (when its name had changed to Sceptune). Then in 1297, Ingram Berenger became the lord of the manor of Shipton and it was he who added his name to the village. Over the years the name has taken on its present day spelling.

During the First World War the army barracks were built in Tidworth, which had an immediate impact on the village and to this day the army presence is very large, with probably about a third to a half of the village being connected with the army in some way. Situated as it is , not really on a main route (although in recent years the A338, on the edge of the village, has seen an increase in traffic from north to south), there are no tales of famous kings taking refuge, nor does it boast any famous inhabitants, but a great feat by the villagers in the 1980s is worth recording.

There had been discussions regarding a village hall in the early 1900s, but when, in 1910, a working men's club was built, the subject of a hall was dropped. However, in 1983, the village having expanded considerably, it was decided that a village hall was needed and talks recommenced. Discussions with the County Council and Test Valley Borough Council proved fruitful as regards obtaining grants and the Parochial Church Council pledged a donation, but there was still the fairly hefty sum of almost £20,000 to be raised by villagers. The mammoth task of raising the balance was then tackled by various means. Finally, the building work was started 18 months after the first discussions and in September 1985 the Village Centre (as it was now named) was opened. It is something of which the villagers are, quite justly, extremely proud. And therein lies the community spirit – a tremendous effort which took just two years from start to finish.

Shirley 🦢

Shirley today is a busy suburb of Southampton, and not many local people can remember when the former village was taken into the city in 1895. However, this is still a close-knit community and many families have memories of times when a large area was made up of farm and common land.

The drinking fountain dating from 1837 is a well known landmark. It used to be in the High Street, but is now in the modern shopping precinct. As well as housing small shops, the pedestrian layout has seats where people can enjoy the sun and pass the time of day with friends and neighbours.

Although many Shirley residents are employed in the city centre or other areas, there are local jobs in shops, small businesses and factories. Probably the largest employer in the area is the Health Authority at the nearby general hospital, which has expanded over the years and is now a teaching hospital taking patients from far and wide. Another well known employer is the Ordnance Survey Office where modern technology is now used in the production of the maps and charts.

A prominent man in Shirley was Robert Claude Ashby, born in 1887.

In 1898 he helped to form the Shirley branch of the Church Lads Brigade. He retired from active Youth Service in 1949. During those 50 years some 1,500 to 2,000 boys came under his influence, and in 1937 he was made a CBE for his youth work. The hall was turned into the Ashby Youth Club. Unfortunately some years ago it was burned down, but a modern youth club arose from the ashes. He died in 1962.

In the early 19th century Shirley villlage centre was further west at the junction of Romsey Road and Winchester Road. At this point was Shirley mill, which was powered by water from three ponds, the mill stream running eventually into the river Test. An iron works making spades and shovels was there until 1880, when it was converted to a brewery, then, after about 20 years, the Royal Mail Line took it over as a laundry to service their ships. Only one pond remains in that area today, but it is popular with bird watchers looking for unusual species.

A reminder of times past is the public house named the Ice House, standing on the site where ice from the ponds which regularly froze in winter was stored. Another nearby public house is the Old Thatched Inn, still a popular rendezvous.

Shirrell Heath

The name Shirrell Heath derives from two features – the hill now known as Gravel Hill, which used to be called Sheer Hill, and the heath. The heath stretched as far as Biddenfield Lane and included Shirrel Fields, Shedfield Common and the cemetery. Described in 1846 as 'a wild heath with here and there a few wretched huts', most of the land was later cleared and used for market gardening or sand pits.

A living was hard to make, particularly in the 19th century, and in November 1830 *The Times* newspaper carried an account of how 300 men met on Shedfield Common 'armed with implements of husbandry' and walked towards Wickham. News of their movements evidently travelled fast for they were soon met by two gentlemen, probably magistrates, with a detachment of military. The report says that at this point some of the men became violent, whereupon three of the ringleaders were arrested and taken to Wickham to stand trial. The rest separated but made their way to Wickham in groups and then reassembled. A certain Major Campbell addressed them and asked what complaints they had. They explained to him very rationally that it was the lowness of their wages, upon which it was impossible to live. On being assured that the matter would be looked into, they dispersed quietly.

By the 20th century, cherry and strawberry growing had become important and the cherry blossom made the village very pretty in spring.

Often the cherries were taken to Portsmouth to be sold and the strawberries were taken to Wickham station, from where many went to London hotels.

In the late 1920s a Mr Clarke from Swanmore ran an Anzac Bus through Shirrell Heath to Fareham for 10d return. On Mondays passengers travelling to Fareham market were allowed to have a crate of rabbits or chickens transported on the roof. Sometimes people stopped the bus and asked the driver if he would do some shopping for them in Fareham, such as buying a tin of paint or matching a roll of wallpaper. He waited in Fareham for about ten minutes or long enough to do any errands which had been requested. The Anzac Bus was eventually taken over by the Hants & Dorset Bus Co, but for service it has never been equalled.

Sopley 🦢

The village is small, straddling the Christchurch/Ringwood road. The inhabitants consist of old-established families whose names appear in the local churchyard and on both World War memorial plaques in the parish church, and newcomers who decided on this lovely spot to live when the commercial upsurge in the South brought new industries into the area.

Since the beginning of the 20th century the composition of the village has changed, from small houses standing close together with public houses at each end of the main thoroughfare, a commercial laundry and at least one general store, to some small dwellings, still close together while larger houses are hidden by trees and swathes of lawn in the general area of former habitation. The one way traffic scheme has isolated the Woolpack on its own little island whilst the Bakers Arms only exists as a name on the brickwork of a private dwelling. The village store also doubles as a post office and an ornamental ironwork establishment stands where perhaps the village forge stood. A garage takes care now of the 'transport' repairs.

The parish church, St Michael and All Angels, stands on the probable site of a Saxon church which was endowed by Earl Godwin, the father of King Harold. Thirty acres of land was included. There is still a local hamlet called Godwinscroft which is close enough to have been included in the original tract of land.

During the Civil War, the vicar was Thomas Lake who made no secret of his sympathy with the Royalist cause by allowing his congregation to celebrate the king's victories and mourn his defeats. Not surprisingly, he was replaced – or ejected – about 1642.

At the beginning of the Second World War local agricultural land was seconded to the Ministry of Defence. Sopley's contribution became known as Sopley Camp which functioned during hostilities as a radar station, attracting many top political visitors. The land remained in Ministry hands until recently and sheltered parties of Vietnamese Boat People until permanent homes could be found for them. Some obviously did not want to leave the area, marrying in Hurn church and settling locally.

Summer visitors who are always welcome are the horses of the Household Cavalry who, with their grooms and handlers, hold an annual Summer Camp where the animals (and men?) enjoy rest and relaxation in the country.

Mrs Barrow, laundress to the local gentry, was a well-known colourful character in the area. She and her donkey and cart could be seen at the beginning of every week collecting from the larger houses. Her work-room was the open air. Tubs of washing seemed to be under all the trees in the garden, each, it seemed, with a different process in operation. The starch bath stood under the lilac bush and was a constant source of attraction to the local children. The ironing was the only activity to be carried out in the house, as the bushes were draped with clothes to dry in the fresh air. At the end of the week Mrs Barrow and donkey would deliver her work – and collect her wages. Unfortunately the way home passed all the local hostelries! Jane, the donkey, was a well loved character in her own right as her mistress would deck her in finery to match every occasion.

South Baddesley

South Baddesley lies between the Forest and the Solent, some two miles east of Lymington. Together with the adjoining hamlets of Norley Wood and East End, it is part of the manor of Pylewell. It has a church, a school and a village hall, all firmly and confidently Victorian; and the confidence is not misplaced since all three play their part not only in Baddesley itself but in Norley Wood and East End.

Apart from these, Baddesley has none of the amenities usually associated with a village – no shops, no post office, and a very limited bus service. But it has a Great House and its Park and it is with these and with their owners throughout the centuries that the village story is largely connected, although it is some time since the estate provided work for the majority of the inhabitants.

Baddesley has several legends, beginning in the 17th century with that of The Wild Beast from which the then owner of Pylewell, Sir James Worsley, was saved. By what means, and from where the beast came, each account differs. Some say it came from the nearby forest, others that it was not in this country at all but in Africa. But wherever it happened, the fact remains that in thanks for his deliverance, Sir James left instructions that every year in March a sermon was to be preached in the nearby church at Boldre, for which the vicar should receive 'A goose and a golden guinea'. This sermon was given until very recently although the goose was latterly replaced by another guinea – a poor exchange.

The second story, that of The Groaning Tree, was retold by William Gilpin in his *Forest Scenery*, published in the 1870s. It is of a tree in Pylewell Park that disturbed everybody by its incessant groaning, until it attracted visitors from miles around, including Frederick William, Prince of Wales (son of George III) who was staying at Pylewell House with his wife the Princess Augusta. The unfortunate tree was eventually cut down.

Finally the story of the Balloon; and for that at least we have a visual record in a delightful drawing by Thomas Rowlandson from his sketch book of *A Journey in a Post Chaise* made in 1784. It shows a balloon floating over Pylewell Park with all the household standing on the lawn waving in great excitement. Recent research shows that this was in fact a balloon carrying Jean de Blanchard on a flight from Chelsea that eventually took him to Romsey, some 15 miles away across the forest.

It was these legends, with inevitable variations, that formed the more spectacular parts of a pageant which the South Baddesley WI, together with some 30 villagers and schoolchildren, presented in the year of the Queen's Jubilee in 1977. It was a happy event played out on the Pylewell lawn against a back-cloth of the Solent with the downs of the Island behind. This was one of many such happy occasions since 1874, when the first William Ingham Whitaker came to Pylewell, thus starting a family connection which persists today. But even before that another village tradition was already established in the Pylewell Park Cricket Club, several times the proud winner of the Stone Cup for New Forest Village Cricket.

It was, however, with the second William Ingham Whitaker that the village enjoyed, from 1893 to 1936, a period which some still look back on as a Golden Age. That he was loved and appreciated is shown by a tablet in his memory put up in St Mary's church by 150 estate workers 'in gratitude for many years of just and liberal treatment'.

South Hayling

The oldest building in South Hayling is the parish church of St Mary the Virgin. Building began in 1225 and the fabric remains today almost as the original builders left it.

One of Hayling's profitable trades in the olden days was smuggling.

They used to start out on a dark night from the ferry in a four-oared gig and row over to France. An old inhabitant said they had specially made canvas bags for brandy and these used to be hung from ladies' crinolines and so transported to their destination.

The number of 'real tennis' courts in the British Isles is small. The one on Hayling opened in 1912, built by Mr R. F. Marshall. There is also a tennis war memorial, now in the gallery of the club house.

A large East Coast oyster company constructed oyster beds at Salterns Creek at the end of the 19th century. The oysters were dredged up from the large beds in the Solent, brought into the creek and preserved there for the winter. A terrible winter in 1901 froze them all and the local industry died out soon after.

After the First World War Commander David Joel and his wife started a business building wooden houses. They were the pioneers of Empire Wood near Hayling station. After many appearances at the Ideal Home exhibitions they left Hayling to open a factory near London.

The golf club was founded in 1883. The Royal Hotel served as the club house until the club was able to build its own. The Hayling Island golf club can boast of having the first lady captain in England. This was Mrs Howard Fairhough, who captained the ladies' golf team in about 1885. She was also the first woman to win a ladies' golf competition in England.

Southwick 🌿

Southwick is a very small, very old village. In 1988 the owner of the village and estate of Southwick, Mrs Eva Borthwick-Norton, died in her nineties and left it complete to a nephew, Mr R. Thistlethwaite. The whole episode was well publicised by the media – bringing this rather shy retiring place into the limelight for a while.

The other major event in the 20th century was the planning of Operation Overlord, D-Day, in 1944 at Southwick House. Southwick House was acquired by the Ministry of Defence and remains as HMS Dryad. HMS Dryad is very much part of Southwick and the Navy and the village work amicably together. Some of Southwick Park has been returned to the District Council. Most of the people of Southwick, both in the old part of the village and in the newer council estate, work either for the estate or at HMS Dryad, but gradually more are having to seek work in the local towns, Portsmouth, Fareham and Havant.

The first mention of Southwick was in 1150 when the Augustinian friars found that the priory they had built at Portchester in 1129 was too small. Southwick priory itself was never very large but it was extremely influential at times, indeed the church which now is incorporated in Portsmouth Cathedral was in the priory's possession. William of Wykeham, founder of Winchester College, paid for masses to be said at Southwick for both his parents and many others did the same.

The village church is known as 'St James without the Priory Gates', which indicates it belonged to Southwick rather than the priory.

At the Dissolution of the Monasteries, the priory and its possessions were given to a John White and the estate has passed down more or less intact since then. By the beginning of the 20th century everything in the village – school, churches, shops, pubs, as well as all the houses, belonged to 'The Squire' and so it has remained. Only the 'Big House' and the Park have gone – to the government.

The village is most attractive. Because of its single ownership all the woodwork of the cottages and smaller houses is painted the same colour. Now it is a red/maroon but at one time it was dark green. There is a disproportionate number of larger houses in the village – these *must* have white paintwork. A stroll down West Street (one of the two streets) takes in five centuries of architecture – from a wattle and daub thatched cottage to Victorian flint houses. There is nothing 20th century in the main part of the village.

The village school is now used as offices; there are very few children in the village although recently the numbers have increased – a good sign.

Most visitors notice the houses by the green – Tudor cottages mainly, and the 'Terrace', which runs from the Old Post Office to the Red Lion. The two pubs are both 'Lions', the Red and the Golden.

The village population is small – less than 200 – with the farms on the estate adding perhaps another 100. There are 550 on the electoral roll but many live much nearer to Purbrook.

Southwick has recently been 'discovered', but for a while at least it seems set to stay unspoilt and dream peacefully on into the 21st century.

South Wonston 🌿

South Wonston is situated four miles north of Winchester, off the old A34 road to the Midlands. It is about 400 ft above sea level, built on chalk downland which for hundreds of years has been known as Wonston Down.

Originally it was a stopping-over place for gypsies on the drove road between the hopfields at Alton and Salisbury. It lacked running water and the land was not rich enough to encourage people to stay permanently, though there is evidence of prehistoric occupation in the form of a long barrow at the eastern end of the village.

There has been sparse but more or less continuous settlement, but it was not until the turn of the century when Henry William Brake bought South Wonston Farm that people began to settle in any number. He divided the land into acre building plots by roughly pacing the land, which were then marked by a furrow made by a horse-drawn plough. These plots cost £10 an acre and the buyers were mainly from Winchester. They would come out from the city and camp at the weekends while building their houses of wood and corrugated iron. Thus the grid system which we still see today in the village was introduced.

The arrival of the Royal Flying Corps at Worthy Down during the First World War provided work locally and the building of a halt on the Didcot, Newbury and Southampton Railway provided easier access and so further encouraged people to settle in the area.

Water has always been a problem. Rain water was stored in tanks, in butts and sometimes in large underground tanks, which it is said became a hazard when cars became popular. A local GP found that the covers were not substantial enough to support the weight of a car and he was left suspended in mid-air during the blackout of the Second World War.

Around 1919 a 200 ft well was sunk, the water being pumped up by an engine now in the ownership of Hampshire County Council Museum Services and stored at Twyford Waterworks. This well, now capped, still exists in the village. The 1950s saw the introduction of mains water and in 1985 problems of low water pressure were addressed by the installation of a large water tower, which has now become a prominent landmark for the village. Electricity came in 1954, precipitating the explosion of development which has continued up until the present time. There are now about 800 households in the village and a population of 3,000.

The area between South Wonston and Worthy Down is open land and was used as a racecourse during the 19th century. Some of the racehorses were stabled at South Wonston Farm. Race meetings were referred to in the *New Sporting Magazine* of 1833 but it is thought to have lost popularity before the First World War. Timbers from the grandstand removed in 1917 were brought to the village and used in a number of buildings.

During the First World War, Worthy Down was used as an airfield by the Royal Flying Corps and later the Royal Air Force, the Fleet Air Arm and then the Royal Army Pay Corps, who are still there today. The black barns used as aircraft hangars, two pilots' cottages and the remains of an ammunition dump are still in existence.

There are still people living in the village who can remember when Downs Road, the main thoroughfare, was only a farm track. They had to wear wellington boots if they went to catch a bus on the A34 carrying their walking shoes with them, putting them on when they got to the bus stop and leaving their wellingtons in the hedge for their return.

There is now one shop in the village, an off licence/general store incorporating a post office. With a much smaller population, though much less mobile, there were at one time four shops and a variety of van rounds.

The village church, St Margaret's, of corrugated iron construction, is the daughter church of Holy Trinity church, Wonston. Alongside is the new village hall, a brick building opened in 1986 after considerable fund raising by the village.

Sparsholt & Lainston 🦢

Through the centuries the histories of Sparsholt and Lainston have always been interwoven. They have supported and relied upon each other in equal measure, but there is one past inhabitant and benefactor who had quite a considerable bearing on the day to day lives of the villagers of these two parishes over the last century or so.

It was a Mr Samuel Bostock, a barrister formerly of Lainston House, who finally managed to organise a reliable water supply for the area. Before this, the villagers obtained their water from a variety of wells in and around the parishes of Sparsholt and Lainston. Some people had their own, but the chief supply came from the village well, which relied upon one or two people walking a treadmill for an arduous 20 minutes or so, to draw water from 247 ft below ground. As if this were not problem enough, long hot summers could cause the well to dry up, and villagers were known to cart barrels into Winchester in order to draw water from the river Itchen. They would do this sometimes twice a day and on returning to the village would sell the water to friends and neighbours.

In 1897, to mark Queen Victoria's Jubilee, a new well house was built which not only disposed of the old well house but also the treadmill within. In its place a brick building was erected to house a wind-assisted pump. However, over the years this still did not prove very satisfactory. Fires were frequent. Several thatched cottages burned down because the water pressure was not strong enough for fire fighting, and so in 1908, Mr Bostock arranged for a piped supply from Crabwood Reservoir to service Sparsholt and Lainston, as well as the neighbouring village of Littleton. The well house can still be seen today, though, opposite the church, and now houses a craft shop.

It is thanks to Mr Bostock and his wife that Sparsholt, and indeed

Hampshire, has a Women's Institute movement. 1917 saw the launch of the movement in Hampshire with Sparsholt as its founder member.

The site of the village hall is again due to the generous benevolence of Samuel Bostock, but for some reason he was against the erection of a brick building, and so an army hut was purchased after the First World War and used for most village gatherings until the new hut was built in the 1980s. Similarly, the land for the village cricket ground was donated in the same way, with the only interruption for its use coming during the war years when it was converted to a bowling green. This was presumably due to the fact that most of the men from the village were away fighting for King and Country. Today, Sparsholt Cricket Club still plays on the same ground in Locks Lane and the traditional English sound of leather on willow is a fitting tribute to this man of Sparsholt and Lainston.

Steep ✍

Steep is a large parish lying at the western end of the Weald and stretching from the summit of the wooded hangers to the boundary of Petersfield and from Stroud to Liss. The richer parts have always been farmed and the less fertile and steep slopes have remained as woodlands, mainly beech and yew trees.

There was no real village until recently but several small settlements, the earliest being Dunhill – a group of farms and probably an inn. The old Stoner Hill road from Alton to Petersfield was turnpiked in 1772, and in 1825 a zigzag road from Island to Weeke Green, Froxfield, was constructed to bypass the very steep climb up Stoner Hill. This road with its magnificent views is often known as Little Switzerland. Nowadays the village stretches along the ridge from the Cricketers Inn at the crossroads to Steep church. Until after the Second World War there was a blacksmith's opposite the Cricketers and Tommy Moss was a well-known character. Now it is a garage.

Ecclesiastically Steep and Froxfield once came under East Meon. Legend has it that they wanted to build a church on the hangers to serve both parishes but mysteriously the work was undone each night and the stones moved to the present site of All Saints' church, Steep.

All Saints' is known to have been built in the 12th century and restored in 1876 and now is a most attractive village church situated with lovely views of the South Downs. In it are a carved oak organ screen by Edward Barnsley who lived locally, and two windows beautifully engraved by Laurence Whistler in memory of the poet, Edward Thomas. Another feature is the kneelers, all different and depicting rural things such as

212

animals, birds, plants and so on, a great many of which were designed by the vicar and embroidered by ladies in the parish. Opposite the church is the village school and a very attractive common where various summer activities are held. To the west of the church there was originally a tithe barn, later converted into cottages and now a private house. To the east, an old timber-framed house was in early days known as Steep Church House, but it was reconstructed about 1905 and is now a private residence.

The river Ashford drains from the hangers and after a series of ponds where watercress used to be grown, there is a waterfall at the old mill site. At one time this was a mill for fulling cloth and later for milling grain and is now one of the beauty spots of Steep. Another is further down the Ashford where several old cottages stand by the bridge across the river at Kettlebrook. The gully followed by the 10th century road to Liss is here, but is mainly the haunt of badgers. This leads to Steep Marsh, another hamlet.

On a less wooded spur of the hangers is a large sarsen stone brought from Somerset and erected as a memorial to the poet, Edward Thomas, who lived in Steep for a time. It commands a superb view of the South Downs from Butser to Chanctonbury Ring in Sussex, with all the lovely countryside in the foreground. Each March the Edward Thomas Society organises a walk to Selborne and back to a memorial service in Steep church.

Steep was essentially an agricultural society of yeomen and labourers but the disastrous agricultural slump of the 1870s brought change. Many farmhouses were replaced by gentlemen's residences and these gave employment to bailiffs, coachmen, gardeners, gamekeepers and domestic workers. Then in 1900 Bedales School, a co-educational boarding school, moved to Steep, taking over some 150 acres of farmland and providing a green belt between Steep and Petersfield. With its progressive ideas it introduced a third element into the social division between the gentry and the locals and its expansion has led to about half the growth of the last 80 years, which has turned central Steep into a long village of scattered houses, with its one village shop and post office. Bedales has brought back work for people in Steep, it has a strong link with the village school and integrates well.

There is a flourishing tennis club and a most enthusiastically supported cricket club which has its headquarters at the Harrow Inn. This is an old inn situated where at one time the old road from Stoner to Sheet crossed the one from Petersfield to Liss. Historically it has always been in Steep but now, for local government purposes it is in Sheet. Unfortunately the peace and quiet of this area will be threatened when the Petersfield bypass is built.

Steventon 🌿

Steventon lies about seven miles south-west of Basingstoke and joins the parish of North Waltham on its southern boundary and the larger village of Overton to the north. It nestles in the heart of the north Hampshire countryside and is reached by a network of narrow, twisty lanes so typical of this part of the county. There are many trees in and around the village and some of these are planted as formal woodland.

In early summer, the hedgerows are white with Queen Anne's Lace or hedge parsley and the air is filled with its pungent scent and the insects which this plant attracts. For the most part, farming is arable, but some cattle and sheep are kept and these add a particularly pastoral feature to the countryside.

There is a timeless quality about Steventon. It is not difficult to imagine that the atmosphere of the countryside in which she was born and lived for more than half her life, influenced Jane Austen when she embarked on her literary career in the 18th century.

Jane Austen was born in Steventon in 1775 and it was here that she spent the first 25 years of her life as the daughter of a country parson. Although more comfortably placed than many of his parishioners, George Austen was not a wealthy man and with eight children to provide for, he took in scholars and farmed land adjoining the rectory to supplement his income. It was at Steventon that Jane wrote *Pride and Prejudice* and *Sense and Sensibility* and they are so descriptive of a particular way of life that she must have drawn on her surroundings and the lives of her neighbours and family for such precise and detailed writing.

Sadly the rectory in which she was born was pulled down in the 19th century and there is no visible evidence of its existence, but from a sketch, and descriptions which have survived, it was a substantial, two-storeyed Georgian building with a garden and a barn in which plays were performed by this talented family.

Were it possible for Jane Austen to return to the village of her birth, she would not see a great deal of change. Of course, houses have come and gone, a modern village hall been built, and a school opened and closed again in less than a century, but the Deane Gate from which she boarded the stage-coach to Bath and London is still there and the church in which her father preached, remains.

She certainly would not recognise Steventon Manor. This has undergone three dramatic changes and many minor ones in its history and a fire in the 1930s caused much devastation.

The church is dedicated to St Nicholas, and the first known recorded mention of it was in 1238. There have been improvements, changes and restoration over the centuries, but much of the original remains and, because of the close associations of the church with the Austen family, it attracts worldwide visitors. In the churchyard there is a tree of great girth, which is reputedly mentioned in Domesday.

The route of the London to Southampton railway through the village must have caused a great stir in the middle of the 19th century, and apparently the event was celebrated by the roasting of an ox at Michel-dever station, part of it being brought back to Steventon to be consumed in North Down Field. The long road tunnel underneath the railway is now lit by electricity, but in 1903 the Parish Council paid a lamplighter three shillings to light the lamps, and he had to provide oil, glasses and wicks out of that amount!

Despite the closure of the village shop and post office, as well as the primary school, there is still a strong sense of community in the village. Mobile shops visit, and twice a month a 'shop' is held in the village hall and local produce is sold and cups of tea served.

Stockbridge ✿

Stockbridge is an interesting village to linger in. Its long street of small shops includes cosy little teashops, and a hotel with a room which projects out into the street over an impressive pillared porch.

Sheep fairs were held here from the time of Henry III until 1932. Stockbridge was on the main route for herds of stock being driven from Wales to Surrey and Kent, but with the coming of the railways these journeys declined.

This is still farming and racing country and St Peter's church has a roundel over the door leading to the choir vestry depicting one notable winner, *The Tetrarch*, always ridden by Steve Donaghue.

Parchment was made here at one time, no doubt helped by water from the river Test, and tanning was another local industry. A local clock-maker named Eack was renowned for producing grandfather clocks with a painted face depicting vessels in full sail. Houghton Fishing Club were equally renowned for their expertise in dry fly fishing on the river Test!

Stockbridge is built upon an artificial causeway thought to have been laid during Roman times to enable the main channel of the Test to be bridged. During the 10th century a frontier stronghold garrisoned by the Saxons was built on the causeway to defend Wessex against the Danes and it later became the main road between Old Sarum and Winchester.

Stroud ❧

Stroud is a small village straddling the A272 Petersfield/Winchester road just west of Petersfield. It comprises some 150 households.

Apart from three or four farmhouses dating from the 16th century or earlier, most of the dwellings were built at the end of the 19th century and in Edwardian times. A new development of 19 houses, built on the site of the old brickyard, has added some much needed new accommodation to the village. As well as housing, there is a village pub, the Seven Stars, an attractive building facing a small village green where the local Women's Institute planted a tree and placed a wooden seat in 1977 to mark the Queen's Silver Jubilee. The village shop and sub post office closed some 20 years ago and the premises are now used as an antiques shop. A petrol filling station and ancillary workshops complete the commercial side of the village.

The village hall is a rather decrepit First World War tin hut. Used as part of a prisoner of war camp for Italians in the Second World War, it now serves a useful purpose providing the venue for meetings, parties etc.

The spiritual needs of the village are served by a small church built to commemorate Queen Victoria's Golden Jubilee, on the Steep/Stroud road. In 1867 a Primitive Methodist church was built at the eastern end of the village. This closed in 1946 and from 1957 until 1975 was used to house hens. It was then converted into an attractive dwelling.

The name Stroud means a wet marshy place and the clay soil in the area provided suitable material for a brickworks which flourished a hundred years ago. Owing to the wet land, all the farms are dairy farms, the cattle being kept under cover in the winter to avoid spoiling the pastures by treading.

Most residents of the village, apart from the retired, commute to London, Portsmouth, Winchester or Petersfield for their employment, a few working in the local garage and on the farms.

To the south-east of the village lies a Roman villa. This was excavated in 1905 and was open to the public for five years before being covered over again.

Stubbington & Crofton ❧

Both Stubbington and the neighbouring hamlet of Crofton are mentioned in the Domesday Book – and were then forgotten for many years.

As small districts of the vast estates of Titchfield Abbey, they were of little interest. Crofton, with its manor house, demesne farm and small chapel of ease, was then the larger of the two, with Stubbington having no more than a few workmen's cottages around a small green.

In the 19th century, Stubbington started to expand and soon absorbed Crofton, together with the little fishing village of Hillhead to the south. A major contribution to this growth was the establishment of Stubbington House Preparatory School, by the Foster family in 1841. Many new buildings were needed for the school and it dominated the village for the next 100 years, providing employment and housing for many of the villagers. The Foster family were generous benefactors, providing a reading room for the men of the village and the land for a new church, which was built in 1878. Even today, long after the school has gone, many of the buildings are still in use as the village hall, community centre, scout hut, and the laundry is now an engineering workshop.

By 1939, Stubbington was a self-contained, self-sufficient little village of 2,500 residents. Around the village green were many small shops, mostly of one room in a cottage, a forge, builder's yard, doctor's surgery in an old thatched cottage, a small telephone exchange and two inns. It is interesting to note there were no less than three boot and shoe repairers.

One state school catered for all ages and up to the 1960s was heated by one tortoise stove, had gas lighting and outside toilets. The public library was housed in cupboards in the village hall.

The considerable development in and around the area in the last 50 years has been of great importance to the village. What was then a truly rural area, has now become urbanised. Gradually more and more houses and bungalows have been built and the population has now grown to over 15,000. The green fields and lanes which abounded then, have mostly disappeared. Lanes, flanked by old hedges and ditches, have become 'B' class roads, losing their rural characteristics for ever. Only the names remind us of the old days.

Stubbington is fortunate in retaining a centre for the village round the village green. In fact shops and businesses in the centre have 'The Green' as their postal address, although there is no road nameplate.

Prominent in the centre is the war memorial and adjacent are the two red-flowered horse chestnut trees, planted there by Stubbington and Hillhead Women's Institute, to commemorate their formation in 1919. When these trees were threatened with removal to make way for a supermarket, the WI led the successful campaign to preserve them and the supermarket was built behind them.

All the old buildings and cottages have been replaced by modern buildings, housing, a post office, four main banks, dental surgery and veterinary practice, as well as a good selection of shops. There are now five schools in the village, all in modern buildings, as well as private schools. This development alone shows how the village has changed. A purpose-built library was opened in 1970 and a new leisure centre has been added to the community centre.

The village also has four churches, including ancient Crofton Old Church. When the Victorian parish church of Holy Rood was gutted by fire a few years ago, the opportunity was taken to modernise the interior, allowing for more flexible use.

Sutton Scotney & Wonston

Sutton Scotney is six miles from Winchester to the south and Andover to the north. There have been many changes in the village since the 1930s. There was plenty of work then to be had on the farms and estates, which supplied houses for the farmhands, butlers, chauffeurs, grooms and gardeners. There was also work on the local watercress beds. There used to be quite a good bus service, so the villagers could do their shopping for clothes, footwear and all household goods. In the village there were three grocer's stores, one butcher's shop, a bakery, coal merchant's, post office and three public houses, as well as the village blacksmith and a shoe repairer. Petrol pumps at Taylor's garage were in the centre of the village.

Mr R. Smith was the wheelwright, so a great asset to the village. He was also carpenter, undertaker, and captain of the bellringers at Holy Trinity church for 50 years.

There were two churches. Holy Trinity, situated in Wonston village just a mile away from Sutton Scotney, was built in the 12th century of flint and stone, with a plain tile roof and a south door. The church was twice restored after disastrous fires in 1714 and 1908. The old house next to the church was formerly the vicarage, but now the vicarage is situated half a mile away, as Lord Rank had a modern house built when he came to the village before the Second World War.

The second church, St Luke's, was in the centre of Sutton Scotney on the main Oxford road. It was built in a Swiss style. Christenings could take place there and also Sunday services, but it was not consecrated for weddings. It had to be demolished a few years ago as it was considered unsafe, and now offices have been built there.

In the late 1930s the fire station was still thatched. It has done a great service to the village, and the part-time firemen are now also called to many accidents on the busy motorways.

Sutton Scotney used to have a railway station, with the trains travelling to Winchester and Newbury on the Great Western Railway every day. There were three porters, two of whom were named Bob Penny and Bob Tanner! The station then won prizes for the Best Kept Station. But sadly it is now gone and office buildings are in its place.

St Luke's church, Sutton Scotney

Lord and Lady J. A. Rank came to live at Sutton Manor just before 1939. They did a great deal for the village and employed a great many people. Lady Rank had a surgery built in 1975, where there are now five doctors practising.

The village is now very changed. There is only one general shop and post office. Taylor's is the one garage, where holidays at home and abroad can be booked, or outings and trips to shows. Taylor's has been a well-known firm for many years. Their coaches take the children to school – as the village school is now closed and sold. It has been made into two houses and an eight room house has been built on the old playground.

There is still the coal merchant, Wheeler's, but now most houses are centrally heated. There are 74 council houses, and special senior citizens' bungalows with a warden were built by Lord Rank. Sutton Manor is a well staffed nursing home, and houses in the grounds have been made into flats for the elderly.

Swanmore 🖋

It is said that the original spelling of Swanmore was Swanmere, conjuring up a picture of lakes and swans. Deeds of older properties show that the land was in fact claimed from the forest of Bishops Chase. St Barnabas' is the beautiful, well cared for parish church, built in 1844. The tower was added in 1877. The Methodist chapel was built in 1863 and there is always a warm welcome in these places of worship.

Mr Myers lived at Swanmore House during the 19th century and employed most of the inhabitants. He married in July 1888 and when he and his bride returned from their wedding tour, the carriage was drawn by the village men from the bottom of the hill a full mile up to the house.

In bygone years the village was self-sufficient, with three bakeries, a blacksmith, a vendor and repairer of bicycles, a brickyard, three butchers, a dressmaker, a fish and chip shop, a haberdashery and clothes shop, an ironmonger's, four dairy farms (two of them delivering fresh milk to the door each day), three sweet shops, and a newsagent's where gentlemen could also get a hair cut! There are now four shops and a post office, and commuting to work is the norm.

Opposite St Barnabas' is the Church of England primary school, and the comprehensive school in New Road serves pupils from surrounding villages. The primary school has been extended and is well equipped, but villagers remember when the classrooms were heated with tortoise stoves, and there were holes in wooden seats over open drains for toilets. The favourite sport of the boys was to creep around the back and tickle the girls' bottoms with nettles, for which they invariably had the cane!

Probably the most famous local inhabitant was the humorist Stephen Leacock, born in 1870. He went to live in Canada and in 1974 some Canadian dignitaries came to unveil a commemorative plaque on Leacock House.

Before the Second World War, each summer children from the East End of London would stay with village families for a country holiday. We called them 'London Bugsquashers' and they called us 'Hampshire Hogs'. Do they remember, we wonder? Then with the war came the evacuees, some of them staying on to become villagers.

The new village hall built in 1980 and the parish rooms are venues for meetings and entertainment of all kinds. The village football and cricket teams have always been well supported, and in recent years a tennis club and bowls club have been formed.

The village has four well supported public houses – the Rising Sun which was an old coaching inn, the Hunters Inn, the New Inn and the Bricklayers Arms which was rebuilt in 1920. A relative of 'mine hosts' of the New Inn from 1924 until 1954 can remember when there were spittoons to be cleaned and gentlemen smoked clay pipes. There are also memories of sitting in the family room, which was like a parlour, endeavouring to understand the meaning of a placard on the wall which said 'Laugh like Helen B. Merry'.

Sway ✒

Estate agents describe Sway as a village in the heart of the New Forest. In fact it sprawls untidily on the southern edge of the forest, with views of the Isle of Wight from elevated land. Old maps indicate the position of the village some distance from today's centre.

For centuries a poor living was scraped from smallholding, farming and seasonal forest work. Smuggling and poaching were rife and in about 1777 the vicar of Boldre, whose parish then included Sway, described his parishioners as 'little better than bandits'.

St Luke's church was built in 1839 to serve some 600 people who previously would have had a journey of several miles to Boldre. There is a mystery about the dedication of the foundation stone. It is inscribed 'St Mark' whereas original documents show that it was always the intention that the church should be called St Luke's.

The opening of the Brockenhurst to Christchurch section of the London & South Western Railway in 1888 changed the village in more ways than one. Prosperity was increased as businessmen moved in. They built houses, providing more local employment for labourers, craftsmen and domestic servants. Also two local roads were renamed Manchester Road and Brighton Road as a reminder of the railway gangs from those towns. Manchester Road certainly sounds incongruous in a Hampshire village until you know the reason!

Sway has grown round the church, railway station and school and has not expanded so much as filled in. It is fortunately limited on two sides by the boundaries of the forest. There are no ancient buildings in the village, though there are a few cob cottages, now modernised. A local landmark is Peterson's Tower, designed by Andrew Peterson on his retirement from India. It is 218 ft high and built of mass concrete by unskilled labourers who were paid five shillings a day. It was finished in 1885 and still stands straight and true.

In the village now there are two pubs and a small hotel. In days gone by there were several more such establishments to cater for a comparatively small population. Some had a dubious reputation for being the haunts of poachers, highwaymen and smugglers. According to local tradition a tunnel led from Keyhaven to Sway Inn, now Sway House.

221

Another house called Kettlethorns is built on the site of an alehouse of that name. It is said that Captain Marryat, when writing *The Children of the New Forest*, had this in mind as the alehouse run by Gossip Allwood.

Local myths associate Sway with docks and treacle mines! Ironic references to these among the older generation can be heard today. The origin of these myths is not known. However, it is interesting to note that there is a house called 'Switchells' built on the site of Switchells coppice and according to Chambers Dictionary the definition of 'switchel' is treacle-beer.

The descendants of the original villagers are now outnumbered. Some families have been in the neighbourhood for at least 300 years. They form a closely knit group, conscious of their own identity but at the same time they are friendly and helpful to the incomers who have come to live among them. The presence of a thriving primary school, medical services and shops sufficient for daily needs ensure a population of all ages and income groups. Sway is by no means a retirement village. Many people earn their living by commuting to Southampton or Bournemouth or even by fast train to London. There are still a few farms and market gardens and a small industrial park.

Sway today is an active, friendly and caring village. There are over 30 clubs and organisations offering a wide range of activities. A voluntary welfare group helps with hospital transport and many other matters. There is little to attract the casual sightseer but visitors are welcomed and come to enjoy the pleasures of the Forest or the sea a few miles away. Sway is situated off a 'B' road so many motorists pass by without noticing it, and all this adds up to a very pleasant place to live.

Thruxton 🌿

Lying just to the north of the busy A303, Thruxton is a name familiar to those interested in gliding or car and motor-cycle racing. These events are held at the former Second World War airfield situated just to the west of the village and where there is also a busy little industrial estate. A few of the businesses have a specific link with the sporting activities; some are highly specialised firms with customers all over the world.

Unlike the racing circuit, the village proper can hardly be seen from the main road. The centre of the village was declared a conservation area in 1985. The oldest dwellings are said to be Gooseacre, the Old Forge and George Cottage – parts of these date from the 16th century – and there are many more Listed buildings, including cob boundary walls tradition-ally capped with thatch or tile. The village green, with the seasonal stream running between it and the street, together with the surrounding houses, look as if they have been there for centuries, thus epitomising the idea of the English Village. In fact there have been many changes in recent years: the green was glebe land until 1978, the money to buy it being raised by events held in the Queen's Silver Juibilee Year; Bridge Cottage, a focal point of picturesque charm, was only restored in the early 1970s; Bray Cottage, formerly the village bakery and a general shop, lost its thatch in a fire in 1985.

Standing boldly in the centre of the village is the chapel of this former Wesleyan stronghold. It was built in 1875 and opinions differ as to its architectural merits. After the First World War it became the village Memorial Hall. It still hosts the full gamut of community activities.

The parish church of St Peter and St Paul is tucked away off School Lane, beside the present manor house, within the ancient manorial fortifications. The church dates back to the 13th century but much of what we see today is a result of 19th century rebuilding and recent restoration. Inside, however, are a few treasures of particular note. There is a magnificent brass portrait of Sir John de Lisle, lord of the manor, who died in 1407. He is shown in plate armour under a rich canopy with his feet resting on a lion and this is the earliest known brass to show the change from chain to plate mail. An Elizabethan lady carved in English oak is thought to be Elizabeth Philpott, lady of the manor, who was buried in April 1616. Her fashionable clothes are beautifully carved but alas the effigy is terribly battered. By no means least, although not visible to the general public, is the oldest bell, given in 1581, which is known to have been rung to warn of the Armada.

Beyond the village there is evidence of Bronze and Iron Age occupation and traces of two Roman buildings have been discovered, the more important at Mullenspond. This was possibly a temple dedicated to Bacchus who is depicted on the mosaic pavement found under the rubble in 1823. In 1899 the owner of the site presented the mosaic and the terracotta candelabrum found at the same time, to the British Museum, where they can still be viewed.

Today it is wildlife found at Mullenspond which is of particular interest and fiercely protected. The present pond was created during the Second World War when gravel was excavated to lay the runways at the airfield. It naturalised quickly to become an outstanding feature of the locality and many villagers monitor the impressive variety of birds who use it as a home, or as a temporary stop.

The buildings remain and so, hopefully, does the natural environment but the people come and go. The chief reason for this is the proximity to garrisons. Service personnel choose to live here but cannot really settle, although a certain number return in retirement. The majority of the working population commute to Andover, Basingstoke or even London, for there is little employment in the parish. Only a few farms remain, a handful of people work at the village school, the pub and the airfield, and there are the self employed working from home in the new 'cottage industries'.

Some of the older residents have lived in or near the village all their lives and remember the old ceremony of 'Skimmington'. To express communal disapproval of some misdeed, two straw effigies were mounted on a donkey and led by villagers rattling trays and tin cans past the houses of the offenders. However, the most notorious event to happen in the parish did not concern a villager. It was in April 1920 when Percy Topliss, better known now as the 'Monocled Mutineer', murdered a Salisbury taxi driver at a point since called Topliss Hill.

Tichborne 🎋

The name Tichborne is thought to derive from the river Itchen which runs through the valley. Indeed, the spelling 'Itchenbourne' is found in ancient documents, with variations.

The church of St Andrew stands on rising ground to the west of the village. It has a Saxon chancel with rare double-splayed windows. The body of the church dates from the 12th and 13th centuries and is filled with Jacobean box pews. The original door is still there, with an iron ring which gave sanctuary to all who grasped it. Another very unusual feature is the north aisle, a Roman Catholic chantry of the Tichborne family, founded in 1338. Even after the Reformation, the records show that the Roman Catholics used the parish church when their religion was proscribed. It has continued in its orginal use and Tichborne is therefore one of only two churches in the country (the other is Arundel) used for worship by both Protestants and Roman Catholics.

Tichborne is famous for its Dole. Every Lady Day, 25th March, the villagers of both Tichborne and Cheriton meet in front of the portico of Tichborne House with pillowcases to collect their dole, one gallon of flour (7 lbs) for each adult and a half gallon for each child, with a maximum of four gallons per family. The ceremony dates from the reign of Henry II when the saintly Lady Mabella, on her deathbed and concerned about the poor people on the estate, begged her husband to distribute the value of a small portion of land annually. Her husband, Sir Roger, being less charitable, replied by offering as much land as she could encompass whilst carrying a burning brand. Lady Mabella rose from her bed and, despite being almost crippled, managed to crawl round 23 acres, still known as 'The Crawls'. With almost her last breath she threatened that, if Sir Roger or his heirs failed to give the value of the land to the poor, there would be a generation of seven daughters and the house would fall down. In 1794 the Dole was stopped because of trouble caused by vagabonds arriving from all over the country. Tragedy followed, the name 'Tichborne' almost died out and the house partly fell down. The Dole was reinstated, continuing to the present day in the form of self-raising flour where once it was bread. During the Second World War villagers gave up their precious coupons so that it could continue.

In 1854 tragedy again struck the family when the male heir, another Sir Roger, was presumed lost at sea off the coast of South America. Eighteen years later Arthur Orton arrived from Australia claiming to be the missing Sir Roger. A civil law suit followed, which he lost. He was then tried in the High Court for perjury in what was, until recently, the longest trial to be held in England,which ended with his conviction and sentence to 14 years in prison. The Tichborne Case almost bankrupted the family.

Tichborne in 1901 had a population of 276, in 1987 it was estimated at 167. Early in the 20th century there was a parsonage for a curate, a school, police station, post office, laundry, forge, several farms and a village pub. The laundry burned down before the First World War and was never replaced. In the 1920s a hut served briefly as a village hall where silent films were shown. Prior to the Second World War the last policeman to be stationed in the village retired and the police station closed.

A serious fire occurred in 1939, gutting the public house and an adjoining cottage. Happily the Tichborne Arms was rebuilt; it is thatched and two bench seats which were rescued were placed in the public bar as a reminder of the former hostelry.

The lady who was postmistress early in the 20th century lived to become one of the oldest postmistresses in England. She was succeeded by her daughter who also lived to a great age, but the post office finally closed in 1968.

Today Tichborne has its church, public house and its farms. Just two houses have been built in recent years and a bus takes shoppers to nearby Alresford each Tuesday morning. Watercress is still grown commercially in the parish and a trout farm has been established. Part of the water-meadows have been designated a Site of Special Scientific Interest. The cricket club has its home ground in Tichborne Park where matches are played regularly every summer. The Alresford Show is held annually in the Park. There are strong links with neighbouring Cheriton, where the people from Tichborne take an active part in the many organisations. With its thatched cottages, the earliest dating from the 15th century, and the surrounding farmland, Tichborne has an air of timelessness which is rare.

Timsbury 🖊️

The old Stockbridge to Romsey road runs through Timsbury and was first constructed of flint and gravel. It crossed the Test by a ford, which came out by the Duke's Head at Greatbridge and you can still see today the opening to it beside the pub. Later the two present-day bridges were built.

Timsbury consists of a green valley of pasture, rich in marshy land and wild flowers. A hundred yards away lies the manor house and close by the church of St Andrew. School House is a lovely building of flint and brick, a gift to the parish by a vicar centuries ago.

The Domesday Book tells us that the Abbey of St Mary in Winchester held Timbreberie and had always held it. By 1212 the church had become a prebend of St Laurence within Romsey Abbey. At the close of the 12th century there was a wave of church building in Hampshire, due to the munificence of Henry de Blois, Bishop of Winchester and brother of King Stephen. It was at this time that a new church was built here, almost certainly on the site of its Saxon predecessor. Two hundred years later, in the time of William of Wykeham (or possibly as a memorial to him) a restoration took place. Very largely the church today is as it was then.

Because it is a private little building in the sense that it is slightly off the beaten track it seems to have escaped both despoliation and the worst excesses of later restoration. Plainly there is some Georgian work to be seen in the interior, but that gives the building much of its charm. There is Victorian work – for instance the floor of the sanctuary – but not enough to affect the general character of the building.

In a case near the screen in the church is a nice copy of a beautiful 17th century Chained Bible (1613), with the chain by which it was secured when books were rare and precious commodities.

On the outskirts of Timsbury at Brook is the oldest reservoir in the county. It dates from Saxon times and retained the water for the fishpond and weir. The stream running through it is now called Fairburn.

The village pub, called the Malthouse, is very old and for years brewed their own beer.

Titchfield 🖊️

Lying at the heart of the growing 'metropolis' of south Hampshire, Titchfield still maintains much of its village charm, its many ancient buildings being immediately obvious.

The highlight of the year in Titchfield is the annual bonfire carnival held on the last Monday of October. The carnival procession, the largest in Hampshire, winds its way round the village in the afternoon, and again in the evening, with many village families entering floats, houses and business premises being decorated, Cole's funfair in attendance and a large bonfire on the recreation ground. As in most villages the origins of the carnival are shrouded in mystery, many believing it to date from the 15th century when the Earl of Southampton ordered the damming of the Meon estuary, thus effectively ending Titchfield's life as a port.

Titchfield Abbey, to the north of the village, became home to the Earls of Southampton after the Dissolution of the Monasteries and it is widely believed that William Shakespeare was a regular visitor.

A prominent feature of the village church of St Peter, which stands next to the river at the end of a narrow street leading from the village square, is the tomb of the Earls of Southampton. The church dates from before the Norman Conquest, and has obviously been enlarged many times, reflecting the days when Titchfield was a more important town than neighbouring Fareham.

Today the church is again undergoing alterations with the construction of the chapter rooms, whilst the vicarage next door is being sold and old people's housing built in the vicarage garden. New houses have been built on many occasions over the years, but the dominant image is of the old houses which remain, the oldest being in South Street and dating from the 14th century.

Within the memory of many of today's villagers great changes have been seen. In the 1940s Titchfield was able to boast having its own brewery, Fielders in Bridge Street, and its own gasworks, in Castle Street (known locally as Frog Lane). The gas showrooms are now the Co-op, whilst on the opposite side of The Square, the former grocery, iron-monger's and butcher's shops of Lankaster and Crooks, have been taken over by a bank, a book shop and an insurance agent.

Titchfield was once at the heart of a flourishing strawberry growing area, and although neighbouring Locksheath has seen its fields covered by housing estates, the farms surrounding Titchfield are still noted for today's Pick Your Own fruit trade. Titchfield was early to this business in the 1960s when local farmer Steve Harris was one of the first to open his fields to the public.

The older village industries, such as the tannery, now converted to small industrial units, have been replaced by new industries. Going up Southampton Hill and following the road towards Southampton are today's two biggest employers – Plessey Aerospace and the Office of Population, Censuses and Surveys (OPCS) from where the national census is conducted.

The winning of the Best Kept Village award is commemorated by a clock mounted in the High Street and plaques mounted on the parish room. The awards are a tribute to the spirit which still exists, and recent Christmases have seen a further tribute to this spirit – the village has been lit up by more than 100 Christmas trees on the outside of houses on every street.

Totton & Redbridge

There has been a settlement here for many centuries. Palaeolithic implements have been found and the nearby Tatchbury Mount Iron Age fort suggests occupation of the area from pre Roman times.

The natural outlet to the sea, with salt-producing marshes, would have made this an ideal place for a community to settle and trade. After the Norman conquest the area was divided into manors. These manors became hamlets and eventually joined to become Totton, which was once regarded as 'the largest village in England' and is now joined with Eling.

At Eling there has been a tide mill for centuries, mentioned in the Domesday Book, for milling the local flour. It is in production today, one of a few such mills in Europe and consequently a tourist attraction. The local wharfs where once ship building thrived now house timber merchants and light industry, while the creek is used also as a leisure amenity for sailing.

St Mary's church on the hill is of Saxon origin and its registers go back to 1537. The church is full of history and well worth a visit if only for the picture of 'The Last Supper' above the altar.

A Fair used to be held at Eling in the 19th century – this was a two day event but was banned from 1892 because of unruly behaviour. It was revived in 1951 as part of the Festival of Britain but has petered out and only the annual carnival now survives.

Rumbridge Street was the main shopping area until quite recently. The blacksmith's shop, carter's and waggonmaker were situated there. At the turn of the century a Mr C. F. Batt bought two cottages at a place where the coaches stopped. He turned these into a general stores and this is still a focal point in the area, known as 'Batt's Corner'.

There was a well known antiques shop in Station Road, where Queen Mary and others shopped – stopping the train and no doubt keeping it waiting. There was also the local Ashby's Brewery. William White's Gazeteer mentioned some three public houses in the area in 1859 and they are still in use: the Red Lion, Elephant and Castle and the Anchor.

Great Testwood House is the only local manor house to have survived until recent years. Queen Elizabeth I stayed there and is purported to have fallen off her horse into the river Test, being rescued by the bailiff.

In thanks she gave permission for cordwood to be taken from the New Forest. Of course, this house had its ghosts – it is said that a monk walks across the drive, disappears and then reappears further along on a path which is said to defy cultivation.

Many people commute to Southampton each day and also to the oil refinery at Fawley and, with the advent of the motorway (M27), further afield. The residential area to the west has expanded considerably – green fields becoming housing estates in almost a matter of months and joining the outlying New Forest villages to make the one-time village of Totton into a large sprawling conurbation.

On the other side of the river Test, across the causeway, is Redbridge. Once known as Reed-bridge, it derived its name from the reeds that grew and still grow in the river. In 1954 it was taken into the City of Southampton, and in recent years the area has been cut in half by the major road leading out to the West Country and by the building of fly-overs and a 20 storey block of flats, Redbridge Towers, which dominates the scene. Of the old buildings, the Ship Inn still exists and reminds one of the more leisurely days when horse-drawn coaches called at the village. This inn is reputed to have been a smugglers' haunt as at one time it had direct access to the river Test. The old bridges still span the river at a lower level than the causeway, and gazing northwards across the reeds and water, the traffic can temporarily be forgotten.

Twyford

Twyford, four miles south of Winchester, gets its name from the two fords across the river Itchen, world famous for its trout fishing. Today the village is bisected by the busy B3335 and villagers would welcome two crossing places. However, the installation of traffic lights in the centre of the village has eased the crossing problem.

Many of the village houses are some 200 years old and are crammed with history. Comparatively little new building has taken place since the completion of the council estate, which includes some sheltered housing.

The present church of St Mary was rebuilt in 1878, but it incorporates the 12th century nave arcades and the font. A window in the north wall dates back to 1520. Under the tower are twelve stones in a circle. These, combined with a well and an ancient yew tree, are said to provide the circle, wood and water needed for Druidic worship. The yew tree was mentioned in the Domesday Book and it provided the name for a flourishing linen embroidery cottage industry between 1926 and 1939. Scattered around the parish are several sarsen stones.

The whole village is full of history. A Roman villa was unearthed, at the top of Roman Road, in 1891. The Dolphin Inn is reputedly an 18th century coaching inn on the London to Southampton route. Twyford House also dates back to the early 18th century. It belonged to the Shipley family. Bishop Jonathan Shipley, Bishop of St Asaph, invited his friend Benjamin Franklin, the American statesman, to stay in 1771 and it was there that he wrote part of his memoirs. The poet Alexander Pope briefly attended a school at Segars Buildings (since destroyed). This school was the forerunner of the present Twyford Preparatory School.

Brambridge House stands on the edge of the village. The avenue of limes leading to the house was planted in the reign of Charles II. Brambridge House was the family home of Maria Smythe who, as the widowed Mrs Fitzherbert, contracted a morganatic marriage with the Prince Regent in December 1785. The original house was burned down in 1872 and the present house and stables have been converted into flats.

There has been a village school since 1834. The first schoolroom was in Hazeley Road and is now in the yard of Mr Lampard, the builder. The present school was built in 1861. The most remarkable teacher was Mr Gilbert who taught there for 47 years, before and during the First World War. He was also organist, choirmaster, leader of the village band and the cycling club and a keen painter.

The village has memories of various wars. The barn at Manor Farm was used to quarter troops during the Civil War. Army Row (next to the post office garden) was built to house veterans of Waterloo. In the First World War troops were encamped on Hazeley Down. There is a monument on the Down to record this. Villagers ran a canteen for the soldiers in the village hall. In the Second World War Canadian soldiers were billeted in the village and joined in village activities.

The only surviving custom is the Bell Ringers' Feast. Legend has it that William Davis was returning home on horseback over the downs when the mist came down. The bells of Twyford church warned him that he was on the edge of a deep chalk pit. In his will he left a guinea to the bell ringers so long as they rang a peal morning and evening on 7th October. The bells are rung accordingly and the bell ringers enjoy supper together afterwards.

It is easier to write of the past than the present. The village is prosperous, the streets full of cars. The three mixed farms and large chicken farm provide some employment, but most people work outside the village. Is it perhaps indicative of the age that there are three pubs, three antiques shops and a hairdresser, but only one grocer, with a post office, one butcher and one ironmonger?

Dutch Elm disease drastically changed the parish landscape and more trees were lost in the 1987 hurricane. Fortunately many trees are now being planted.

The footpaths by the Itchen Navigation Canal and others leading up over the chalk downs reveal a wealth of plants, birds and insects and contribute to the pleasure of living in Twyford.

Upper Clatford 🌿

Upper Clatford lies one and a quarter miles south of Andover. It is a most delightful village with a beautiful church and the river Anton flowing through the valley.

It was probably during the reign of Henry I (1100–1135) that the church of All Saints was first built. Its massive columns and round arches are typical of the first half of the 12th century. A little of this style can still be seen in the south wall and in the north-east corner of the tower, as well as on the large round stone, and two half-round pillars dividing the nave from the chancel. This was rebuilt in the 16th century and the building transformed into an 'auditory church' in the 17th century. Even so a large proportion of the congregation still cannot see the altar.

The fine house known as Red Rice stands in the parish of Upper Clatford, having been built by General Webb in about 1740. General Webb was one of the Duke of Marlborough's subordinates, and it is said that the trees in the park surrounding the house represent the troop line-up at the battle of Malplaquet in 1709.

Bury Hill hill fort has no known history, unlike its famous neighbour Danebury Ring four miles away. Some exploration was carried out in the 1930s but did not bring forth much information, and another dig is to take place in the near future.

A famous feature of Anna Valley (also part of the parish) was the well-known firm of Taskers which for more than 160 years provided employment for many local people. Founded in 1873 by three brothers, the foundry manufactured cottage pumps, agricultural machinery, steam engines, iron bridges (one is still in use today in the village by Fishing Cottage) and, during the Second World War, aeroplane trailers large enough to carry completed aeroplanes for the RAF.

The Tasker brothers provided housing, a school, church and a workman's rest for the people of Anna Valley. The school house can still be seen, called the Lodge. The left-hand side of the Lodge was the dwelling place of the schoolmistress and over the arch to the other side was the schoolroom. The Lodge has recently been repaired and is said to be one of only a few of this design of building. It has become one of the many Listed properties in the parish, many being beautiful thatched cottages several hundred years old, including the post office and the village pub, the Crook and Shears.

231

Sadly, the Anna Valley area has altered dramatically with Taskers having been replaced by a modern housing estate. Very little is left to show what was there in the past. Brook House, the home of the Taskers, still remains and again has been renovated recently.

At the beginning of the 20th century, Clatford was a farming community with many people working on the land. It had many shops, and transport to town by horse and cart. However, change has taken place and it is rapidly losing its rural feel. Although it has been designated a conservation area, one feels it gets closer to Andover all the time.

There is still farming, but this employs very few people today. Recently a vineyard has been planted out in the village which is an encouragement to rural life and may reduce the fear of more housing development taking place. There is other work in the village, which includes a rubber stamp company, chick rearing, watercress beds and a few other small industrial companies.

Upper Clatford is still, however, a village with a heart. Its three churches are all well attended each week with a good congregation, and an active community spirit. It is also lucky to have a very good village school shared with Goodworth Clatford, a post office, village shop and village pub.

Upton Grey

Upton Grey is one of Hampshire's most attractive villages, a pond at the junction of the village street and the Weston Patrick road, with its ducks donated by a local resident, being a feature which identifies the village for many people from local towns.

The residents comprise a few only who have lived all their lives in the village and on them the village depends for continuity and its history. Most of the other residents are commuters to London or some of the larger towns in the area or are people who have retired to the village. Very few earn their livelihood in the village.

Known in Saxon times as Aoltone, and later as Upetone and Upetona, it was owned for 200 years by the De Grey family. In olden times the village was served by a baker, a blacksmith, a carpenter, a cordwainer, a maltster, a tailor and a wheelwright. Farming was the main industry.

St Mary's church dates back to Norman times, although there was a church on the site in Saxon times. The vicar now has to serve five parishes. There is a village shop which caters for all requests, a pub (the Hoddington Arms), a post office and a village hall, but sadly the school has closed. There are also some fine old houses, one or two being 16th century and thatched. One is said to house the ghost of a monk, seen by various people over its 400 years.

The Pond House once housed the tailor, whose lamp lit up the pond. In those days it froze over in winter so the locals would skate on it by the light of the tailor's lamp. In another old house it is said that the men of the adjoining cottages met over a fence in their respective cellars for a glass of beer!

The main village events revolve round the church and the village hall, such as the annual fete, cheese and wine parties and jumble sales. As the community is small, fund raising in such ways is essential. Happily the village still has its Flower Show on the second Saturday in August and the WI holds an annual party for pensioners each December. All these events bring together the long established and the new residents.

Wallington 🦢

Wallington is an old village situated on the east bank of the river Wallington, which flows through the length of the village. It is over-looked by Fort Wallington, one of the chain of forts which were built along Portsdown Hill as a result of the Royal Commission of 1859.

The river is well known for its coarse fish such as carp, roach and dace, and there are many native trees such as oak, ash, hazel and field maple. There is a thriving badger population, plus urban foxes and deer, and this in spite of the presence of the M27 which crosses the northern end of the village. There is no church, but the two pubs, the White Horse and the Cob and Pen, are always busy, especially on Sunday mornings! A popular village shop is also part of the life of the community.

In 1784 William Thresher of Fareham built a tannery in Wallington, which in later years was run by the Sharland family. The production of high quality leather gave employment to many local men. The work must have been hard and laborious, starting at 6 am and finishing at 5.30 pm; all for under £1 a week for the majority of the workers. The tannery continued to produce good quality hides until about 1910 when it was closed down.

The present day villagers consist of the descendants of the old rural, farming and tanning families, together with many new arrivals who have moved into the village over the past 30 years or so, and today between them run a successful Wallington Village Community (WVC). This is directed by an Executive Committee and a busy, imaginative social committee.

There is also a programme of environmental improvement which includes coppicing of trees on the riverbanks, siting of bat and dormouse boxes, and tree planting. Ducks and geese have been introduced to the river and a badger survey (now the subject of lectures) has been carried out by two members of the community. The river is partly tidal, so over the years there has been occasional heavy flooding; however, with modern river management this rarely happens today.

Waltham Chase 🦚

A Chase (or Chace) was a piece of land reserved by the Crown or a local lord for hunting. After the Bishop's Palace had been built at Waltham in the 12th century, Waltham Chase was used as a hunting ground by successive bishops. The chase began at Waltham Park and ran to the south and east, stretching as far as the Bere Forest at Soberton, covering a much larger area than the present village of the same name. Waltham Chase is now part of the ancient Chase, formerly of Droxford parish and now of Shedfield parish.

The deer with which the Chase had been stocked were a nuisance to the labouring tenants whose crops they ate, but it was not until the 18th century that the Waltham Blacks appeared. They were young men who blacked their faces, disguised themselves and stole the bishop's deer. Further, they went on to rob stagecoaches and were much feared by travellers.

In 1722 Parliament, having been urged to do so by Bishop Trimmell, passed a Black Act which listed hundreds of offences, many punishable by death. A gibbet was erected by the roadside hedge of what is now the Triangle Recreation Ground. Although scholars believe the Black Act was not called into use, the gibbet was used more than once. However in 1742 when Bishop Hoadley was asked to restock the Chase with deer, he refused, saying it had done enough harm already.

Waltham Chase village was enclosed, with Droxford parish, in 1855. After that the forest was gradually cut down. At the turn of the century a sawmill was built in Brooklynn Meadow, near the brook. This large black shed stood for about 90 years but had ceased to be used. In 1989 it was demolished, prior to houses being built on the meadow.

Following enclosures, common wasteland was sold for seven shillings an acre. Market gardening became important and there were many smallholders. Strawberry growing was an important industry by the turn of the century, until the Second World War. Many growers took their fruit by horse and van to Botley station where they queued up for their turn to unload. The growers' carriage charges helped the railway and the service provided by the railway helped the growers. Much of the fruit was sent to London hotels.

234

Since the 1940s Waltham Chase has had more than its fair share of building and most of the meadows have disappeared under houses. The resultant newcomers have been good for the village however, and Waltham Chase is a lively village with a good community spirit.

Warnford ఇఫ్చిం

One and a half miles south of West Meon lies the small village of Warnford. Its main claim to fame is the watercress beds fed from artesian wells deep in the chalk, but behind the quiet façade lies a thriving village. Many of the redundant farm buildings have been converted for rural industries, namely a cracker factory, car repair workshop, decorative blacksmith, garden fencing and garden machinery companies, a printer, trout farm, the Meon Valley Study Centre and an engineering company specialising in such things as farm gates.

In the centre of the village is the George and Falcon, which Charles II is said to have visited on his way down to Shoreham to cross to France.

On the east side of the A32 lies Warnford Park and hidden behind the trees is the church of Our Lady. Founded in AD 682 by St Wilfred and rebuilt by the Normans, it is well worth a visit. (Please note that there is only a right-of-way on foot.)

In the churchyard is the grave of George Lewis, carpenter-handyman to the estate, who died on 17th December 1830, aged 41 years. Carved on the gravestone is a tree with a saw lying against it. The legend is that George was working on a Sunday, sawing down trees and incurring the Lord's wrath. A limb fell on him and he consequently died.

Warsash ఇఫ్చిం

Warsash is situated on the eastern bank of the river Hamble, near the entrance of the river into Southampton Water, and opposite the village of Hamble. The parish is known as Hook-with-Warsash because of the links with the nearby village of Hook. The church and the old school are between the two villages, and about a mile from the centre of present day Warsash, where you will find the shops and three public houses.

Modern building and development have covered up many traces of what used to be, and have made the whole area south of the A27, from Sarisbury and Park Gate to Warsash and Locks Heath, seem like a large dormitory town. However, Warsash was a busy and popular village extending from the seashore and riverbank inland for about a mile, and today the village community spirit in this area is strong.

By the crossroads in the centre of the village is the clock tower, which was built as a water tower to supply Warsash House and estate with water. King Edward VII used to visit Warsash House when he was Prince of Wales. The big house was pulled down and a modern estate built just before the Second World War, but the water tower and model farmhouse remain. The clock on the tower struck ship's bell time until an electric clock was installed in 1945.

Ship-building and fishing were very important occupations – crabs, lobsters and shellfish provided the living for several families. Crab teas were provided near the shore and became famous locally. People travelled by horse bus from Gosport and Fareham to sample them down by the Hamble shore. The Rising Sun (where teas were once served) is still a very popular public house – even if it does face west and not east! – but the fishing trade and teas, although gone, are not forgotten.

The land in this area is very stony and is ideal for growing strawberries. Twenty years ago, on a fine summer's day the smell of strawberries was all pervading. The trade has been important to the area for many years, the fruit being taken in special baskets, by horse and cart, to Swanwick station and thence to London and other big cities. Strawberries are still sold at the side of the road in season, but most of this land is now occupied by houses.

The College of Maritime Studies, situated where the old coastguard station used to be, has trained countless Merchant Navy seamen from all over the world, from the young to the experienced. It is possible to steer one of the world's largest oil tankers and bring it into port and never leave the college buildings, thanks to modern technology!

Yet, very near here, a century or more ago, salt was collected from the salterns after the sea water had evaporated. Wooden posts can still be seen at low tide marking this area. Later, live fish were kept in a fish pond until sold, and crabs were kept in special boxes with holes drilled in the sides so that they could be kept alive and fresh in sea water. Later still, towards the end of the Second World War, Royal Marines in a fleet of small boats went across the Channel from here to take part in the Normandy landings. A footpath follows the bank of the river Hamble from Warsash Hard to the Point where it joins the sea, past and through where all these activities took place.

A ferry runs regularly across the river Hamble to Hamble village. Some people travel to work that way, and it is very popular with holidaymakers. Once it was a rowing boat but is now a small purpose-built ferry carrying adults, children, dogs and bicycles. It operates all year round and the ferryman is a fount of local knowledge.

Wellow ✍

Wellow covers a large area, divided by the river Blackwater into two parts known as East and West Wellow. The village has become increasingly populated in the lifetime of some of the older inhabitants, and now has the modern amenities of mains water, electricity and sewerage. All of which these villagers had earlier to live without. Water was from wells and tanks, lighting by lamps and candles, while the privy was a wooden-seated earth closet, with seats for two or more at a time!

The church, St Margaret's, stands in a more remote situation. It was built by 1216, and it is thought that at one time it was probably in the middle of the village, before the evacuation of people due to the plague in 1665. The church is well known and is visited by many people, especially nurses, from all parts of the world, who come to see the grave of Florence Nightingale in the churchyard. The tomb bears a very simple inscription, 'F.N. 1820–1910', in accordance with her wishes. Many villagers recall the actual funeral, which must have been a momentous occasion for Wellow. Inside the church there are mementoes of Florence Nightingale's life, including a lamp.

Florence Nightingale lived at Embley Park during her childhood. The large brick house is now a public school for boys. The park and gardens contain many varieties of large rhododendrons and azaleas. The farmland around it has changed somewhat in the last few years, as it has been planted with vines by Wellow Vineyards. The house also now overlooks man-made fishing lakes. Certainly a change of landscape.

Connecting part of the Embley estate was a carriage driveway over a bridge on a roadway beneath. This was known as Sounding Arch, a very substantial construction of stonework. It was in a deep cutting and the actual archway was quite long, hence the name because noises echoed – horses' hooves, shouting, and later car horns. Stories were told of ghostly coaches passing over, past the iron railings on the top, at midnight on New Year or Christmas nights.

The Sounding Arch was demolished, as road widening became a necessary safety factor. A seat was made from some of the stone, and now marks the spot where once it stood. One stone was used in the churchyard to mark the grave of a young lad killed on the road. There is also a wooden cross by a roadside to mark the first fatal car accident in Wellow in 1911. It is sad to think that the busy A36 has claimed several victims since, and how many accidents occur nowadays. But the small roads and lanes about the village are still pleasant. One has a ford with a footbridge; this is Rix's Ford, and is a lovely quiet spot. In flood many cars get stuck, as the water can be quite deep and wide. The local farmer has to come to the rescue with his tractor, after the hapless motorist has waded, barefoot, from his car.

There were village shops, a bakery, a wheelwright's, a brickworks and many local industries, replaced now with the necessary shops for everyday life. There remains one character equal to the personalities of the past – Carlo, who makes his famous home-made ice cream and sells it from his small home.

The village, in common with many nowadays, has a very practical, purpose-built village hall, but before this there were two previous reading rooms. This name was carried on from the first wooden building, which was a men's club. Women, drink and gambling were forbidden! Subscription was 2/-, to read books, or newspapers, and enjoy a game of billiards. In 1898 a new building, 'a picturesque structure of the Swiss chalet order', was erected on a different site, brought by horse-drawn cart from Romsey railway station. This was the new reading room, and for 82 years it was well used for lectures, concerts, film shows, and by local organisations.

Wellow has two pubs, although it used to have many more. The oldest surviving one is the Red Rover, which was a coaching inn and was named after one of the famous stage-coaches. The Rockingham Arms started out as a chapel, it is believed, but, never completed, it was sold to a brewery and became a pub.

West End

If you drive on the B3035 from east to west and pass through West End High Street, you might be forgiven for thinking that the village comprises just some post-war shops and one or two pubs. How wrong you would be. As far back as 1320 Hatch Grange was recorded as the home of John de Hache, when the area was mainly heath and open fields. Hatch Grange woods and meadows still exist.

In the living memory of those over 50 years old, the village was still very much a country place. Yet by 1993 West End will be well and truly upon the map as the new home of the Hampshire County Cricket Ground. This will be developed, together with a nine-hole golf course and other facilities upon Hickley Farm, where in the 19th century an enterprising farmer introduced the commercial growing of tomatoes. But at first the suspicious villagers would not eat them!

West End (originally Westend) was on the main turnpike road from Portsmouth to Romsey, via Botley and Swaythling, and the mail coaches went through to Poole. It is on a high ridge and has views across the Itchen valley – indeed, the main entrance to the Itchen Valley Country

Park is on the eastern boundary of the village in Allington Lane. Armies have camped on the high places, particularly in the time of Napoleon, and the roads named Beacon Road and Telegraph Road indicate older beacons and the telegraph station which sent messages from Portsmouth to London.

The high and the lowly knew West End. The South Stoneham Institute (the workhouse) was erected in 1848 but an even earlier poorhouse existed. The buildings, together with extensions, now comprise Moorgreen Hospital and the Countess Mountbatten Hospice, the latter one of the pioneers of the hospice concept.

In the 19th century the very large estate of Harefield was owned by Edwin Jones (founder and owner of a large department store in Southampton, now known as Debenhams). Although Harefield was acquired from West End by Southampton in 1954 for the building of a large housing estate, many trees still remain and the roads take the original paths through the estate.

Quality paper was made until recent years at Gater's Mill. Henry Portal was originally apprenticed here and moved to north Hampshire with some West End men to start up the now famous Portal Bank Note Company at Laverstoke.

The New Inn (now renamed the Lamp and Mantle) was a central point in the village, having a large green in front of it. Parties were held here or a circus might come. The animals grazed on land which is now Swan Nurseries. In more recent years, the large house and garden called The Wilderness on the corner of West End Road (opposite St James's church) was the centre for the carnival. This is now held on Hatch Grange every June.

West End today is still known to the residents as 'the village'. Relatively few still work in the village, most travelling east and west on the motorway or even to London via Parkway/Eastleigh. Inevitably, new building keeps taking place but the recently formed Friends of Hatch Grange are successfully preserving that part of the village for future generations.

West Meon 🐚

Like many Hampshire villages, West Meon suffers the disadvantage of a surfeit of traffic. The main A23 road divides the west from the east. Cars, lorries and juggernauts thunder through – many ignoring the 30 mph signs. However, for its 700 inhabitants there are many advantages. The village boasts a school, a village hall, a post office, a doctors' surgery, plus two pubs, a grocer's shop and an excellent butcher. The knapped flint church of St John built in 1846 has a fine set of eight bells. The river Meon runs through an area of outstanding natural beauty, and timbered and thatched houses add to the village's rural charm.

Mr Gardiner was the verger at St John's church. He mended shoes in the house now known as Warnford Corner, and before the house was altered there was a hole in the wall on Church Path where the villagers would put their boots and shoes for repair. He was very strict and in the days when everybody went to church, including the children, he would rap the boys with his long staff if they misbehaved themselves. The boys of the village had their revenge. Late in life he married a widow at St John's and dressed in his best smock for the occasion. As he was returning from church with his bride all the boys of the village hid behind the wall and pelted them with clods of earth.

Opposite Warnford Corner is a house called Rose Cottage, which has had its staircase in three different places. Many, many years ago an old gentleman died there and the staircase then was so narrow that the coffin had to be lowered out of a bedroom window to the waiting bearers below. In another cottage in the village there is a 'coffin door' on the staircase to allow a coffin to be manoeuvred round the narrow, twisting stairs.

Although there are now many people using the village as a dormitory, there is still a strong sense of community. Clubs and social activities catering for all ages abound. Sadly there is as yet no provision for housing for those youngsters who would like to marry and spend the rest of their days in this delightful part of the Meon Valley.

Weston Patrick
& Weston Corbett

If you look in the churchyard at Weston Patrick, you will find a number of tombstones to the memory of the Green family. In the church itself, hanging on the wall by the font is part of an altar frontal dated 1682 with the initials G. G. and I. R., which stand for George Green and Isaac Round, who were the churchwardens at that time. The Greens were an important family, owning land in both Weston Corbett and Weston Patrick.

Their farming must have been prosperous as at some time in the 17th century Weston Corbett House must have been built. The family continued living there until the middle of the 19th century, when the last George Green died, leaving the house to his two maiden sisters. On their death the house was left to Thomas Henry Wyatt and the Wyatt family lived there until the 1920s.

The main room of the house was known as the 'houseplace' and all the cooking was done in the original fireplace. When T. H. Wyatt first visited the house in 1848, the farmworkers slept in the attics and they and the family all had their meals in the 'houseplace'!

The kitchen was one of the finest and most complete of the period. Above the fireplace were racks with the old fowling pieces, whose barrels were some eight to ten feet long, together with the shot moulds and powder flasks. Then there were the spits and jack for roasting the meat, the large iron pots and the beautiful copper vessels. The furniture was simple, consisting of a refectory table and simple chairs and stools. Also, there were the usual household items, such as goffering irons, candle snuffers, a warming pan, a leather bottle and many other bits and pieces.

It is still possible to see the kitchen today, complete but slightly rearranged, at Sulgrave Manor, the George Washington Memorial Home near Banbury. One point, perhaps, that should be mentioned, is that the mousetrap on the table at Sulgrave did not come from Weston Corbett!

Wherwell ✦

Wherwell, with the hamlet of Fullerton to the west, is approximately one mile wide and three miles long. It is a village in northern Hampshire with a population of 500. Situated on the river Test, a chalk stream rising at Overton and flowing into Southampton Water at Redbridge, it is renowned for its fly fishing for trout. Occasionally salmon come this far up river to spawn.

When Winchester was the capital of England, Wherwell was a royal hunting lodge. Part of Harewood Forest is still in the parish. In the 10th century Elfrida married King Edgar, who owned the manor, but after his death she murdered his son at Corfe Castle. In expiation of this crime she founded the abbey of Wherwell and ended her life in penance. Nothing remains today, but 'The Priory' was built on the same site. The church, which was not the original church for the abbey but stood very close to it, was destroyed in 1858. The present church of St Peter and Holy Cross was built on the same site. A painting of the original church hangs there today.

Until recently Easter cakes were made and marked with an ancient seal of the priory. An interesting charity recorded in the church is that in 1691 Philadelphia Whitehead, out of the yearly rent of the White Lion, made available twelve shillings a year for ever, to be paid to twelve of the oldest parishioners. Until recently this was still paid by the brewers, who now own the White Lion. Today the brewers give a lump sum of money to be invested. A previous Oxford College charity which gave a yearly income to any man who lived alone, and was a deserving case for help, has also invested the money. Trustees from the village meet three times a year to assess if anyone has a particular need.

In the centre of the lawn at The Priory is a tree stump. The tree was blown down some years ago, and under the roots was found the body of a man covered by a hurdle. Legend says a great treasure is buried there, but anyone trying to recover it would pay the penalty of sudden death.

A weather vane depicting a cockatrice used to be fixed on the church spire but it is now in Andover Museum. The story goes that many years ago, in a dungeon beneath the priory, a duck laid an egg, which was hatched by a toad and produced a cockatrice, a fearsome monster. A reward of four acres of land was offered to anyone who could slay the monster and various people lost their lives trying. A servant at the priory called Green obtained a large steel mirror, which was lowered into the dungeon. The cockatrice, seeing another of its kind, exhausted himself trying to kill the newcomer, whereupon the valiant Green descended into the dungeon and slew it with a spear. In Harewood Forest today there is a piece of land, exactly four acres, known as Green's Acres.

At Fullerton, by the old canal and the river Anton are the remains of a Roman villa. A large corner of mosaic floor was found and is now in the hall of a local house.

A cannon ball fired by Oliver Cromwell's men against the priory is kept at the White Lion, where it is supposed to have fallen down its chimney.

On the approach to the village from Winchester is Toll Cottage, reputed to be one of the oldest cottages in Hampshire. A great many cottages in Wherwell are thatched, with timbering and wattle and daub walls.

Until the late 1920s there was a station with a direct line to Waterloo, and with a junction at Fullerton to Southampton, Andover and Gloucester. Buses started running from Andover to Romsey in 1936. Now only a few run to Andover which is four miles away.

Whitchurch

Whitchurch is tucked in a fold of the hills where the river Test meanders. It had three old watermills, harnessing the water to run machinery for the making of silk cloth, and a fulling mill for the washing and thickening of woollen cloth.

The silk mill has recently been restored and works regularly weaving silk. A shop sells the finished product to the many visitors. The church of All Hallows was founded early and has additions of various periods, from the 13th to the 19th centuries. There is also a Methodist chapel, a modern Roman Catholic church and a very old Baptist chapel.

In the 16th century Whitchurch was one of the largest towns in Hampshire, on land with evidence of human habitation since Neolithic times. The White Hart Inn in the centre was on old coaching inn on the road to Salisbury. Then the railways came, bringing navvies to dig the cuttings and build the bridges that are still used by the London to Salisbury line. The men got thirsty so there were a large number of pubs, some of which are still functioning. Others are known now only by their names, such as the Pineapple. After the Second World War new housing estates were built and Whitchurch grew.

Although fishing on the Test has become a pastime for the rich, everyone can enjoy feeding the ducks from one or other of the bridges that cross the river in the area. The silk mill bridge or the town bridge are restful reminders that there is still wonderful country around Whitchurch.

Whitehill

Whitehill is a comparatively new village, but there is evidence to show that there were inhabited settlements in the area as far back as Stone Age times. In 1867 at Hogmoor Enclosure, part of Whitehill village, the largest hoard of Roman relics ever discovered in Great Britain was unearthed. This find included bronze swords, bladed spearheads and Roman coins, now on display at the British Museum. There have been many Roman 'finds' in this area, probably due to the fact that the Roman road from the fort at Portchester through to Aldershot runs through Blackmoor and the edge of Whitehill village.

It was in 1866, however, that a small flint and stone house was built and later that year the first person was born in Whitehill. She was christened with the new village in her name: Alice Whitehill Lemon.

In 1902 Bordon Camp came into being and a military railway line was built from Longmoor to Bordon, which ran through Whitehill. During the transportation of sheds from Longmoor to Bordon Camp, one fell off the line at Whitehill and this was used as a police station.

On 3rd July 1905 the first sitting of the Whitehill Petty Sessions took place. One of the first cases it heard was of an offender begging alms at Whitehill and he was sentenced to seven days hard labour!

Whitehill Working Men's Club was built in 1902. Members were not allowed to bring guests into the club and everyone was limited to two pints of beer a night! Many Canadian troops stationed in Bordon during the war used Whitehill Club's facilities and helped the club to level the ground for a cricket pitch to be laid. In appreciation Whitehill Club named it the Maple Leaf Cricket Ground and so it is still named today.

When Whitehill Parish Council was formed in 1928 one of their earlier tasks was to organise the King George V's Jubilee celebrations. These took place on Lovell's Field, on 6th May 1935. There were fancy dress competitions, children's and old folk's tea parties, sports races (which included one for errand boys), and a special prize of ten shillings was given to the oldest and youngest parishioner on the field at 4 pm.

Whitehill village hall was built in the early 1970s and together with the working men's club has become the meeting point for many local people. In the last 20 years or so a great number of new houses have been built in Whitehill and this has brought many new people to the village. It is hoped that the new facilities planned for the area will continue to bring the people of Whitehill together as a community.

Wickham 🦢

The lovely village of Wickham has a large square, said to be the second largest in the country. Shops surround the square, along with Georgian houses, and there are 16th century houses just around the corner. The population of the village is over 4,000.

Wickham was the birthplace of William of Wykeham, Bishop of Winchester and founder of Winchester College, in the 14th century.

The mound on which the church is built was used by Celts and Saxons for burial or religious rites. St Nicholas' was built by the Normans in 1120, but has been thoroughly altered since. Inside there is a large memorial to the Uvedale family, once lords of the manor.

In 1268 King Henry III granted a charter to the lord of the manor, Roger de Scures, to hold an annual fair. One has been held every year since – even during wartime.

At the turn of the century a railway was constructed, but it was closed in 1955. In those days one could catch a train from Wickham to London.

The old Victory Hall, now being made into flats, beside the river Meon, was once a busy tannery where men from the village worked. Later it became a brewery, with heavy horses coming and going, pulling great drays loaded with barrels. What horror was felt by the villagers when part of the building caught fire and the horses perished. But it was rebuilt and there is still a plaque on the rear of the building saying 'Wickham Brewery rebuilt ANO DMI 1887 being the Jubilee Year of the Reign of H.M. Queen Victoria'. The brewery closed in 1910 and later the Victory Club was formed to commemorate victory in the First World War. It was used in the Second World War as home and refuge for many evacuees from Portsmouth and Southampton.

Village life in the 1930s presented a very different picture from today. If you had walked into the square then, you would have seen only two cars! During the Second World War things changed drastically. 'Beverley' was used as a Naval maternity hospital and there were large influxes of evacuees. There was an army headquarters in the Kings Head public house, Canadian soldiers at Rookesbury School, and army engineers took over part of a garage along the Fareham road. A great many of the engineers married local girls and settled here after the war.

There were soldiers everywhere – they lined the roads ready for transportation to the French coast. One soldier scratched an incription on the Rookesbury wall which was sadly destroyed during the hurricane of 1987. Just behind this wall , it is said, there is the 'Ghost of Rookesbury' – a lady who rides around the estate on a white horse.

Wield ✤

Wield comprises the two villages of Upper Wield and Lower Wield, the first being a 'green' village with the houses formally arranged round a green and the latter a 'street' village with the houses mainly along a single lane.

Upper Wield's most notable building is its 12th century church of St James. This is always open to the visitor. It still retains most of its Norman architecture and there are many vestiges of wall paintings which date from medieval times to Queen Anne's reign. Her royal coat of arms can be seen above the chancel arch. The church also contains a large memorial to Henry Wallop and his wife. This is not only a beautiful piece of alabaster carving but the inscription is a remarkable piece of snobbery which eulogises Henry's brother and appears to mention the deceased almost as an afterthought.

Immediately outside the churchyard is the small post office which has a seasonal succession of flowers growing throughout the year.

Looking from the green there is a charming scene of a group of thatched cottages with the church behind them. This is best seen in the early morning when the sun glints on the golden weathercock on the wooden church spire. Only one cottage is still thatched in the 'longstraw' or 'Hampshire' thatch, the others favouring the 'wheat reed' style which is more hard-wearing.

There is a small manor house, in the grounds of which can be seen the remains of the village well. Next to the green is a large house built on the foundations of a great Tudor house, one of many visited by Queen Elizabeth I on her royal progresses.

There is a tiny Primitive Methodist chapel, which speaks of dissension in the village 100 years ago. Religion caused great disruption in 1851 when William Budge, a Mormon, came from America looking for converts. They were baptised in Wield Wood pond and some emigrated to Utah. Between 1851 and 1861 the population of the village dropped by over a quarter. Some of these probably emigrated, while others went to work in factory towns hoping for better wages.

The census of 1881 shows that 90 per cent of the population were engaged in agricultural or allied jobs. Today the percentage has dropped to less than 0.5 per cent as mechanisation has altered farming methods and people have moved into the village from surrounding towns.

Lower Wield may not have a church or a chapel but it does contain the Yew Tree pub, which is now a popular place to eat. It is directly opposite one of the prettiest cricket fields in the county. This is a pleasant place to have a picnic on a summer Sunday. Straying from the match and walking through the village will reward you with the sight of some very attractive houses.

Wolverton ✤

Wolverton is a scattered community of some 70 houses set in beautiful open farmland, interspersed with fine woodlands, under the north Hampshire downs.

It has a church, two large houses worthy of note, two inns, a forge and a thatched village hall. Once it had a school, several little shops and a much larger population. Many of the larger residences of the present day were once rows of cottages housing several families.

The church is dedicated to St Catherine and it is thought that there has been a church on the site since 1286. In 1717 it was reconstructed by a pupil of Sir Christopher Wren, who encased the existing structure in brick. In 1872 it was restored again, not very tastefully. A beautiful white marble vase font was thrown out into the churchyard and replaced with a modern one. This fell to pieces in 1920 and the old vase font was put back. The church has boxed pews, and, amongst its treasures, a handsome Dutch candelabra which was found in the old rectory attic. This is thought to have been a gift from Charles Van Notten, who purchased the manor in 1782.

The original rectory was The Old House in what is still called Rectory Lane. It is a very attractive building, part Elizabethan and part Georgian, and its grounds possess some very fine trees. The present rectory, near the church, was built in 1926.

The other house of some significance is the Park House and there is evidence that Queen Eleanor lived in a house on the site for some time while her husband Henry II was in Normandy. The house eventually became the property of the Duke of Wellington. In the early 20th century it was rented out to Squire Wallace Walker, a much loved man, who lived there until his death in 1937. The Duke of Wellington sold his estates in Wolverton to pay death duties and during the Second World War the Park House was used as army headquarters. It is now once again in private ownership.

Of the two inns the Hare and Hounds was built first, in the late 16th century. It was owned for generations by the Davis family. The last Mr Davis ran a horse and cart carrier service twice a week to Basingstoke and once a week to Newbury. These journeys took all day, as much shopping was done for the villagers. In 1920 Mr Davis ran a 14 seater bus to the towns, giving the villagers a chance to do their own shopping.

The George and Dragon was built in 1760 in the days of coaches and still has a whip rack in the parlour used by the coachmen while they slaked their thirst. When the inn was undergoing alterations a matchbox of polished boxwood, dated 1768, was found. This contained matches as fine as hairpins which struck perfectly.

The forge was built in 1750 and has been in the Wiggins family for many years. In the heyday of the horse, six men worked there in two forges. Now, instead of the horses coming to him, the farrier travels many miles to the racing stables that abound in north Hampshire and neighbouring Berkshire.

The village hall was built in the early part of the 20th century on a site donated by the Duke of Wellington. Villagers made the bricks from clay dug from the field behind the site. These were dried in the sun. Squire Walker and his men laid the wooden floor on top of larch poles, and the estate carpenter made the doors and window frames. The roof was thatched. The mud bricks eventually disintegrated and were replaced by concrete blocks at the end of the Second World War.

Before the post office was opened the mail was collected from Baughurst, some miles away, and delivered on foot by Mr Froome. Mr Froome lived in one of four small cottages known as Poors Cottages. They were built by Sir George Brown, a resident of the village until his death in 1685, when under his will a trust fund was started for the benefit of the poor. This trust still exists today and village pensioners benefit as the result of his generosity. Poors Cottages have been sold and converted into one house which is in private ownership.

Woodgreen ✦

In the north-west corner of the New Forest, the woods slope gently down to the river Avon; a quiet secluded place for anyone avoiding authority. And so the early settlement was formed, by proud, independent people with no lord of the manor or vicar.

As transport improved, more people came and more sophisticated houses were built; also a modern church and chapel. Woodgreen was now a real village. Like many villages it has houses of all dates and materials – from the Elizabethan cottage, now a garden shed, through lath and plaster, bricks and mortar, to one apparently built entirely of glass.

The village green with its dells and hillocks has its own cricket pitch, lovingly maintained. Cricket matches and teas served from the thatched pavilion, are a feature of week-ends throughout the summer, while ponies and foals, cows and calves graze happily round the common.

A local shop with the post office is an important part of the village, and the Horse and Groom, the village 'local', is in the centre of the village.

Before the village hall was built in 1932, meetings took place in a wooden hut on the green. This had a tin roof and the village lads would throw stones on to it during meetings. Vaughan Nash, who lived in the village, was a friend of the principal of the London Art College. He suggested that he send down students to paint murals on the walls of the new village hall, as he was worried about the art dying out. As a result, Mr Baker and Mr Payne came down and painted murals depicting village life throughout the year, using the local people as models. The TV show *All Our Yesterdays* took these murals for the subject of one of their programmes entitled 'The Village On the Wall'. Since then many people have come to the village to see them. If they are lucky they are given an excellent talk on the murals, including many interesting and amusing anecdotes, by Jim Hooper. Jim was one of the children on the wall in the Sunday school mural. He is now Chairman of the Woodgreen Council.

Over the past 50 years changes have come about in the village. More people have come to live here, so there are retired people and young ones who go daily to work in Salisbury or further afield. But still there are many activities. The Cricket Club is flourishing, the Red Cross members do much fund raising and also run a very successful club for the handicapped, the Horticultural Society unites with the neighbouring village of Hale and has over 100 members. There is no Morris dancing now, but an active group of hand bell ringers entertains locally and round the district.

Woodgreen cannot boast any large or famous buildings but, across the water meadows, past the ancient mill by the river Avon, is the village of Breamore. Woodgreen children once went to school there, a mile walk in each direction, or by horse and cart if the river was flooded. Breamore village has a beautiful Elizabethan manor house, Saxon church and a countryside museum with a collection of treasures showing the life of the past.

The population of Woodgreen is changing slowly, with more weekenders coming to live here and old houses being enlarged, but the forest animals still roam freely through the village and the stories of the village live on in the murals of the 'Village on the Wall'.

Woodlands 🐚

Where on earth is Woodlands? Originally a small part of the parish of Eling, it is now in the parish of Netley Marsh, which was formed from Eling in 1894.

Woodlands was originally merely a wooded area, part of a primeval forest possibly 10,000 years old. The area is still rich in lichens. Gradually parts of the woodlands were cleared for small dwellings. To the north of what is now Woodlands Road the fields today still bear witness to this haphazard development. The boundaries are irregular and have often caused controversy. The areas to the south of the road are more regular, having been sold over the years, many by Winchester College, and the boundaries drawn and decided on maps.

The hamlet of Woodlands over the years was merely a cluster of thatched cottages. The thatcher's materials were readily available at Reedbridge (Redbridge) just a mile or two towards Southampton. These reed beds have a preservation order on them and still flourish today.

The Woodlands of today is a Victorian creation. Three large houses were built in the mid 19th century. What is now Busketts Lawn Hotel, built in the 1860s, was originally the country seat of wealthy landowners and village squires. These properties created a fair amount of local employment. The mother of one present elderly resident worked for two of these families – asking 6d from one but only 5d from the other as she liked them better and felt they could afford no more. In the 1920s her son played in the Woodlands Road, then a gravel track, with his metal hoop or wooden top and whip.

Today, although some of Netley Marsh and Bartley may use Woodlands as part of their postal address, the actual hamlet of Woodlands is barely half a mile long. Bordering on the New Forest, it is an area of mixed housing, served by one public house and a small general store. Two of the three larger houses are now residential homes for the elderly, the other a family run hotel. The old lodge, stables and so on have become very desirable properties, and modern houses blend in well with the old.

Woodley & Crampmoor

Today Woodley and Crampmoor forms the eastern boundary as one travels out of Romsey. It consists of several housing estates and estate shops. There is a school, church, public house and two halls. The Hunter's Inn is the focal point for many locals and passing travellers. The main social centre is Woodley village hall, which is in daily use.

Woodley and Crampmoor in the 1930s were vastly different, with lovely green fields where now so many estates abound. A scattering of small semi-detached buildings housed gardeners and farm workers. There were some large houses, such as Woodley Court which is now a nursing home and Woodley Grange, now a rest home.

A gravel road from Crampmoor, with open fields on either side to the Winchester road (no bungalows then), went to St Swithun's church (1856), which had then just closed as a church school. The sanctuary was partitioned off during school days and opened up for Sunday services. A door where the lectern stood led to the headmistress's small home. This is now the vestry. Before crossing the road to go to the new school, a visit to Miss Roberts' sweet shop was obligatory if you had a penny or two to spend. This is now a private house.

The Hunter's Inn was there but no other building except a semi-detached just by the new school. This was very much a 'Miss Read'

St Swithun's church, Woodley & Crampmoor

school, necessary because there were so many children! Small cottages housed anything up to ten children in some cases. How did they manage? Very well really – they all seemed healthy, probably due to the lovely cold well water and fresh vegetables from the garden. They used oil lamps and wood for the black-leaded stoves and open fires. Of course there was no mains drainage, no bathrooms and life was very hard. The school has since been demolished and is the site of the Woodley village hall.

The Worldhams 🎋

Near Alton lies the village of East Worldham, situated dramatically on the top of an escarpment. The old road from Selborne to Binsted, now visible as two lanes, crosses the Kingsley to Alton road at East Worldham.

Philippa Chaucer, wife of the poet Geoffrey Chaucer, is said to be buried in the pretty church at East Worldham, and the coffin lid from her tomb, found in the chancel, is in a niche in the church. Chaucer's son was lord of the manor at Worldham and Keeper of Woolmer Forest. A wooded mound, visible from the main road and called King John's Hill, is the site of a royal huting lodge.

Away from the main road and about a mile and a half through peaceful countryside is West Worldham. Here the little church, medieval in origin, adjoins a 16th century manor farmhouse. There is more history at Hartley Mauditt, still within the parish, where a few mounds in the soil mark a vanished village. St Leonard's church remains with its Norman architecture, delightfully situated beside a lake.

Before the Second World War, the area was entirely agricultural with two village schools, now both shut. Only two farms, out of the four which were hop producers, still grow hops. There are quite a lot of new houses, and farm buildings have been put to industrial uses.

The Worldhams still cherish a strong sense of identity. Highlight of the year is the Fete and Flower Show. A Parish Walk takes place on Rogation Sunday. April 1950 saw the formation of the Worldhams' WI. More recently, and thanks to the enthusiasm of a new resident, a village map was compiled.

The Worthys 🎋

The four Worthys (Headbourne, King's, Abbot's and Martyr) are spread along the north bank of the river Itchen, north-east of Winchester. The source of the suffix, Worthy, is uncertain – it may be derived from 'wordig' indicating a boundary. The villages and hamlets are listed in the Domesday Book, though not by their modern names. Kings Worthy was king's land, while the other villages belonged to the church.

In the mid 1920s the Blake brothers, owners of Woodhams Farm at Kings Worthy, began excavating to try to discover the source of mortared flints they found in one of their fields. Their first efforts uncovered an abandoned grain-store pit of an Iron Age settlement. Further excavation eventually revealed a Roman villa. For many years a battered stone head of a woman was kept at the farmhouse. At a distance from the site of the villa, there was subsequently found the portrait head of a boy. Both these heads have recently been authenticated by the British Museum as Roman. Other finds, including a fine table top, are in Winchester museum.

During the Second World War when Nissen huts were being erected in the grounds of Worthy Park, a burial ground of Saxon origin was discovered. In 1985–86 evidence of a riverside Saxon settlement was uncovered during the building of a section of the M3 motorway.

In medieval times, the river Itchen played a much bigger part in the life of the community than in more recent centuries. It was then navigable up to Alresford and was used for the transport of goods. There were a number of mills in the villages along the river, one of which (the fulling mill) remains now as a private dwelling at Abbots Worthy.

Springvale was also a small waterway, but the flow of water disappeared after the sinking of boreholes further up stream.

The road from Winchester to London passes through Headbourne Worthy and Kings Worthy, where the Cart and Horses has provided refreshment since at least the 18th century. The northern end of the Winchester by-pass terminates at Kings Worthy and that stretch of the road was closed off to be used as a vehicle park during the Second World War and a gathering point prior to the D-Day landings in June 1944.

The railway came to the Worthys in about 1909, when the Didcot, Newbury and Southampton line was opened and a station built. The railway did not survive beyond 1960 and the A34 now runs along part of the track which passed through the villages. Another line from Winchester to Alton, known as the Watercress Line, ran along the north of the area and succumbed to the Beeching axe.

The villages depended mainly on farming until the 19th century, when they began to attract business people and others as residents. One of the most notable was C.W. Benny, twice mayor of Winchester and a considerable landowner and entrepreneur. In the 1880s, Kings Worthy acquired a foundry, which came to be known as the Vulcan Iron Works. The chief product of the iron works was the hydraulic ram for raising water. The rams were exported all over the world where they gave sturdy service for many years in developing countries and put Kings Worthy on the world map. The business survived a disastrous fire in 1907, recorded by a Winchester photographer, whose pictures were reproduced as postcards.

The churches in the villages are of varying ages. St Swithun's, Headbourne Worthy, is Saxon and is one of the oldest churches in Hampshire. It has a Saxon rood. St Mary's, Kings Worthy, was much restored and extended twice in the 19th century, but shows evidence of its earlier provenance in a Norman doorway and a 14th century font. St Swithun's, Martyr Worthy, dates from the 12th century.

Though inhabited for so many centuries, the Worthys seem to have remained small and under the shadow of the big city, Winchester, until the 19th century. Then with the arrival of more wealthy residents, larger houses were built, a number of which though still existing are no longer in residential use.

The largest house, Worthy Park, in its present guise was started in 1820, but there was a house on the site previously, when William Evelyn, cousin of John Evelyn the diarist, built there in 1722. There is said to have been a house on the site since Saxon times, when the king (of the West Saxons) granted the manor of Worthy to the church in Winchester.

The population began to increase in the 19th century and since 1945 has exploded so that the villages are now effectively a dormitory area. There is a small industrial estate on the site of the old Vulcan Iron Works and some thriving watercress beds at Headbourne Worthy. The best known business in Kings Worthy is probably Conder Engineering, which started its enterprise in a small workshop a little distance from some of its present offices. Though the Worthys are no longer truly rural, they still retain their identity as villages with their various community activities.

Worting 🦋

Worting today is just part of the great conurbation of Basingstoke, which threw out its tentacles, grasped and enclosed it. But once it was a lovely, busy, friendly village in the heart of beautiful countryside.

It is a place with a long history, for evidence has been found of the work of early Britons, Romans, Saxons and Danes here. The earliest direct reference to Worting is in an 11th century manuscript at the British Museum. Another reference is made in the Domesday Book of 1086, and Worting is described as a territory of five ploughlands, worth five hides.

There was a church in Worting in 1086 and the present parish church of St Thomas of Canterbury which was built in 1848 is the fourth on this site. Parish registers go back to 1604.

There are some amusing entries in church records, such as 'December 7, 1763. The sink at sesspool in Ye Parsonage Yard, about a foot and a half in diameter was cleaned and covered with Plank. However, it ought to be examined into 20 years hence if not before.'

On 9th May, 1655 a great fire destroyed the parish church, a farmhouse adjacent to the parsonage, the White Horse Inn, six dwelling houses, eleven barns and many goods. The inhabitants of Worting lost £2,000 and were destitute. They appealed to the Justices of the Peace for leave to make a public collection and a brief to pass through Hampshire and other counties for charitable relief. An Order in Council was issued for a collection in Hampshire, Wiltshire, Sussex and Dorset.

Jane Austen was born in the nearby village of Steventon and during her girlhood was a frequent visitor to Manydown Park near Worting. She also visited Worting House for, in writing to her sister Cassandra in 1798, she described how, after dining at Worting House she joined a party for a ball in Basingstoke Assembly Rooms.

A hundred and fifty years ago Worting was full of life. There were four schools, two blacksmiths, a butcher, a tailor and breeches maker, a shoemaker and a rat catcher.

The railway first came through the village in 1840 when the line from Basingstoke to Winchester was laid. Worting now hosts an important and famous railway junction. In 1897 the two tracks from Basingstoke were doubled and a fly-over junction with high speed crossovers to and from the fast lines at Worting replaced the former flat junction at Battledown a mile to the west.

A railway bridge crosses the main Basingstoke to Andover road, and double-decker buses occasionally get stuck there when drivers keep too close to the left.

What remains of Worting village now? The village shop/post office thrives, the church is well attended, and Worting House is occupied by a firm of naval architects and marine consultants. There is still a blacksmith.

The reading room where Worting WI have held their meetings since July 1918 was a gift to the village by Miss Louisa Worsam in 1908. It is constantly under threat of demolition and replacement by a modern community centre. This is sad. It is a 'funny little hall' with structurally only the bare essentials. But is has a lovely old village atmosphere which could never be recaptured in a new building.

Even those who never knew Worting as a true village sigh for the old days, and wish they could put back the clock.

Index